TEAS V
STUDY GUIDE 2016

TEAS TEST PREP AND PRACTICE QUESTIONS FOR THE
TEAS VERSION 5 EXAM

FREE *FROM STRESS TO SUCCESS* DVD FROM TRIVIUM TEST PREP

Dear Customer,

Thank you for purchasing from Trivium Test Prep! Whether you're looking to join the military, get into college, or advance your career, we're honored to be a part of your journey.

To show our appreciation (and to help you relieve a little of that test-prep stress), we're offering a **FREE *From Stress to Success* DVD** by Trivium Test Prep. Our DVD includes 35 test preparation strategies that will help keep you calm and collected before and during your big exam. All we ask is that you email us your feedback and describe your experience with our product. Amazing, awful, or just so-so: we want to hear what you have to say!

To receive your **FREE *From Stress to Success* DVD**, please email us at 5star@triviumtestprep. com. Include "Free 5 Star" in the subject line and the following information in your email:

1. The title of the product you purchased.

2. Your rating from 1 – 5 (with 5 being the best).

3. Your feedback about the product, including how our materials helped you meet your goals and ways in which we can improve our products.

4. Your full name and shipping address so we can send your **FREE *From Stress to Success* DVD**.

If you have any questions or concerns please feel free to contact me directly.

Thank you, and good luck with your studies!

Alyssa Wagoner
Quality Control
alyssa.wagoner@triviumtestprep.com

TABLE OF CONTENTS

INTRODUCTION

Congratulations on your decision to join the field of nursing—few other professions are so rewarding! By purchasing this book, you've already taken the first step towards succeeding in your career. The next step is to do well on the TEAS exam, which will require you to demonstrate knowledge of high school-level reading, writing, math, and science.

This book will walk you through the important concepts in each of these subjects and also provide you with inside information on test strategies and tactics. Even if it's been years since you graduated from high school or cracked open a textbook, don't worry—this book contains everything you'll need for the TEAS V.

ABOUT TRIVIUM TEST PREP

Trivium Test Prep uses industry professionals with decades' worth of knowledge in their fields, proven with degrees and honors in law, medicine, business, education, the military, and more, to produce high quality test prep books for students.

Our study guides are specifically designed to increase any student's score, regardless of his or her current skill level. Our books are also shorter and more concise than typical study guides, so you can increase your score while significantly decreasing your study time.

HOW TO USE THIS GUIDE

This guide is not meant to waste your time on superfluous information or concepts you've already learned. Instead, we hope you use this guide to focus on the concepts YOU need to master for the test and to develop critical test-taking skills. To support this effort, the guide provides:

- organized concepts with detailed explanations
- practice questions with worked-through solutions
- key test-taking strategies
- simulated one-on-one tutor experience
- tips, tricks, and test secrets

Because we have eliminated *filler* or *fluff*, you'll be able to work through the guide at a significantly faster pace than you would with other test prep books. By allowing you to focus only on those concepts that will increase your score, we'll make your study time shorter and more effective.

ABOUT THE TEST

The TEAS V exam is three hours and thirty minutes long and is divided into the following sections:

SUBJECT	TIME LIMIT
Reading 48 questions: paragraph and passage comprehension and informational source comprehension	58 minutes
Mathematics 34 questions: numbers and operations, measurement, data interpretation, and algebra	51 minutes
Science 54 questions: scientific reasoning, human body science, life science, earth science, and physical science	66 minutes
English and Language Arts 34 questions: grammar, punctuation, spelling, word meaning, and sentence structure	34 minutes
Total: 170 questions	3 hours 29 minutes

There are a total of 170 questions on the TEAS exam; however twenty of them are unscored and used only by the test makers to gather information. That means 150 of the questions you answer will count toward your score.

Scoring

You cannot pass or fail the TEAS exam. Instead, you will receive a score report that details the number of questions you got right in each section and also gives your percentile rank, which shows how you did in comparison with other test takers. Each school has its own entrance requirements, so be sure to check the requirements of the institutions you want to attend, so you can set appropriate goals for yourself.

How This Book Works

The chapters in this book are divided into a review of the topics covered on the exam. This is not intended to teach you everything you'll see on the test: there is no way to cram all of that material into one book! Instead, we are going to help you recall information that you've already learned, and even more importantly, we'll show you how to apply that knowledge.

Each chapter includes an extensive review with practice questions at the end to test your knowledge. With time, practice, and determination, you'll be well-prepared for test day.

PART I: READING

48 questions | 58 minutes

The TEAS Reading section will require you to read both non-fiction and fiction passages and then answer questions about them. These questions will fall into three main categories:

ABOUT THE AUTHOR: The question will ask about the author's attitude, thoughts, and opinions. When encountering a question asking specifically about the author, pay attention to context clues in the article. The answer may not be explicitly stated, but instead conveyed in the overall message.

PASSAGE FACTS: You must distinguish between facts and opinions presented in the passage. You may also be asked to identify specific information supplied by the author of the passage.

ADDITIONAL INFORMATION: These questions will have you look at what kind of information could be added to or was missing from the passage. They may also ask in what direction the passage was going. Questions may ask what statement could be added to strengthen the author's statement, or weaken it; they may also provide a fill-in-the-blank option to include a statement that is missing from, but fits with, the rest of the passage.

The Reading section will also include informational source comprehension questions. These questions don't refer back to a text passage; instead, they will ask you to interpret an informational source like a nutrition label, map, or thermometer (these questions are covered in in the chapter titled *Informational Sources*).

STRATEGIES

Despite the different types of questions you will face, there are some strategies for reading comprehension which apply across the board:

- Read the answer choices first, then read the passage. This will save you time, as you will know what to look out for as you read.
- Use the process of elimination. Some answer choices are obviously incorrect and are relatively easy to detect. After reading the passage, eliminate those blatantly incorrect answer choices; this increases your chance of finding the correct answer much more quickly.

- Avoid negative statements. Generally, test-makers will not make negative statements about anyone or anything. Statements will be either neutral or positive, so if it seems like an answer choice has a negative connotation, it is very likely that the answer is false.

READING PASSAGES

THE MAIN IDEA

The main idea of a text is the purpose behind why a writer would choose to write a book, article, story, etc. Being able to find and understand the main idea is a critical skill necessary to comprehend and appreciate what you're reading.

Consider a political election. A candidate is running for office and plans to deliver a speech asserting her position on tax reform. The topic of the speech—tax reform—is clear to voters, and probably of interest to many. However, imagine that the candidate believes that taxes should be lowered. She is likely to assert this argument in her speech, supporting it with examples proving why lowering taxes would benefit the public and how it could be accomplished. While the topic of the speech would be tax reform, the benefit of lowering taxes would be the main idea. Other candidates may have different perspectives on the topic; they may believe that higher taxes are necessary, or that current taxes are adequate. It is likely that their speeches, while on the same topic of tax reform, would have different main ideas: different arguments likewise supported by different examples. Determining what a speaker, writer, or text is asserting about a specific issue will reveal the MAIN IDEA.

One more quick note: the TEAS may also ask about a passage's THEME, which is similar to, but distinct from its topic. While a TOPIC is usually a specific *person, place, thing,* or *issue,* the theme is an *idea* or *concept* that the author refers back to frequently. Examples of common themes include ideas like the importance of family, the dangers of technology, and the beauty of nature.

There will be many questions on the TEAS that require you to differentiate between the topic, theme, and main idea of a passage.

Topic: The subject of the passage.
Theme: An idea or concept the author refers to repeatedly.
Main idea: The argument the writer is making about the topic.

Let's look at an example passage to see how you would answer these questions:

> Babe Didrikson Zaharias, one of the most decorated female athletes of the twentieth century, is an inspiration for everyone. Born in 1911 in Beaumont, Texas, Zaharias lived in a time when women were considered second-class to men, but she never let that stop her from becoming a champion. Babe was one of seven children in a poor immigrant family and was competitive from an early age. As a child she excelled at most things she tried, especially sports, which continued into high school and beyond. After high school, Babe played amateur basketball for two years, and soon after began training in track and field. Despite the fact that women were only allowed to enter in three events, Babe represented the United States in the 1932 Los Angeles Olympics, and won two gold medals and one silver for track and field events.
>
> In the early 1930s, Babe began playing golf, which earned her a legacy. The first tournament she entered was a men's only tournament; however she did not make the cut to play. Playing golf as an amateur was the only option for a woman at this time, since there was no professional women's league. Babe played as an amateur for a little over a decade, until she turned pro in 1947 for the Ladies Professional Golf Association (LPGA) of which she was a founding member. During her career as a golfer, Babe won eighty-two tournaments, amateur and professional, including the U.S. Women's Open, All-American Open, and British Women's Open Golf Tournament. In 1953, Babe was diagnosed with cancer, but fourteen weeks later, she played in a tournament. That year she won her third U.S. Women's Open. However by 1955, she didn't have the physicality to compete anymore, and she died of the disease in 1956.

The topic of this paragraph is obviously Babe Zaharias—the whole passage describes events from her life. Determining the main idea, however, requires a little more analysis. The passage describes Babe Zaharias' life, but the main idea of the paragraph is what it says about her life. To figure out the main idea, consider what the writer is saying about Babe Zaharias. The writer is saying that she's someone to admire—that's the main idea and what unites all the information in the paragraph. Lastly, what might the theme of the passage be? The writer refers to several broad concepts, including never giving up and overcoming the odds, both of which could be themes for the passage.

Two major indicators of the main idea of a paragraph or passage follow:

- It is a general idea; it applies to the more specific ideas in the passage. Every other sentence in a paragraph should be able to relate in some way to the main idea.
- It asserts a specific viewpoint that the author supports with facts, opinions, or other details. In other words, the main idea takes a stand.

Example

From so far away it's easy to imagine the surface of our solar system's planets as enigmas—how could we ever know what those far-flung planets really look like? It turns out, however, that scientists have a number of tools at their disposal that allow them to paint detailed pictures of many planets' surfaces. The topography of Venus, for example, has been explored by several space probes, including the Russian Venera landers and NASA's Magellan orbiter. These craft used imaging and radar to map the surface of the planet, identifying a whole host of features including volcanoes, craters, and a complex system of channels. Mars has similarly been mapped by space probes, including the famous Mars Rovers, which are automated vehicles that actually landed on the surface of Mars. These rovers have been used by NASA and other space agencies to study the geology, climate, and possible biology of the planet.

In addition to these long-range probes, NASA has also used its series of orbiting telescopes to study distant planets. These four massively powerful telescopes include the famous Hubble Space Telescope as well as the Compton Gamma Ray Observatory, Chandra X-Ray Observatory, and the Spitzer Space Telescope. Scientists can use these telescopes to examine planets using not only visible light but also infrared and near-infrared light, ultraviolet light, x-rays, and gamma rays.

Powerful telescopes aren't just found in space: NASA makes use of Earth-bound telescopes as well. Scientists at the National Radio Astronomy Observatory in Charlottesville, VA, have spent decades using radio imaging to build an incredibly detailed portrait of Venus' surface. In fact, Earth-bound telescopes offer a distinct advantage over orbiting telescopes because they allow scientists to capture data from a fixed point, which in turn allows them to effectively compare data collected over a long period of time.

Which of the following sentences best describes the main idea of the passage?

A) It's impossible to know what the surfaces of other planets are really like.

B) Telescopes are an important tool for scientists studying planets in our solar system.

C) Venus' surface has many of the same features as the Earth's, including volcanoes, craters, and channels.

D) Scientists use a variety of advanced technologies to study the surface of the planets in our solar system.

Answer A) can be eliminated because it directly contradicts the rest of the passage. Answers B) and C) can also be eliminated because they offer only specific details from the passage—while both choices contain details from the passage, neither is general enough to encompass the passage as a whole. **Only answer D) provides an assertion that is both backed up by the passage's content and general enough to cover the entire passage.**

Topic and Summary Sentences

The main idea of a paragraph usually appears within the topic sentence. The TOPIC SENTENCE introduces the main idea to readers; it indicates not only the topic of a passage, but also the writer's perspective on the topic.

Notice, for example, how the first sentence in the example paragraph about Babe Zaharias states the main idea: *Babe Didrikson Zaharias, one of the most decorated female athletes of the twentieth century, is an inspiration for everyone.*

Even though paragraphs generally begin with topic sentences due to their introductory nature, on occasion writers build up to the topic sentence by using supporting details in order to generate interest or build an argument. Be alert for paragraphs when writers do not include a clear topic sentence at all; even without a clear topic sentence, a paragraph will still have a main idea. You may also see a SUMMARY SENTENCE at the end of a passage. As its name suggests, this sentence sums up the passage, often by restating the main idea and the author's key evidence supporting it.

Example

In the following paragraph, what are the topic and summary sentences?

The Constitution of the United States establishes a series of limits to rein in centralized power. Separation of powers distributes federal authority among three competing branches: the executive, the legislative, and the judicial. Checks and balances allow the branches to check the usurpation of power by any one branch. States' rights are protected under the Constitution from too much encroachment by the federal government. Enumeration of powers names the specific and few powers the federal government has. These four restrictions have helped sustain the American republic for over two centuries.

The topic sentence is the first sentence in the paragraph. It introduces the topic of discussion, in this case the constitutional limits aimed at restricting centralized power. **The summary sentence is the last sentence in the paragraph.** It sums up the information that was just presented: here, that constitutional limits have helped sustain the United States of America for over two hundred years.

Implied Main Idea

A paragraph without a clear topic sentence still has a main idea; rather than clearly stated, it is implied. Determining the IMPLIED MAIN IDEA requires some detective work: you will need to look at the author's word choice and tone in addition to the content of the passage to find his or her main idea. Let's look at a few example paragraphs.

Examples

One of my summer reading books was *Mockingjay*. I was captivated by the adventures of the main character and the complicated plot of the book. However, I felt like the ending didn't reflect the excitement of the story. Given what a powerful personality the main character has, I felt like the ending didn't do her justice.

1. Even without a clear topic sentence, this paragraph has a main idea. What is the writer's perspective on the book—what is the writer saying about it?

    A) *Mockingjay* is a terrific novel.

    B) *Mockingjay* is disappointing.

    C) *Mockingjay* is full of suspense.

    D) *Mockingjay* is a lousy novel.

    The correct answer is B): the novel is disappointing. How can you tell that this is the main idea? First, you can eliminate choice C) because it's too specific to be a main idea. It only deals with one specific aspect of the novel (its suspense).

    Sentences A), B), and D), on the other hand, all express a larger idea about the quality of the novel. However, only one of these statements can actually serve as a "net" for the whole paragraph. Notice that while the first few sentences praise the novel, the last two criticize it. Clearly, this is a mixed review.

    Therefore, the best answer is B). Sentence A) is too positive and doesn't account for the *letdown* of an ending. Sentence D), on the other hand, is too negative and doesn't account for the reader's sense of suspense and interest in the main character. But sentence B) allows for both positive and negative aspects—when a good thing turns bad, we often feel disappointed.

Fortunately, none of Alyssa's coworkers have ever seen inside the large filing drawer in her desk. Disguised by the meticulous neatness of the rest of her workspace, there was no sign of the chaos beneath. To even open it, she had to struggle for several minutes with the enormous pile of junk jamming the drawer, until it would suddenly give way, and papers, folders, and candy wrappers spilled out of the top and onto the floor. It was an organizational nightmare, with torn notes and spreadsheets haphazardly thrown on top of each other, and melted candy smeared across pages. She was worried the odor would soon permeate to her coworkers' desks, revealing her secret.

2. Which sentence best describes the main idea of the paragraph above?

   A) Alyssa wishes she could move to a new desk.

   B) Alyssa wishes she had her own office.

   C) Alyssa is glad none of her coworkers know about her messy drawer.

   D) Alyssa is sad because she doesn't have any coworkers.

Clearly, Alyssa has a messy drawer, and C) is the right answer. The paragraph begins by indicating her gratitude that her coworkers do not know about her drawer (*Fortunately, none of Alyssa's coworkers have ever seen inside the large filing drawer in her desk.*) Plus, notice how the drawer is described: *it was an organizational nightmare*, and it apparently doesn't even function properly: *to even open the drawer, she had to struggle for several minutes.* The writer reveals that it has an odor, with melted candy inside. Alyssa is clearly ashamed of her drawer and fearful of being judged by her coworkers about it.

SUPPORTING DETAILS

SUPPORTING DETAILS provide more support for the author's main idea. For instance, in the Babe Zaharias example, the writer makes the general assertion that *Babe Didrikson Zaharias, one of the most decorated female athletes of the twentieth century, is an inspiration for everyone.* The rest of the paragraph provides supporting details with facts showing why she is an inspiration: the names of the illnesses she overcame, and the specific years she competed in the Olympics.

Be alert for SIGNAL WORDS, which can be helpful in identifying supporting details. These signal words tell you that a supporting fact or idea will follow, and so can be helpful in identifying supporting details. Signal words can also help you rule out sentences that are not the main idea or topic sentence: if a sentence begins with one of these phrases, it will likely be too specific to be a main idea.

⚠

SIGNAL WORDS
- for example
- specifically
- in addition
- furthermore
- for instance
- others
- in particular
- some

Examples

From so far away it's easy to imagine the surface of our solar system's planets as enigmas—how could we ever know what those far-flung planets really look like? It turns out, however, that scientists have a number of tools at their disposal that allow them to paint detailed pictures of many planets' surfaces. The topography of Venus, for example, has been explored by several space probes, including the Russian Venera landers and NASA's Magellan orbiter. These craft used imaging and radar to map the surface of the planet, identifying a whole host of features including volcanoes, craters, and a complex system of channels. Mars has similarly been mapped by space probes, including the famous Mars Rovers, which are automated vehicles that actually landed on the surface of Mars. These rovers have been used by NASA and other space agencies to study the geology, climate, and possible biology of the planet.

In addition to these long-range probes, NASA has also used its series of orbiting telescopes to study distant planets. These four massively powerful telescopes include the famous Hubble Space Telescope as well as the Compton Gamma Ray Observatory, Chandra X-Ray Observatory, and the Spitzer Space Telescope. Scientists can use these telescopes to examine planets using not only visible light but also infrared and near-infrared light, ultraviolet light, x-rays, and gamma rays.

Powerful telescopes aren't just found in space: NASA makes use of Earth-bound telescopes as well. Scientists at the National Radio Astronomy Observatory in Charlottesville, VA, have spent decades using radio imaging to build an incredibly detailed portrait of Venus' surface. In fact, Earth-bound telescopes offer a distinct advantage over orbiting telescopes because they allow scientists to capture data from a fixed point, which in turn allows them to effectively compare data collected over a long period of time.

1. Which sentence from the text best develops the idea that scientists make use of many different technologies to study the surfaces of other planets?

   A) These rovers have been used by NASA and other space agencies to study the geology, climate, and possible biology of the planet.

   B) From so far away it's easy to imagine the surface of our solar system's planets as enigmas—how could we ever know what those far-flung planets really look like? ✗

   C) In addition to these long-range probes, NASA has also used its series of orbiting telescopes to study distant planets. ✗

   D) These craft used imaging and radar to map the surface of the planet, identifying a whole host of features including volcanoes, craters, and a complex system of channels.

You're looking for details from the passage that supports the main idea—scientists make use of many different technologies to study the surfaces of other planets. Answer A) includes a specific detail about rovers, but does not offer any details that support the idea of multiple technologies being used. Similarly, answer D) provides another specific detail about space probes. Answer B) doesn't provide any supporting details; it simply introduces the topic of the passage. **Only answer C) provides a detail that directly supports the author's assertion that scientists use multiple technologies to study the planets.**

2. If true, which detail could be added to the passage above to support the author's argument that scientists use many different technologies to study the surface of planets?

   A) Because the Earth's atmosphere blocks x-rays, gamma rays, and infrared radiation, NASA needed to put telescopes in orbit above the atmosphere.

   B) In 2015, NASA released a map of Venus which was created by compiling images from orbiting telescopes and long-range space probes.

   C) NASA is currently using the Curiosity and Opportunity rovers to look for signs of ancient life on Mars.

   D) NASA has spent over $2.5 billion to build, launch, and repair the Hubble Space Telescope.

   You can eliminate answers C) and D) because they don't address the topic of studying the surface of planets. Answer A) can also be eliminated because it only addresses a single technology. **Only choice B) would add support to the author's claim about the importance of using multiple technologies.**

3. The author likely included the detail *Earth-bound telescopes offer a distinct advantage over orbiting telescopes because they allow scientists to capture data from a fixed point* in order to:

   A) explain why it has taken scientists so long to map the surface of Venus

   B) suggest that Earth-bound telescopes are the most important equipment used by NASA scientists

   C) prove that orbiting telescopes will soon be replaced by Earth-bound telescopes

   D) demonstrate why NASA scientists rely on many different types of scientific equipment

   Only answer D) speaks directly to the author's main argument. The author doesn't mention how long it has taken to map the surface of Venus (answer A), nor does he say that one technology is more important than the others (answer B). And while this detail does highlight the advantages of using Earth-bound telescopes, the author's argument is that many technologies are being used at the same time, so there's no reason to think that orbiting telescopes will be replaced (answer C).

FACTS VS. OPINIONS

On TEAS reading passages you might be asked to identify a statement in a passage as either a fact or an opinion, so you'll need to know the difference between the two. A FACT is a statement or thought that can be proven to be true. The statement *Wednesday comes after Tuesday* is a fact—you can point to a calendar to prove it. In contrast, an OPINION is an assumption that is not based in fact and cannot be proven to be true. The assertion that *television is more entertaining than feature films* is an opinion—people will disagree on this, and there's no reference you can use to prove or disprove it.

Example

Exercise is critical for healthy development in children. Today, there is an epidemic of unhealthy children in the United States who will face health problems in adulthood due to poor diet and lack of exercise as children. This is a problem for all Americans, especially with the rising cost of health care.

It is vital that school systems and parents encourage their children to engage in a minimum of thirty minutes of cardiovascular exercise each day, mildly increasing their heart rate for a sustained period. This is proven to decrease the likelihood of developmental diabetes, obesity, and a multitude of other health problems. Also, children need a proper diet rich in fruits and vegetables so that they can grow and develop physically, as well as learn healthy eating habits early on.

Which of the following is a fact in the passage, not an opinion?

A) Fruits and vegetables are the best way to help children be healthy.

B) Children today are lazier than they were in previous generations.

C) The risk of diabetes in children is reduced by physical activity.

D) Children should engage in thirty minutes of exercise a day.

Answer C) is a simple fact stated by the author; it's introduced by the word *proven* to indicate that you don't need to just take the author's word for it. Choice B) can be discarded immediately because it is not discussed anywhere in the passage, and also because it is negative. Answers A) and D) are both opinions—the author is promoting exercise, fruits, and vegetables as a way to make children healthy. (Notice that these incorrect answers contain words that hint at being an opinion such as *best, should,* or other comparisons.)

MAKING INFERENCES

In addition to understanding the main idea and factual content of a passage, you'll also be asked to take your analysis one step further and anticipate what other information could logically be added to the passage. In a non-fiction passage, for example, you might be asked which statement the author of the passage would agree with. In an excerpt from a fictional work, you might be asked to anticipate what the character would do next.

To answer these questions, you need to have a solid understanding of the topic, theme, and main idea of the passage; armed with this information, you can figure out which of the answer choices best

✔ _____

Which of the following words would be associated with opinions?

- for example
- studies have shown
- I believe
- in fact
- the best/worst
- it's possible that

fits within those criteria (or alternatively, which ones do not). For example, if the author of the passage is advocating for safer working conditions in textile factories, any supporting details that would be added to the passage should support that idea. You might add sentences that contain information about the number of accidents that occur in textile factories or that outline a new plan for fire safety.

Example

Exercise is critical for healthy development in children. Today, there is an epidemic of unhealthy children in the United States who will face health problems in adulthood due to poor diet and lack of exercise as children. This is a problem for all Americans, especially with the rising cost of health care.

It is vital that school systems and parents encourage their children to engage in a minimum of thirty minutes of cardiovascular exercise each day, mildly increasing their heart rate for sustained period. This is proven to decrease the likelihood of developmental diabetes, obesity, and a multitude of other health problems. Also, children need a proper diet rich in fruits and vegetables so that they can grow and develop physically, as well as learn healthy eating habits early on.

What other information might the author have provided to strengthen the argument?

A) an example of how fruits and vegetables can improve a child's development

B) how much health insurance costs today vs. ten years ago

C) a detailed explanation of how diabetes affects the endocrine and digestive systems

D) how many calories the average person burns during thirty minutes of exercise

All of the choices would provide additional information, **but only one pertains specifically to the improvement of health in children: choice A).**

TYPES OF PASSAGES

Whenever an author writes a text, she always has a purpose, whether that's to entertain, inform, explain, or persuade. A short story, for example, is meant to entertain, while an online news article would be designed to inform the public about a current event.

Each of these different types of writing has a specific name. On the TEAS, you will be asked to identify which of these categories a passage fits into:

- **NARRATIVE WRITING** tells a story (novel, short story, play).
- **EXPOSITORY WRITING** informs people (newspaper and magazine articles).

- **TECHNICAL WRITING** explains something (product manual, directions).
- **PERSUASIVE WRITING** tries to convince the reader of something (opinion column on a blog).

You may also be asked about primary and secondary sources. These terms describe not the writing itself but the author's relationship to what's being written about. A **PRIMARY SOURCE** is an unaltered piece of writing that was composed during the time when the events being described took place; these texts are often written by the people involved. A **SECONDARY SOURCE** might address the same topic but provides extra commentary or analysis. These texts can be written by people not directly involved in the events. For example, a book written by a political candidate to inform people about his or her stand on an issue is a primary source; an online article written by a journalist analyzing how that position will affect the election is a secondary source.

Example

Elizabeth closed her eyes and braced herself on the armrests that divided her from her fellow passengers. Take-off was always the worst part for her. The revving of the engines, the way her stomach dropped as the plane lurched upward: it made her feel sick. Then, she had to watch the world fade away beneath her, getting smaller and smaller until it was just her and the clouds hurtling through the sky. Sometimes (but only sometimes) it just had to be endured. She focused on the thought of her sister's smiling face and her new baby nephew as the plane slowly pulled onto the runway.

The passage above is reflective of which type of writing?

A) narrative

B) expository

C) technical

D) persuasive

The passage is telling a story—we meet Elizabeth and learn about her fear of flying—so **it's a narrative text.** There is no factual information presented or explained, nor is the author trying to persuade the reader.

TEXT STRUCTURE

Authors can structure passages in a number of different ways. These distinct organizational patterns, referred to as **TEXT STRUCTURE**, use the logical relationships between ideas to improve the readability and coherence of a text. The most common ways passages are organized include:

- **PROBLEM-SOLUTION**: the author presents a problem and then discusses a solution.

- **COMPARISON-CONTRAST:** the author presents two situations and then discusses the similarities and differences.

- **CAUSE-EFFECT:** the author presents an action and then discusses the resulting effects.

- **DESCRIPTIVE:** an idea, object, person, or other item is described in detail.

Example

The issue of public transportation has begun to haunt the fast-growing cities of the southern United States. Unlike their northern counterparts, cities like Atlanta, Dallas, and Houston have long promoted growth out and not up—these are cities full of sprawling suburbs and single-family homes, not densely concentrated skyscrapers and apartments. What to do then, when all those suburbanites need to get into the central business districts for work? For a long time it seemed highways were the answer: twenty-lane wide expanses of concrete that would allow commuters to move from home to work and back again. But these modern miracles have become time-sucking, pollution-spewing nightmares. They may not like it, but it's time for these cities to turn toward public transport like trains and buses if they want their cities to remain livable.

The organization of this passage can best be described as:

A) a comparison of two similar ideas

B) a description of a place

C) a discussion of several effects all related to the same cause

D) a discussion of a problem followed by the suggestion of a solution

You can exclude answer choice C) because the author provides no root cause or a list of effects. From there this question gets tricky, because the passage contains structures similar to those described above. For example, it compares two things (cities in the North and South) and describes a place (a sprawling city). However, if you look at the overall organization of the passage, you can see that it starts by presenting a problem (transportation) and then presents a solution (trains and buses), **making answer D) the only choice that encompasses the entire passage.**

VOCABULARY

On the Reading section you may also be asked to provide definitions or intended meanings for words within passages. You may have never encountered some of these words before the test, but there are tricks you can use to figure out what they mean.

Context Clues

The most fundamental vocabulary skill is using the context in which a word is used to determine its meaning. Your ability to observe sentences closely is extremely useful when it comes to understanding new vocabulary words.

There are two types of context that can help you understand the meaning of unfamiliar words: situational context and sentence context. Regardless of which context is present, these types of questions are not really testing your knowledge of vocabulary; rather, they test your ability to comprehend the meaning of a word through its usage.

SITUATIONAL CONTEXT is context that is presented by the setting or circumstances in which a word or phrase occurs. SENTENCE CONTEXT occurs within the specific sentence that contains the vocabulary word. To figure out words using sentence context clues, you should first determine the most important words in the sentence.

There are four types of clues that can help you understand the context, and therefore the meaning of a word:

- RESTATEMENT clues occur when the definition of the word is clearly stated in the sentence.
- POSITIVE/NEGATIVE CLUES can tell you whether a word has a positive or negative meaning.
- CONTRAST CLUES include the opposite meaning of a word. Words like *but, on the other hand*, and *however* are tip-offs that a sentence contains a contrast clue.
- SPECIFIC DETAIL CLUES provide a precise detail that can help you understand the meaning of the word.

It is important to remember that more than one of these clues can be present in the same sentence. The more there are, the easier it will be to determine the meaning of the word. For example, the following sentence uses both restatement and positive/negative clues: *Janet suddenly found herself destitute, so poor she could barely afford to eat.* The second part of the sentence clearly indicates that *destitute* is a negative word. It also restates the meaning: very poor.

> **Examples**
>
> *Select the answer that most closely matches the definition of the underlined word or phrase as it is used in the sentence.*
>
> **1.** I had a hard time reading her <u>illegible</u> handwriting.
>
> **A)** neat
>
> **B)** unsafe
>
> **C)** sloppy
>
> **D)** educated

Already, you know that this sentence is discussing something that is hard to read. Look at the word that *illegible* is describing: handwriting. Based on context clues, you can tell that *illegible* means that her handwriting is hard to read.

Next, look at the answer choices. Choice A), *neat,* is obviously a wrong answer because neat handwriting would not be difficult to read. Choices B) and D), *unsafe* and *educated,* don't make sense. **Therefore, choice C), *sloppy*, is the best answer.**

2. The dog was <u>dauntless</u> in the face of danger, braving the fire to save the girl trapped inside the building.

    A) difficult

    B) fearless

    C) imaginative

    D) startled

    Demonstrating bravery in the face of danger would be B) *fearless*. In this case, the restatement clue (braving the fire) tells you exactly what the word means.

3. Beth did not spend any time preparing for the test, but Tyrone kept a <u>rigorous</u> study schedule.

    A) strict

    B) loose

    C) boring

    D) strange

    In this case, the contrast word *but* tells us that Tyrone studied in a different way than Beth, which means it's a contrast clue. If Beth did not study hard, then Tyrone did. **The best answer, therefore, is choice A).**

Analyzing Words

As you no doubt know, determining the meaning of a word can be more complicated than just looking in a dictionary. A word might have more than one DENOTATION, or definition; which one the author intends can only be judged by looking at the surrounding text. For example, the word *quack* can refer to the sound a duck makes, or to a person who publicly pretends to have a qualification which he or she does not actually possess.

A word may also have different CONNOTATIONS, which are the implied meanings and emotion a word evokes in the reader. For example, a cubicle is simply a walled desk in an office, but for many the word implies a constrictive, uninspiring workplace. Connotations can vary greatly between cultures and even between individuals.

Lastly, authors might make use of FIGURATIVE LANGUAGE, which is the use of a word to imply something other than the word's literal definition. This is often done by comparing two things. If you say *I felt like a butterfly when I got a new haircut*, the listener knows you don't resemble an insect but instead felt beautiful and transformed.

Examples

Select the answer that most closely matches the definition of the underlined word or phrase as it is used in the sentence.

1. The uneven <u>pupils</u> suggested that brain damage was possible.

    A) part of the eye

    B) student in a classroom

    C) walking pace

    D) breathing sounds

    Only answer choice A (part of the eye) matches both the definition of the word and context of the sentence. Choice B is an alternative definition for pupil, but does not make sense in the sentence. Both C and D could be correct in the context of the sentence, but neither is a definition of pupil.

2. Aiden examined the antique lamp and worried that he had been <u>taken for a ride</u>. He had paid a lot for the vintage lamp, but it looked like it was worthless.

    A) transported

    B) forgotten

    C) deceived

    D) hindered

    It's clear from the context of the sentence that Aiden was not literally taken for a ride. Instead, this phrase is an example of figurative language. **From context clues it can be figured out that Aiden paid too much for the lamp, so he was deceived (answer choice C).**

Word Structure

Although you are not expected to know every word in the English language for your test, you will need the ability to use deductive reasoning to find the choice that is the best match for the word in question, which is why we are going to explain how to break a word into its parts to determine its meaning. Many words can be broken down into three main parts:

PREFIX — ROOT — SUFFIX

ROOTS are the building blocks of all words. Every word is either a root itself or has a root. Just as a plant cannot grow without roots, neither can vocabulary, because a word must have a root to give it meaning. The root is what is left when you strip away all the prefixes and suffixes from a word. For example, in the word *unclear*, if you take away the prefix *un-*, you have the root *clear*.

Check out the chapter *Human Body Science* for a list of medical roots and prefixes that are commonly tested on the TEAS V.

Can you figure out the definitions of the following words using their parts?

- ambidextrous
- anthropology
- diagram
- egocentric
- hemisphere
- homicide
- metamorphosis
- nonsense
- portable
- rewind
- submarine
- triangle
- unicycle

Roots are not always recognizable words, because they generally come from Latin or Greek words, such as *nat*, a Latin root meaning born. The word *native*, which means a person born in a referenced place, comes from this root; so does the word *prenatal*, meaning *before birth*. It's important to keep in mind, however, that roots do not always match the exact definitions of words, and they can have several different spellings.

PREFIXES are syllables added to the beginning of a word and SUFFIXES are syllables added to the end of the word. Both carry assigned meanings and can be attached to a word to completely change the word's meaning or to enhance the word's original meaning.

Let's use the word *prefix* itself as an example: *fix* means to place something securely and *pre-* means before. Therefore, *prefix* means to place something before or in front of. Now let's look at a suffix: in the word *feminism*, *femin* is a root which means female. The suffix *-ism* means act, practice, or process. Thus, *feminism* is the process of establishing equal rights for women.

Although you cannot determine the meaning of a word by a prefix or suffix alone, you can use this knowledge to eliminate answer choices; understanding whether the word is positive or negative can give you the partial meaning of the word.

Table 1.1. Common roots and affixes

ROOT	DEFINITION	EXAMPLE
ast(er)	star	asteroid, astronomy
audi	hear	audience, audible
auto	self	automatic, autograph
bene	good	beneficent, benign
bio	life	biology, biorhythm
cap	take	capture
ced	yield	secede
chrono	time	chronometer, chronic
corp	body	corporeal
crac or crat	rule	autocrat
demo	people	democracy
dict	say	dictionary, dictation
duc	lead or make	ductile, produce
gen	give birth	generation, genetics
geo	earth	geography, geometry
grad	step	graduate
graph	write	graphical, autograph
ject	throw	eject
jur or jus	law	justice, jurisdiction
log or logue	thought	logic, logarithm
luc	light	lucidity
man	hand	manual
mand	order	remand
mis	send	transmission
mono	one	monotone
omni	all	omnivore
path	feel	pathology
phil	love	philanthropy
phon	sound	phonograph
port	carry	export
qui	rest	quiet
scrib or script	write	scribe, transcript
sense or sent	feel	sentiment
tele	far away	telephone
terr	earth	terrace
uni	single	unicode
vac	empty	vacant
vid	see	video
vis	see	vision

Table 1.2. Common prefixes

PREFIX	DEFINITION	EXAMPLE
a- (also an-)	not, without; to, towards; of, completely	atheist, anemic, aside, aback, anew, abashed
ante-	before, preceding	antecedent, ante-room
anti-	opposing, against	antibiotic, anticlimax
com- (also co-, col-, con-, cor-)	with, jointly, completely	combat, codriver, collude, confide
dis- (also di-)	negation, removal	disadvantage, disbar
en- (also em-)	put into or on; bring into the condition of; intensify	engulf, entomb
hypo-	under	hypoglycemic, hypothermia
in- (also il-, im-, ir-)	not, without; in, into, towards, inside	infertile, impossible, influence, include
intra-	inside, within	intravenous, intrapersonal
out-	surpassing, exceeding; external, away from	outperform, outdoor
over-	excessively, completely; upper, outer, over, above	overconfident, overcast
pre-	before	precondition, pre-adolescent, prelude
re-	again	reapply, remake
semi-	half, partly	semicircle, semi-conscious
syn- (also sym-)	in union, acting together	synthesis, symbiotic
trans-	across, beyond	transatlantic
trans-	into a different state	translate
under-	beneath, below	underarm, undersecretary
under-	not enough	underdeveloped

Examples

Select the answer that most closely matches the definition of the underlined word or phrase as it is used in the sentence.

1. The _bellicose_ dog will be sent to training school next week.

   A) misbehaved

   B) friendly

   C) scared

   D) aggressive

Both misbehaved and aggressive look like possible answers given the context of the sentence. **However, the prefix *belli*, which means warlike, can be used to confirm that aggressive (choice D) is the right answer.**

2. The new menu <u>rejuvenated</u> the restaurant and made it one of the most popular spots in town.

   A) established

   B) invigorated

   C) improved

   D) motivated

All of the answer choices could make sense in the context of the sentence, so it's necessary to use word structure to find the definition. The root *juven* means young and the prefix *re* means again, so *rejuvenate* means to be made young again. **The answer choice with the most similar meaning is *invigorated*, which means to give something energy.**

INFORMATIONAL SOURCES

On the TEAS V exam, you will encounter questions designed to test your comprehension of sources that convey all sorts of information. These sources may be visual (e.g., maps, graphs), textual (e.g., directions, indices), or both (e.g., labels, telephone listings).

SETS OF DIRECTIONS

Completing certain tasks requires you to follow directions. These directions can be given in a paragraph format or list format. Usually, each step, or direction, includes specific instructions that must be remembered in order to complete the subsequent steps.

⚠️ Write out the new answer for each step as you finish it so you can easily check your work.

Examples

1. You start with three red apples and one green apple in a basket. After following the directions below, how many apples are in the basket?

   Remove one red apple.

   Add one green apple.

   Add one red apple.

   Add one green apple.

   Remove two red apples.

   Remove one green apple.

   Add three red apples.

   Add two green apples.

   After following these directions, you have four red apples and four green apples in the basket.

2. You have twelve gallons of fuel in your tank. After following the directions below, how many gallons of fuel are left in the tank?

Use one gallon to drive to work.

Use one gallon to drive home.

Use half a gallon to drive the kids to soccer practice.

Use half a gallon to drive to the grocery store.

Use two gallons to drive back home.

After following these directions, you have seven gallons of fuel in your tank.

LABEL INGREDIENTS AND DIRECTIONS

Reading a label is crucial for extracting critical information such as ingredients in food or side effects and dosage requirements on a prescription label.

Examples

Use the nutrition label below to answer the following questions.

Nutrition Facts

Serving Size 172 g

Amount Per Serving

Calories 200   Calories from Fat 8

% Daily Value*

Total Fat 1g	1%
Saturated Fat 0g	1%
Trans Fat	
Cholesterol 0g	0%
Sodium 7mg	0%
Total Carbohydrate 36g	12%
Dietary Fiber 11g	45%
Sugars 6g	
Protein 13g	

Vitamin A	1%	Vitamin B	1%
Calcium	4%	Iron	24%

*Percent Daily Values are based on a 2,000 calorie diet. Your daily values may be higher or lower depending on your calorie needs.

NutritionData.com

1. If a man is monitoring his fat intake, would the above product be acceptable to consume?

Yes, as this product has only two hundred calories and one gram of total fat per serving.

2. If a man wants to build muscle, would the above product help him achieve his goal?

Yes. Protein aids muscle production, and this product has thirteen grams of protein per serving.

PRINTED COMMUNICATIONS

Printed communications such as invitations, advertisements, and memos contain quite a bit of information. It is good practice to read through the document once to understand its general purpose, then re-read the document to obtain specific information.

Examples

1. What is the general purpose and tone of this memo?

MEMO

To: Human Resources Department

From: Corporate Management

Date: December 6, 2013

Subject: Personal Use of Computers

The corporate office has been conducting standard monitoring of computer usage, and we have been quite dismayed at the amount of personal use occurring during business hours. Employee computers are available for the sole purpose of completing company business, nothing else. These rules must be respected. If not, steps will be taken to ensure maximum productivity. Personal use should occur only in emergency situations and should be limited to thirty minutes per day. Please communicate these requirements to lower management and personnel.

The purpose is to address personal use of company computers and to correct the misuse of them. The overall tone is negative, almost threatening.

2. What are the specific instructions given to the Human Resources Department?

The Human Resources Department is to communicate to lower management and personnel that personal use of company computers is to occur only in emergency situations and should be limited to thirty minutes per day.

The strategies you learned for reading passages will help you answer questions about printed communications. For example, you might need to find the main idea of a memo or identify opinions in an advertisement.

→

CONTINUE

INDEXES AND TABLES OF CONTENTS

When would it be appropriate to use an index but not a table of contents?

An **INDEX** is an alphabetical list of topics, and their associated page numbers, covered in a text. A **TABLE OF CONTENTS** is an outline of a text that includes topics and page numbers. Both of these can be used to look up information, but each has a slightly different purpose. An index helps the reader determine where in the text he or she can find specific details. A table of contents shows the reader the general arrangement of the text.

Examples

Use the examples below to answer the following questions.

Nursing, 189 – 296
certification, 192 – 236
code of ethics, 237 – 291
Procedure, 34 – 55

1. According to the index above, where might the reader find information about the nursing code of ethics?

   This information can be found from pages 237 – 291.

Chapter 1: Algebra...5
Chapter 2: Geometry.. 15
Chapter 3: Pre-calculus.. 32
Chapter 4: Chemistry..55

2. According to the table of contents above, in which chapter would the reader find information about the circumference of a circle?

   The circumference of a circle is part of geometry, so that information would be found in Chapter 2.

PRODUCT INFORMATION

When purchasing a product, you typically see an advertised base price. However, shipping and handling fees and taxes are also applied to the purchase. The sum of the base price, shipping and handling fees, and taxes equals the total cost of a product. When considering a purchase, be sure to compare the total cost, not simply the base price, at different retailers.

Examples

Use the chart below to answer the following questions.

Table 2.1. Shoe prices

RETAILER	BASE PRICE	SHIPPING & HANDLING	TAXES
Wholesale Footwear	$59.99	$10.95	$7.68
Bargain Sales	$65.99	$5.95	$5.38
Famous Shoes	$79.99	$0.00	$4.89

1. Rachel wants to buy shoes and can't spend more than 75 dollars. Which retailer must she avoid?

When you add the base price, shipping and handling fees, and taxes, **Famous Shoes is the only retailer that sells shoes that cost more than 75 dollars in total, so she cannot buy from them.**

2. Donald needs shoes and has only 78 dollars to spend. From which retailer can he buy without borrowing money?

When you add the base price, shipping and handling fees, and taxes, **Bargain Sales is the only retailer that sells shoes at a total cost under 78 dollars.**

You will be required to perform basic arithmetic for some of the problems in this section.

INFORMATION FROM A TELEPHONE BOOK

The phone book, often called the yellow pages, lists businesses according to industry. This list usually includes a company's name, phone number, and physical address. Aside from being included in the generic list, businesses can also pay for other options, including bolded or enlarged text and full-page advertisements. These advertisements can provide extra information, such as store hours and email addresses, and can help you form an opinion of the business.

CONTINUE

Examples

Use the excerpt below to answer the following questions.

| L | 272 | LAUNDRIES | To Advertise Call 1-555-929-1255 · Area Code is 555 Unless Otherwise Specified |

LAUNDRIES

A+ Laundry & Cleaners
1279 S Parkfield Dr.............................**121-7755**

Coin City Laundry
1662 Crown Pkwy...............................**999-3232**

Daily Spin Quality Cleaners
3773 Bell Springs Dr..........................**117-1958**

Magic Coin Laundry
9722 S Parkfield Dr.............................**151-0003**

Opal's Cleaners
4355 Central Park Dr..........................**121-7825**

Satin Touch Laundry Center
1116 Bathaven Ct................................**533-1115**

LAUNDRIES-SELF SVCE.

Quik-E-Wash
7879 Springfield Dr............................**111-1985**

Royal Cleaners
1492 Columbus Ct...............................**567-0010**

Spin Cycle Laundry
Self Service Coin Laundromat
Full Service Wash n' Fold
Advanced Washers and Dryers
3475 Baythorne Dr..............................**567-0010**

Super Spin Laundry
4789 Iron Clark Dr..............................**122-1811**

Total Clean Laundry Center
9134 Bay Breeze Cir............................**145-8889**

Wash Center USA
415 Purple Park Dr..............................**555-1212**

LAWN & GARDEN EQUIP.

AAA Lawn Service and Sales
1212 Greenleaf Dr...............................**311-1218**

Bard's Stone & Feed
1117 Maple Crossing..........................**757-0110**

Calm Winds Nursery
47134 N Lakeville Dr...........................**729-1991**

Earth Friendly Gardeners
5234 Orchard Valley Dr......................**445-3335**

Palm Planet
1410 Elm St...**131-1571**

Summer Stone Outdoors
525 Parkside Dr...................................**888-3995**

LAWN & GROUNDS MAINT.

ALL SEASON LAWN MAINTENANCE
Lawn & Grounds Maintenance
Tree Removal
Landscape Design
Stonework & Fencing
Call **555-123-7879**

American Landscape
9822 Dreamy Lane...............................**121-7755**

Capitol Lawn and Design
1237 Georgia Crest Dr.........................**912-3200**

Edward's Irrigation Repair
2010 Blue Jay Ln.................................**151-0003**

GARDENSCAPE
Mowing, Maintenance & Landscaping
Residential and Commercial
1105 Spring Creek Dr..........................**615-1001**

Green Giant Lawncare
0427 Phoenix St...................................**227-1368**

Happy Plant Lawnworks
8081 Red Bird Ct..................................**151-0003**

JTW Landscape Service
39009 Williamsburg Dr.......................**227-1368**

Perfecto Lawncare & Maintenance
0320 Kendrix Ct....................................**431-2906**

Stonewall Complete Landscapes
0525 E Penny Lane...............................**391-5580**

1. If a man needs his suit dry-cleaned for a job interview and is unable to do it himself, how many businesses are available to complete the task for him?

   There are three businesses that can dry-clean the man's suit: A+ Laundry & Cleaners, Daily Spin Quality Cleaners, and Opal's Cleaners. The other related businesses are either laundry-only centers or self-service cleaners.

2. A woman wants to hire a landscaping company this winter to improve her yard's appearance. Which company should she contact?

   She should contact All Season Lawn Maintenance because that company specifically states that it works year-round. Since the woman wants the work done in the winter, this company can accommodate her.

SOURCES FOR LOCATING INFORMATION

The Internet has made information more accessible than ever before, but it has also increased the difficulty of finding valid and appropriate information. To find suitable information, first locate a source that discusses specifically what or who you are investigating. Secondly, locate a source that is credible, or not directly related to what or who you are investigating.

Examples

1. Daniel wants to look up horsepower figures for a brand new car he wants to buy. In terms of specificity, which source would be most likely to provide this information?

   A) Eco-Auto newsletter

   B) Hot Rod Heaven magazine

   C) The manufacturer's website

   All three sources are related to vehicles in one way or another, but **the manufacturer's website is the only source in which Daniel could find horsepower numbers for the vehicle he wants to buy.**

2. Cynthia wants to research the effectiveness of soap from different manufacturers. In terms of credibility, which source would be best to use to look up information?

   A) An online blog

   B) The manufacturer's website

   C) An independent research firm's report

   All three sources might discuss different soaps, but **an independent research firm is the most credible because it is a professional firm and isn't related to the manufacturer.**

LISTINGS OF ITEMS AND COSTS

When making a purchase, you must contend with several factors that could possibly affect your decision. Before selecting a specific brand of a particular product, consider the following steps. First, identify the product features most important to you. Second, gather product information from three to five competitors. Third, sort through this information and select the product that best matches your preferred features.

→

CONTINUE

Examples

Table 2.2. Tee prices

COMPANY	PRICE	COLOR	SIZE
Maximum Tees	$15.99/dozen	red	M
Wholesale Tees	$12.99/dozen	blue	L
Total Tees	$19.99/dozen	green	XL

1. Ben needs to buy shirts for his youth baseball team. The team color is red, the players all wear medium-sized shirts, and they would prefer to spend less than 12 dollars. Which company best meets Ben's requirements?

   Ben's requirements are best met by Maximum Tees. Although the price is higher than desired, the color and size match Ben's needs exactly. Often, you won't find a company or product that matches your requirements exactly.

2. Sarah is buying shirts for her church group. She would like them to be green, large-sized, and 15 dollars or less. Which company best suits Sarah's requirements?

   Sarah's requirements are not met by any one company. Wholesale Tees offers shirts that are blue (not green), large-sized, and 12 dollars and 99 cents. Total Tees offers shirts that are green, extra-large-sized (not large-sized), and 19 dollars and 99 cents (not 15 dollars or less). **Because Wholesale Tees matches two of Sarah's three requirements, compared to Total Tees, which only matches one requirement, Wholesale Tees best suits Sarah's needs.**

GRAPHIC REPRESENTATIONS OF INFORMATION

Information is usually represented as text, but it can also be represented graphically. Types of graphic information include charts, maps, graphs, drawings, and photographs. Graphic representations are used to quickly visualize an idea or compare bits of information. They are typically accompanied by a legend or additional information that aids comprehension.

Examples

Use the pie chart below to answer the following questions about Wholesale Electronics' sales.

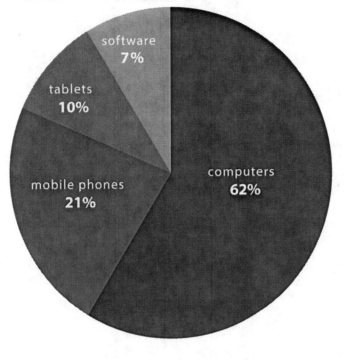

1. Which product accounts for most of Wholesale Electronics' total sales?

    At 62 percent, computers account for most of Wholesale Electronics' total sales.

2. Mobile phones and tablets comprise what percentage of Wholesale Electronics' total sales?

    Mobile phones and tablets comprise 31 percent of Wholesale Electronics' total sales.

SCALE READINGS

A scale reading is simply a numerical value collected from a scale, or measurement device such as a weight scale or thermometer. To accurately interpret a scale reading, you must know the maximum and minimum values of the measurement device; otherwise, the measurement limits of the device can be misinterpreted as a genuine reading.

CONTINUE →

Examples

Use the thermometer below to answer the following questions.

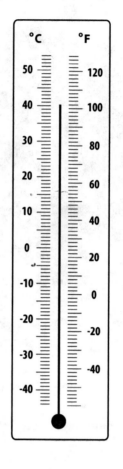

1. The current temperature is approximately 105°F. What is the approximate temperature in degrees Centigrade?

   105°F is approximately 40°C.

2. If the thermometer indicated a temperature of 15°C, what would the temperature be in degrees Fahrenheit?

   15°C is approximately 60°F.

MAP LEGENDS AND KEYS

The LEGEND or KEY of a map explains the various symbols used on a map as well as their meanings and measurements. These symbols typically include a compass rose and a distance scale. A compass rose indicates the four cardinal directions (north, south, west, and east) and the four intermediate directions (northwest, northeast, southwest, and southeast). A distance scale is used to show the ratio of the distance on the page to the actual distance between objects, usually in miles or kilometers.

Examples

Use the map of Gemstone State Park below to answer the following questions.

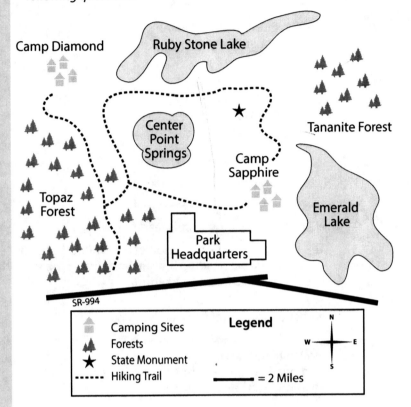

1. From Park Ranger Headquarters, in which direction is Ruby Stone Lake?

   Ruby Stone Lake is north of Park Ranger Headquarters.

2. Approximately how many miles is it from the state monument to the center of Tananite Forest?

   The center of Tananite Forest is approximately four miles from the state monument.

HEADINGS AND SUBHEADINGS

In a long printed work, a general topic or subject is usually divided into categories and sections so the text can be easily navigated and read. A **HEADING** is a subcategory of the subject, and a **SUBHEADING** is a subcategory of a heading. Both types of headings preview what will be covered in their respective sections, but a heading usually encompasses a broader range of information than a subheading does. The font for headings is typically larger than the font for subheadings.

CONTINUE

Examples

Use the example below to answer the following questions.

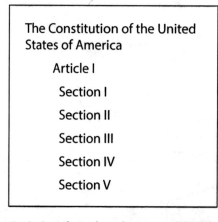

The Constitution of the United States of America

    Article I

      Section I

      Section II

      Section III

      Section IV

      Section V

1. Is Article I a heading or subheading?

The subject is the Constitution of the United States of America. Since a heading is a subcategory of the subject, **Article I is classified as a heading.**

2. Is Section III a heading or subheading?

You already know that the subject is the Constitution of the United States of America. You also know that Article I is a heading. Since a subheading is a subcategory of a heading, **Section III is classified as a subheading.**

TEXT FEATURES

TEXT FEATURES are stylistic elements used to clarify, add meaning, or differentiate. Examples of text features include bold, italicized, or underlined fonts, and bulleted or numbered lists. The general rule of thumb for text features is to use them consistently. Inconsistency can confuse the reader and distort the intended purpose of a text feature.

Example

Use the example below to answer the following question.

I'm glad you have accepted my invitation to meet with me. Directions to my office are below.

1. Head north on IH-10.
2. Take the Woodview exit.
3. Turn right onto Woodview.
4. After 1.3 miles, turn left onto East Glen Street.

What is the purpose of writing the directions as a numbered list?

Bulleted and numbered lists are quite helpful in identifying sequential items, especially travel directions.

PART II: MATHEMATICS

34 questions | 51 minutes

THE MOST COMMON MISTAKES

People make little mistakes all the time, but during a test those tiny mistakes can make the difference between a good score and a poor one. Watch out for these common mistakes that people make on the math section of the TEAS:

- answering with the wrong sign (positive/negative)
- mixing up the order of operations
- misplacing a decimal
- not reading the question thoroughly (and therefore providing an answer that was not asked for)
- circling the wrong letter or filling in wrong circle choice

If you're thinking, *those ideas are just common sense*, that's exactly the point. Most of the mistakes made on the TEAS are simple ones. But no matter how silly the mistake, a wrong answer still means a lost point on the test.

STRATEGIES FOR THE MATHEMATICS SECTION

Go Back to the Basics

First and foremost, practice your basic skills: sign changes, order of operations, simplifying fractions, and equation manipulation. These are the skills used most on the TEAS, though they are applied in different contexts. Remember that when it comes down to it, all math problems rely on the four basic skills of addition, subtraction, multiplication, and division. All you need to figure out is the order in which they're used to solve a problem.

Don't Rely on Mental Math

Using mental math is great for eliminating answer choices, but ALWAYS WRITE DOWN YOUR WORK! This cannot be stressed enough. Use whatever paper is provided; by writing and/or drawing out the problem, you are more likely to catch any mistakes. The act of writing things down also forces you to organize your calculations, leading to an improvement in your TEAS score.

The Three-Times Rule

You should read each question at least three times to ensure you're using the correct information and answering the right question:

Step one: Read the question and write out the given information.

Step two: Read the question, set up your equation(s), and solve.

Step three: Read the question and check that your answer makes sense (is the amount too large or small; is the answer in the correct unit of measure, etc.).

Make an Educated Guess

Eliminate those answer choices which you are relatively sure are incorrect, and then guess from the remaining choices. Educated guessing is critical to increasing your score.

NUMBERS AND OPERATIONS

ROMAN NUMERALS

The roman numeral system uses letters to represent numerical values, as shown below.

Table 3.1. Roman numerals

ROMAN NUMERAL	VALUE
I	1
V	5
X	10
L	50
C	100
D	500
M	1000

These seven numerals are combined to form numbers. Numerals are always arranged from greatest to least in value starting with the largest possible number. For example, the number 157 would be written as: 100 + 50 + 5 + 1 + 1 = CLVII, and the number 3,621 is written as 1000 + 1000 + 1000 + 500 + 100 + 10 + 10 + 1 = MMMDCXXI.

To avoid adding four of the same numeral in a row, subtraction is used. If a numeral with a smaller value is placed before a numeral with a larger value, the smaller number is subtracted from the bigger number. For example, the number 9 is written as IX (10 – 1 = 9). Since I has a value of 1 and it is placed before X, which has a value of 10, the number is found by subtracting 1 from 10.

1. Express the number 538 in roman numerals.

   $538 = 500 + 30 + 8$

   $538 = 500 + 10 + 10 + 10 + 5 + 1 + 1 + 1$

   $538 = $ **DXXXVIII**

2. What number is expressed by the roman numeral CDVII?

   $C = 100, D = 500, V = 5, I = 1, I = 1$

   Since C comes before D, 100 is subtracted from 500.

   $500 - 100 + 5 + 1 + 1 = $ **407**

POSITIVE AND NEGATIVE NUMBER RULES

Adding, multiplying, and dividing numbers can yield positive or negative values depending on the signs of the original numbers. Knowing these rules can help determine if your answer is correct.

$(+) + (-) = $ the sign of the larger number

$(-) + (-) = $ negative number

$(-) \times (-) = $ positive number

$(-) \times (+) = $ negative number

$(-) \div (-) = $ positive number

$(-) \div (+) = $ negative number

Examples

1. Find the product of −10 and 47.

   $(-) \times (+) = (-)$

   $-10 \times 47 = $ **−470**

2. What is the sum of −65 and −32?

   $(-) + (-) = (-)$

   $-65 + -32 = $ **−97**

3. Is the product of −7 and 4 less than −7, between −7 and 4, or greater than 4?

   $(-) \times (+) = (-)$

   $-7 \times 4 = -28$, which is **less than −7**

4. What is the value of −16 divided by 2.5?

   $(-) \div (+) = (-)$

   $-16 \div 2.5 = $ **−6.4**

ORDER OF OPERATIONS

Operations in a mathematical expression are always performed in a specific order, which is described by the acronym PEMDAS:

1. Parentheses
2. Exponents
3. Multiplication
4. Division
5. Addition
6. Subtraction

Perform the operations within parentheses first, and then address any exponents. After those steps, perform all multiplication and division. These are carried out from left to right as they appear in the problem.

Finally, do all required addition and subtraction, also from left to right as each operation appears in the problem.

Can you come up with a mnemonic device to help yourself remember the order of operations?

Examples

1. Solve: $[-(2)^2 - (4 + 7)]$

   First, complete operations within parentheses:

   $-(2)^2 - (11)$

   Second, calculate the value of exponential numbers:

   $-(4) - (11)$

   Finally, do addition and subtraction:

   $-4 - 11 = \mathbf{-15}$

2. Solve: $(5)^2 \div 5 + 4 \times 2$

   First, calculate the value of exponential numbers:

   $(25) \div 5 + 4 \times 2$

   Second, calculate division and multiplication from left to right:

   $5 + 8$

   Finally, do addition and subtraction:

   $5 + 8 = \mathbf{13}$

3. Solve the expression: $15 \times (4 + 8) - 3^3$

   First, complete operations within parentheses:

   $15 \times (12) - 3^3$

   Second, calculate the value of exponential numbers:

   $15 \times (12) - 27$

   Third, calculate division and multiplication from left to right:

   $180 - 27$

   Finally, do addition and subtraction from left to right:

   $180 - 27 = \mathbf{153}$

4. Solve the expression: $\left(\frac{5}{2} \times 4\right) + 23 - 4^2$

First, complete operations within parentheses:

$(10) + 23 - 4^2$

Second, calculate the value of exponential numbers:

$(10) + 23 - 16$

Finally, do addition and subtraction from left to right:

$(10) + 23 - 16$

$33 - 16 = \mathbf{17}$

GREATEST COMMON FACTOR

The greatest common factor (GCF) of a set of numbers is the largest number that can evenly divide into all of the numbers in the set. To find the GCF of a set, find all of the factors of each number in the set. A factor is a whole number that can be multiplied by another whole number to result in the original number. For example, the number 10 has four factors: 1, 2, 5, and 10. (When listing the factors of a number, remember to include 1 and the number itself.) The largest number that is a factor for each number in the set is the GCF.

Examples

1. Find the greatest common factor of 24 and 18.

   Factors of 24: 1, 2, 3, 4, 6, 8, 12, 24

   Factors of 18: 1, 2, 3, 6, 9, 18

   The greatest common factor is 6.

2. Find the greatest common factor of 121 and 44.

   Since these numbers are larger, it's easier to start with the smaller number when listing factors.

   Factors of 44: 1, 2, 4, 11, 22, 44

   Now, it's not necessary to list all of the factors of 121. Instead, we can eliminate those factors of 44 which do not divide evenly into 121:

   121 is not evenly divisible by 2, 4, 22, or 44 because it is an odd number. This leaves only 1 and 11 as common factors, so the **GCF is 11.**

3. First aid kits are being assembled at a summer camp. A complete first aid kit requires bandages, sutures, and sterilizing swabs, and each of the kits must be identical to other kits. If the camp's total supplies include 52 bandages, 13 sutures, and 39 sterilizing swabs, how many complete first aid kits can be assembled without having any leftover materials?

This problem is asking for the greatest common factor of 52, 13, and 39. The first step is to find all of the factors of the smallest number, 13.

Factors of 13: 1, 13

13 is a prime number, meaning that its only factors are 1 and itself. Next, we check to see if 13 is also a factor of 39 and 52:

$13 \times 2 = 26$

$13 \times 3 = 39$

$13 \times 4 = 52$

We can see that 39 and 52 are both multiples of 13. This means that **13 first aid kits can be made without having any leftover materials.**

4. Elena is making sundaes for her friends. She has 20 scoops of chocolate ice cream and 16 scoops of strawberry. If she wants to make identical sundaes and use all of her ice cream, how many sundaes can she make?

   Arranging things into identical groups with no leftovers is always a tip that the problem calls for finding the greatest common factor. To find the GCF of 16 and 20, the first step is to factor both numbers:

   Factors of 16: 1, 2, 4, 8, 16

   Factors of 20: 1, 2, 4, 5, 10, 20

   From these lists, we see that **4 is the GCF**. Elena can make 4 sundaes, each with 5 scoops of chocolate ice cream and 4 scoops of strawberry. Any other combination would result in leftover ice cream or sundaes that are not identical.

COMPARISON OF RATIONAL NUMBERS

Number comparison problems present numbers in different formats and ask which is larger or smaller, or whether the numbers are equivalent. The important step in solving these problems is to convert the numbers to the same format so that it is easier to see how they compare. If numbers are given in the same format, or after they have been converted, determine which number is smaller or if the numbers are equal. Remember that for negative numbers, higher numbers are actually smaller.

The strategies for comparing numbers can also be used to put numbers in order from least to greatest (or vice versa).

Examples

1. Is $4\frac{3}{4}$ greater than, equal to, or less than $\frac{18}{4}$?

   These numbers are in different formats—one is a mixed fraction and the other is just a fraction. So, the first step is to convert the mixed fraction to a fraction:

   $$4\frac{3}{4} = 4 \times \frac{4}{4} + \frac{3}{4} = \frac{19}{4}$$

   Once the mixed number is converted, it is easier to see that $\frac{19}{4}$ **is greater than** $\frac{18}{4}$.

2. Which of the following numbers has the greatest value: 104.56, 104.5, or 104.6?

These numbers are already in the same format, so the decimal values just need to be compared. Remember that zeros can be added after the decimal without changing the value, so the three numbers can be rewritten as:

104.56

104.50

104.60

From this list, it is clearer to see that **104.60 is the greatest** because 0.60 is larger than 0.50 and 0.56.

3. Is 65% greater than, less than, or equal to $\frac{13}{20}$?

The first step is to convert the numbers into the same format. 65% is the same as $\frac{65}{100}$.

Next, the fractions need to be converted to have the same denominator. It is difficult to compare fractions with different denominators. Using a factor of $\frac{5}{5}$ on the second fraction will give common denominators:

$\frac{13}{20} \times \frac{5}{5} = \frac{65}{100}$.

Now, it is easy to see that **the numbers are equivalent**.

UNITS OF MEASUREMENT

You are expected to memorize some units of measurement. These are given below. When doing unit conversion problems (i.e., when converting one unit to another), find the conversion factor, then apply that factor to the given measurement to find the new units.

You'll be given conversion factors if they're needed for a problem, but it's still good to familiarize yourself with common ones before the test.

Table 3.2. Unit prefixes

PREFIX	SYMBOL	MULTIPLICATION FACTOR
tera	T	1,000,000,000,000
giga	G	1,000,000,000
mega	M	1,000,000
kilo	k	1,000
hecto	h	100
deca	da	10
base unit	--	--
deci	d	0.1
centi	c	0.01
milli	m	0.001
micro	μ	0.0000001
nano	n	0.0000000001
pico	p	0.0000000000001

Table 3.3. Units and conversion factors

DIMENSION	AMERICAN	SI
length	inch/foot/yard/mile	meter
mass	ounce/pound/ton	gram
volume	cup/pint/quart/gallon	liter
force	pound-force	newton
pressure	pound-force per square inch	pascal
work and energy	cal/British thermal unit	joule
temperature	Fahrenheit	kelvin
charge	faraday	coulomb

CONVERSION FACTORS

1 in. = 2.54 cm	1 lb. = 0.454 kg
1 yd. = 0.914 m	1 cal = 4.19 J
1 mi. = 1.61 km	$1°F = \frac{5}{9}(°F - 32°C)$
1 gal. = 3.785 L	$1 cm^3 = 1 mL$
1 oz. = 28.35 g	1 hr = 3600 s

Examples

1. A fence measures 15 ft. long. How many yards long is the fence?

1 yd. = 3 ft.

$\frac{15}{3} =$ **5 yd.**

2. A pitcher can hold 24 cups. How many gallons can it hold?

1 gal. = 16 cups

$\frac{24}{16} =$ **1.5 gallons**

3. A spool of wire holds 144 in. of wire. If Mario has 3 spools, how many feet of wire does he have?

12 in. = 1 ft.

$\frac{144}{12} = 12$ ft.

12 ft. × 3 spools = **36 ft. of wire**

4. A ball rolling across a table travels 6 inches per second. How many feet will it travel in 1 minute?

This problem can be worked in two steps: finding how many inches are covered in 1 minute, and then converting that value to feet. It can also be worked the opposite way, by finding how many feet it travels in 1 second and then converting that to feet traveled per minute. The first method is shown below.

1 min. = 60 sec.

(6 in.)/(sec.) × 60 s = 360 in.

1 ft. = 12 in.

(360 in.)/(12 in.) = **30 ft.**

5. How many millimeters are in 0.5 m?

1 meter = 1000 mm

0.5 meters = **500 mm**

6. A lead ball weighs 38 g. How many kilograms does it weigh?

1 kg = 1000 g

$\frac{38}{1000}$ g = **0.038 kg**

7. How many cubic centimeters are in 10 L?

1 L = 1000 ml

10 L = 1000 ml × 10

10 L = **10,000 ml or cm³**

8. Jennifer's pencil was initially 10 centimeters long. After she sharpened it, it was 9.6 centimeters long. How many millimeters did she lose from her pencil by sharpening it?

1 cm = 10 mm

10 cm − 9.6 cm = 0.4 cm lost

0.4 cm = 10 × .4 mm = **4 mm were lost**

DECIMALS AND FRACTIONS

Adding and Subtracting Decimals

When adding and subtracting decimals, line up the numbers so that the decimals are aligned. You want to subtract the ones place from the ones place, the tenths place from the tenths place, etc.

Examples

1. Find the sum of 17.07 and 2.52.

```
  17.07
+  2.52
= 19.59
```

2. Jeannette has 7.4 gallons of gas in her tank. After driving, she has 6.8 gallons. How many gallons of gas did she use?

```
  7.4
− 6.8
= 0.6 gal.
```

Multiplying and Dividing Decimals

When multiplying decimals, start by multiplying the numbers normally. You can then determine the placement of the decimal point in the result by adding the number of digits after the decimal in each of the numbers you multiplied together.

When dividing decimals, you should move the decimal point in the divisor (the number you're dividing by) until it is a whole. You can then move the decimal in the dividend (the number you're dividing into) the same number of places in the same direction. Finally, divide the new numbers normally to get the correct answer.

Examples

1. What is the product of 0.25 and 1.4?

$25 \times 14 = 350$

There are 2 digits after the decimal in 0.25 and one digit after the decimal in 1.4. Therefore the product should have 3 digits after the decimal: **0.350** is the correct answer.

2. Find $0.8 \div 0.2$.

Change 0.2 to 2 by moving the decimal one space to the right.

Next, move the decimal one space to the right on the dividend. 0.8 becomes 8.

Now, divide 8 by 2. $8 \div 2 = $ **4**

3. Find the quotient when 40 is divided by 0.25.

First, change the divisor to a whole number: 0.25 becomes 25.

Next, change the dividend to match the divisor by moving the decimal two spaces to the right, so 40 becomes 4000.

Now divide: $4000 \div 25 = $ **160**

Working with Fractions

FRACTIONS are made up of two parts: the NUMERATOR, which appears above the bar, and the DENOMINATOR, which is below it. If a fraction is in its SIMPLEST FORM, the numerator and the denominator share no common factors. A fraction with a numerator larger than its denominator is an IMPROPER FRACTION; when the denominator is larger, it's a PROPER FRACTION.

Improper fractions can be converted into proper fractions by dividing the numerator by the denominator. The resulting whole number is placed to the left of the fraction, and the remainder becomes the new numerator; the denominator does not change. The new number is called a MIXED NUMBER because it contains a whole number and a fraction. Mixed numbers can be turned into improper fractions through the reverse process: multiply the whole number by the denominator and add the numerator to get the new numerator.

CONTINUE

Examples

1. Simplify the fraction $\frac{121}{77}$.

    121 and 77 share a common factor of 11. So, if we divide each by 11 we can simplify the fraction:

    $$\frac{121}{77} = \frac{11}{11} \times \frac{11}{7} = \frac{11}{7}$$

2. Convert $\frac{37}{5}$ into a proper fraction.

    Start by dividing the numerator by the denominator:

    $37 \div 5 = 7$ with a remainder of 2

    Now build a mixed number with the whole number and the new numerator:

    $$\frac{37}{5} = 7\frac{2}{5}$$

Multiplying and Dividing Fractions

To multiply fractions, convert any mixed numbers into improper fractions and multiply the numerators together and the denominators together. Reduce to lowest terms if needed.

To divide fractions, first convert any mixed fractions into single fractions. Then, invert the second fraction so that the denominator and numerator are switched. Finally, multiply the numerators together and the denominators together.

> ⚠
>
> Inverting a fraction changes multiplication to division:
> $$\frac{a}{b} \div \frac{c}{d} = \frac{a}{b} \times \frac{d}{c} = \frac{ad}{bc}$$

Examples

1. What is the product of $\frac{1}{12}$ and $\frac{6}{8}$?

    Simply multiply the numerators together and the denominators together, then reduce:

    $$\frac{1}{12} \times \frac{6}{8} = \frac{6}{96} = \frac{1}{16}$$

    Sometimes it's easier to reduce fractions before multiplying if you can:

    $$\frac{1}{12} \times \frac{6}{8} = \frac{1}{12} \times \frac{3}{4} = \frac{3}{48} = \frac{1}{16}$$

2. Find $\frac{7}{8} \div \frac{1}{4}$.

    For a fraction division problem, invert the second fraction and then multiply and reduce:

    $$\frac{7}{8} \div \frac{1}{4} = \frac{7}{8} \times \frac{4}{1} = \frac{28}{8} = \frac{7}{2}$$

> ⚠
>
> The quotient is the result you get when you divide two numbers.

3. What is the quotient of $\frac{2}{5} \div 1\frac{1}{5}$?

    This is a fraction division problem, so the first step is to convert the mixed number to an improper fraction:

    $$1\frac{1}{5} = \frac{5 \times 1}{5} + \frac{1}{5} = \frac{6}{5}$$

Now, divide the fractions. Remember to invert the second fraction, and then multiply normally:

$$\frac{2}{5} \div \frac{6}{5} = \frac{2}{5} \times \frac{5}{6} = \frac{10}{30} = \mathbf{\frac{1}{3}}$$

4. A recipe calls for $\frac{1}{4}$ cup of sugar. If 8.5 batches of the recipe are needed, how many cups of sugar will be used?

   This is a fraction multiplication problem: $\frac{1}{4} \times 8\frac{1}{2}$.

   First, we need to convert the mixed number into a proper fraction:

   $$8\frac{1}{2} = \frac{8 \times 2}{2} + \frac{1}{2} = \frac{17}{2}$$

   Now, multiply the fractions across the numerators and denominators, and then reduce:

   $$\frac{1}{4} \times 8\frac{1}{2} = \frac{1}{4} \times \frac{17}{2} = \mathbf{\frac{17}{8}} \textbf{ cups of sugar}$$

Adding and Subtracting Fractions

Adding and subtracting fractions requires a COMMON DENOMINATOR. To find the common denominator, you can multiply each fraction by the number 1. With fractions, any number over itself (e.g., $\frac{5}{5}$, $\frac{12}{12}$, etc.) is equivalent to 1, so multiplying by such a fraction can change the denominator without changing the value of the fraction. Once the denominators are the same, the numerators can be added or subtracted.

To add mixed numbers, you can first add the whole numbers and then the fractions. To subtract mixed numbers, convert each number to an improper fraction, then subtract the numerators.

Examples

1. Simplify the expression $\frac{2}{3} - \frac{1}{5}$.

   First, multiply each fraction by a factor of 1 to get a common denominator. How do you know which factor of 1 to use? Look at the other fraction and use the number found in that denominator:

   $$\frac{2}{3} - \frac{1}{5} = \frac{2}{3}\left(\frac{5}{5}\right) - \frac{1}{5}\left(\frac{3}{3}\right) = \frac{10}{15} - \frac{3}{15}$$

   Once the fractions have a common denominator, simply subtract the numerators:

   $$\frac{10}{15} - \frac{3}{15} = \mathbf{\frac{7}{15}}$$

2. Find $2\frac{1}{3} - \frac{3}{2}$.

   This is a fraction subtraction problem with a mixed number, so the first step is to convert the mixed number to an improper fraction:

   $$2\frac{1}{3} = \frac{2 \times 3}{3} + \frac{1}{3} = \frac{7}{3}$$

The phrase *simplify the expression* just means you need to perform all the operations in the expression.

Next, convert each fraction so they share a common denominator:

$$\frac{7}{3} \times \frac{2}{2} = \frac{14}{6}$$

$$\frac{3}{2} \times \frac{3}{3} = \frac{9}{6}$$

Now, subtract the fractions by subtracting the numerators:

$$\frac{14}{6} - \frac{9}{6} = \frac{5}{6}$$

3. Find the sum of $\frac{9}{16}$, $\frac{1}{2}$, and $\frac{7}{4}$.

For this fraction addition problem, we need to find a common denominator. Notice that 2 and 4 are both factors of 16, so 16 can be the common denominator:

$$\frac{1}{2} \times \frac{8}{8} = \frac{8}{16}$$

$$\frac{7}{4} \times \frac{4}{4} = \frac{28}{16}$$

$$\frac{9}{16} + \frac{8}{16} + \frac{28}{16} = \frac{45}{16}$$

4. Sabrina has $\frac{2}{3}$ of a can of red paint. Her friend Amos has $\frac{1}{6}$ of a can. How much red paint do they have combined?

To add fractions, make sure that they have a common denominator. Since 3 is a factor of 6, 6 can be the common denominator:

$$\frac{2}{3} \times \frac{2}{2} = \frac{4}{6}$$

Now, add the numerators:

$$\frac{4}{6} + \frac{1}{6} = \frac{5}{6} \text{ of a can}$$

Converting Fractions to Decimals

Calculators are not allowed on the TEAS V, which can make handling fractions and decimals intimidating for many test takers. However, there are several techniques you can use to help you convert between the two forms.

The first thing to do is simply memorize common decimals and their fractional equivalents; a list of these is given in Table 3.4. With these values, it's possible to convert more complicated fractions as well. For example, $\frac{2}{5}$ is just $\frac{1}{5}$ multiplied by 2, so $\frac{2}{5} = 0.2 \times 2 = 0.4$.

Table 3.4. Common decimals and fractions

FRACTION	DECIMAL
$\frac{1}{2}$	0.5
$\frac{1}{3}$	$0.\overline{33}$
$\frac{1}{4}$	0.25
$\frac{1}{5}$	0.2
$\frac{1}{6}$	$0.1\overline{66}$
$\frac{1}{7}$	$0.\overline{142857}$
$\frac{1}{8}$	0.125
$\frac{1}{9}$	$0.\overline{11}$
$\frac{1}{10}$	0.1

Knowledge of common decimal equivalents to fractions can also help you estimate. This skill can be particularly helpful on multiple-choice tests like the TEAS, where excluding incorrect answers can be just as helpful as knowing how to find the right one. For example, to find $\frac{5}{8}$ in decimal form for an answer, you can eliminate any answers less than 0.5 because $\frac{4}{8}$ = 0.5. You may also know that $\frac{6}{8}$ is the same as $\frac{3}{4}$ or 0.75, so anything above 0.75 can be eliminated as well.

Another helpful trick can be used if the denominator is easily divisible by 100: in the fraction $\frac{9}{20}$, you know 20 goes into 100 five times, so you can multiply the top and bottom by 5 to get $\frac{45}{100}$ or 0.45.

If none of these techniques work, you'll need to find the decimal by dividing the denominator by the numerator using long division.

Examples

1. Write $\frac{8}{18}$ as a decimal.

The first step here is to simplify the fraction:
$$\frac{8}{18} = \frac{4}{9}$$
Now it's clear that the fraction is a multiple of $\frac{1}{9}$, so you can easily find the decimal using a value you already know:
$$\frac{4}{9} = \frac{1}{9} \times 4 = 0.\overline{11} \times 4 = \mathbf{0.\overline{44}}$$

2. Write the fraction $\frac{3}{16}$ as a decimal.

None of the tricks above will work for this fraction, so you need to do long division:

CONTINUE

```
        0.1875
16 ) 3.0000
    − 1 6
      1 40
    − 1 28
        120
    −   112
          80
    −     80
           0
```

The decimal will go in front of the answer, so now you know that $\frac{3}{16}$ = **0.1875**.

Converting Decimals to Fractions

Converting a decimal into a fraction is more straightforward than the reverse process is. To convert a decimal, simply use the numbers that come after the decimal as the numerator in the fraction. The denominator will be a power of 10 that matches the place value for the original decimal. For example, the numerator for 0.46 would be 100 because the last number is in the tenths place; likewise, the denominator for 0.657 would be 1000 because the last number is in the thousandths place. Once this fraction has been set up, all that's left is to simplify it.

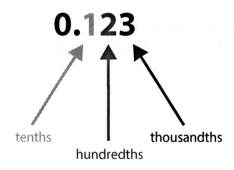

Figure 3.1. Simplified decimal

Example

Convert 0.45 into a fraction.

The last number in the decimal is in the hundredths place, so we can easily set up a fraction:

$0.45 = \frac{45}{100}$

The next step is to simply reduce the fraction down to the lowest common denominator. Here, both 45 and 100 are divisible by 5: 45 divided by 5 is 9, and 100 divided by 5 is 20. Therefore, you're left with:

$\frac{45}{100} = \frac{9}{20}$

RATIOS

A **RATIO** tells you how many of one thing exists in relation to the number of another thing. Unlike fractions, ratios do not give a part relative to a whole; instead, they compare two values. For example, if you have 3 apples and 4 oranges, the ratio of apples to oranges is 3 to 4. Ratios can be written using words (3 to 4), fractions $\left(\frac{3}{4}\right)$, or colons (3:4).

In order to work with ratios, it's helpful to rewrite them as a fraction expressing a part to a whole. For example, in the example above you have 7 total pieces of fruit, so the fraction of your fruit that are apples is $\frac{3}{7}$, and oranges make up $\frac{4}{7}$ of your fruit collection.

One last important thing to consider when working with ratios is the units of the values being compared. On the TEAS, you may be asked to rewrite a ratio using the same units on both sides. For example, you might have to rewrite the ratio 3 minutes to 7 seconds as 180 seconds to 7 seconds.

Examples

1. There are 90 voters in a room, and each is either a Democrat or a Republican. The ratio of Democrats to Republicans is 5:4. How many Republicans are there?

    We know that there are 5 Democrats for every 4 Republicans in the room, which means for every 9 people, 4 are Republicans.

    $5 + 4 = 9$

    Fraction of Democrats: $\frac{5}{9}$

    Fraction of Republicans: $\frac{4}{9}$

    If $\frac{4}{9}$ of the 90 voters are Republicans, then:

    $\frac{4}{9} \times 90 =$ **40 voters are Republicans**

2. The ratio of students to teachers in a school is 15:1. If there are 38 teachers, how many students attend the school?

    To solve this ratio problem, we can simply multiply both sides of the ratio by the desired value to find the number of students that correspond to having 38 teachers:

    $\frac{15 \text{ students}}{1 \text{ teacher}} \times 38 \text{ teachers} = 570 \text{ students}$

    The school has **570 students**.

PROPORTIONS

A **PROPORTION** is an equation which states that 2 ratios are equal. Proportions are usually written as 2 fractions joined by an equal sign $\left(\frac{a}{b} = \frac{c}{d}\right)$, but they can also be written using colons ($a : b :: c : d$). Note that in a proportion, the units must be the same in both numerators and in both denominators.

Often you will be given 3 of the values in a proportion and asked to find the 4th. In these types of problems, you can solve for the missing variable by cross-multiplying—multiply the numerator of each fraction by the denominator of the other to get an equation with no fractions as shown below. You can then solve the equation using basic algebra. (For more on solving basic equations, see *Algebraic Expressions and Equations*.)

$$\frac{a}{b} = \frac{c}{d} \rightarrow ad = bc$$

You'll see ratios written using fractions and colons on the test.

Examples

1. A train traveling 120 miles takes 3 hours to get to its destination. How long will it take for the train to travel 180 miles?

   Start by setting up the proportion:

   $$\frac{120 \text{ miles}}{3 \text{ hours}} = \frac{180 \text{ miles}}{x \text{ hours}}$$

   Note that it doesn't matter which value is placed in the numerator or denominator, as long as it is the same on both sides. Now, solve for the missing quantity through cross-multiplication:

   120 miles × x hours = 3 hours × 180 miles

   Now solve the equation:

   $$x \text{ hours} = \frac{(3 \text{ hours}) \times (180 \text{ miles})}{120 \text{ miles}}$$

   x = 4.5 hours

2. One acre of wheat requires 500 gallons of water. How many acres can be watered with 2600 gallons?

   Set up the equation:

   $$\frac{1 \text{ acre}}{500 \text{ gal.}} = \frac{x \text{ acres}}{2600 \text{ gal.}}$$

   Then solve for x:

   $$x \text{ acres} = \frac{1 \text{ acre} \times 2600 \text{ gal.}}{500 \text{ gal.}}$$

   $x = \frac{26}{5}$ or **5.2 acres**

3. If 35 : 5 :: 49 : x, find x.

   This problem presents two equivalent ratios that can be set up in a fraction equation:

   $$\frac{35}{5} = \frac{49}{x}$$

   You can then cross-multiply to solve for x:

   $35x = 49 \times 5$

   $x = 7$

PERCENTAGES

A **PERCENT** is the ratio of a part to the whole. Questions may give the part and the whole and ask for the percent, or give the percent and the whole and ask for the part, or give the part and the percent and ask for the value of the whole. The equation for percentages can be rearranged to solve for any of these:

$$percent = \frac{part}{whole}$$

$$part = whole \times percent$$

$$whole = \frac{part}{percent}$$

In the equations above, the percent should always be expressed as a decimal. In order to convert a decimal into a percentage value, simply multiply it by 100. So, if you've read 5 pages (the part) of a 10-page article (the whole), you've read $\frac{5}{10} = 0.5$ or 50%. (The percent sign (%) is used once the decimal has been multiplied by 100.)

Note that when solving these problems, the units for the part and the whole should be the same. If you're reading a book, saying you've read 5 pages out of 15 chapters doesn't make any sense.

Examples

1. 45 is 15% of what number?

   Set up the appropriate equation and solve. Don't forget to change 15% to a decimal value:

   $$whole = \frac{part}{percent} = \frac{45}{0.15} = \textbf{300}$$

2. Jim spent 30% of his paycheck at the fair. He spent $15 for a hat, $30 for a shirt, and $20 playing games. How much was his check? (Round to nearest dollar.)

   Set up the appropriate equation and solve:

   $$whole = \frac{part}{percent} = \frac{15 + 30 + 20}{.30} = \textbf{\$217.00}$$

3. What percent of 65 is 39?

   Set up the equation and solve:

   $$percent = \frac{part}{whole} = \frac{39}{65} = \textbf{0.6 or 60\%}$$

4. Greta and Max sell cable subscriptions. In a given month, Greta sells 45 subscriptions and Max sells 51. If 240 total subscriptions were sold in that month, what percent were not sold by Greta or Max?

   You can use the information in the question to figure out what percentage of subscriptions were sold by Max and Greta:

   $$percent = \frac{part}{whole} = \frac{(51 + 45)}{240} = \frac{96}{240} = 0.4 \text{ or } 40\%$$

However, the question asks how many subscriptions weren't sold by Max or Greta. If they sold 40%, then the other salespeople sold 100% − 40% = **60%**.

5. Grant needs to score 75% on an exam. If the exam has 45 questions, at least how many does he need to answer correctly?

Set up the equation and solve. Remember to convert 75% to a decimal value:

part = *whole* × *percent* = 45 × 0.75 = 33.75, so he needs to answer at least **34 questions correctly**.

⚠

Words that indicate a percent change problem:
- discount
- markup
- sale
- increase
- decrease

PERCENT CHANGE

PERCENT CHANGE problems will ask you to calculate how much a given quantity changed. The problems are solved in a similar way to regular percent problems, except that instead of using the *part* you'll use the *amount of change*. Note that the sign of the *amount of change* is important: if the original amount has increased the change will be positive, and if it has decreased the change will be negative. Again, in the equations below the percent is a decimal value; you need to multiply by 100 to get the actual percentage.

$$percent\ change = \frac{amount\ of\ change}{original\ amount}$$

$$amount\ of\ change = original\ amount \times percent\ change$$

$$original\ amount = \frac{amount\ of\ change}{percent\ change}$$

⚠

The same steps shown here can be used to find percent change for problems that don't involve money as well.

Examples

1. A computer software retailer marks up its games by 40% above the wholesale price when it sells them to customers. Find the price of a game for a customer if the game costs the retailer $25.

Set up the appropriate equation and solve:

amount of change = original amount × percent change = 25 × 0.4 = 10

If the amount of change is 10, that means the store adds a markup of $10, so the game costs:

$25 + $10 = **$35**

2. A golf shop pays its wholesaler $40 for a certain club, and then sells it to a golfer for $75. What is the markup rate?

First, calculate the amount of change:

75 − 40 = 35

Now you can set up the equation and solve. (Note that *markup rate* is another way of saying *percent change*):

$$percent\ change = \frac{amount\ of\ change}{original\ amount} = \frac{35}{40} = 0.875 = \textbf{87.5\%}$$

3. A store charges a 40% markup on the shoes it sells. How much did the store pay for a pair of shoes purchased by a customer for $63?

You're solving for the original price, but it's going to be tricky because you don't know the amount of change; you only know the new price. To solve, you need to create an expression for the amount of change:

If *original amount* = x

Then *amount of change* = $63 - x$

Now you can plug these values into your equation:

$$original\ amount = \frac{amount\ of\ change}{percent\ change}$$

$$x = \frac{63 - x}{0.4}$$

The last step is to solve for x:

$$0.4x = 63 - x$$

$$1.4x = 63$$

$$x = 45$$

The store paid **$45 for the shoes**.

4. An item originally priced at $55 is marked 25% off. What is the sale price?

You've been asked to find the sale price, which means you need to solve for the amount of change first:

amount of change = *original amount* × *percent change* →
$$55 \times 0.25 = 13.75$$

Using this amount, you can find the new price. Because it's on sale, we know the item will cost less than the original price:

$$55 - 13.75 = 41.25$$

The sale price is $41.25.

5. James wants to put in an 18 foot by 51 foot garden in his backyard. If he does, it will reduce the size of this yard by 24%. What will be the area of the remaining yard?

This problem is tricky because you need to figure out what each number in the problem stands for. 24% is obviously the percent change, but what about the measurements in feet? If you multiply these values you get the area of the garden (for more on area see *Area and Perimeter*):

$$18\ ft. \times 51\ ft. = 918\ ft.^2$$

This 918 ft.^{2} is the amount of change—it's how much smaller the lawn is. Now we can set up an equation:

$$original\ amount = \frac{amount\ of\ change}{percent\ change} = \frac{918}{.24} = 3825$$

If the original lawn was 3825 ft.^{2} and the garden is 918 ft.^{2}, then the remaining area is

$$3825 - 918 = 2907$$

The remaining lawn covers **2907 ft.^{2}**

PROBABILITIES

A **PROBABILITY** is found by dividing the number of desired outcomes by the number of total possible outcomes. As with percentages, a probability is the ratio of a part to a whole, with the whole being the total number of things that could happen, and the part being the number of those things that would be considered a success. Probabilities can be written using percentages (40%), decimals (0.4), fractions $\left(\frac{2}{5}\right)$, or in words (probability is 2 in 5).

$$probability = \frac{desired\ outcomes}{total\ possible\ outcomes}$$

Examples

1. A bag holds 3 blue marbles, 5 green marbles, and 7 red marbles. If you pick one marble from the bag, what is the probability it will be blue?

   Because there are 15 marbles in the bag (3 + 5 + 7), the total number of possible outcomes is 15. Of those outcomes, 3 would be blue marbles, which is the desired outcome. With that information you can set up an equation:

   $$probability = \frac{desired\ outcomes}{total\ possible\ outcomes} = \frac{3}{15} = \frac{1}{5}$$

   The probability is **1 in 5 or 0.2 that a blue marble is picked.**

2. A bag contains 75 balls. If the probability that a ball selected from the bag will be red is 0.6, how many red balls are in the bag?

   Because you're solving for desired outcomes (the number of red balls), first you need to rearrange the equation:

   $$probability = \frac{desired\ outcomes}{total\ possible\ outcomes} \rightarrow$$
   $$desired\ outcomes = probability \times total\ possible\ outcomes$$

   In this problem, the desired outcome is choosing a red ball, and the total possible outcomes are represented by the 75 total balls.

   $$desired\ outcomes = 0.6 \times 75 = 45$$

   There are **45 red balls in the bag.**

3. A theater has 230 seats: 75 seats are in the orchestra area, 100 seats are in the mezzanine, and 55 seats are in the balcony. If a ticket is selected at random, what is the probability that it will be for either a mezzanine or balcony seat?

   In this problem, the desired outcome is a seat in either the mezzanine or balcony area, and the total possible outcomes are represented by the 230 total seats, so the equation should be written as:

   $$probability = \frac{desired\ outcomes}{total\ possible\ outcomes} = \frac{100 + 55}{230} = \textbf{0.67}$$

4. The probability of selecting a student whose name begins with the letter *s* from a school attendance log is 7%. If there are 42 students whose names begin with *s* enrolled at the school, how many students attend the school?

Because you're solving for total possible outcomes (total number of students), first you need to rearrange the equation:

$$total\ possible\ outcomes = \frac{desired\ outcomes}{probability}$$

In this problem, you are given a probability (7% or 0.07) and the number of desired outcomes (42). These can be plugged into the equation to solve:

$$total\ possible\ outcomes = \frac{42}{0.07} = \textbf{600 students}$$

4

ALGEBRA

ALGEBRAIC EXPRESSIONS AND EQUATIONS

Algebraic expressions and equations include a VARIABLE, which is a letter standing in for a number. These expressions and equations are made up of TERMS, which are groups of numbers and variables (e.g., $2xy$). An EXPRESSION is simply a set of terms (e.g., $3x + 2xy$), while an EQUATION includes an equal sign (e.g., $3x + 2xy = 17$). When simplifying expressions or solving algebraic equations, you'll need to use many different mathematical properties and operations, including addition, subtraction, multiplication, division, exponents, roots, distribution, and the order of operations.

Evaluating Algebraic Expressions

To evaluate an algebraic expression, simply plug the given value(s) in for the appropriate variable(s) in the expression.

Example

Evaluate $2x + 6y - 3z$ if , $x = 2$, $y = 4$, and $z = -3$.

Plug in each number for the correct variable and simplify:

$2x + 6y - 3z = 2(2) + 6(4) - 3(-3) = 4 + 24 + 9 = \mathbf{37}$

Adding and Subtracting Terms

Only LIKE TERMS, which have the exact same variable(s), can be added or subtracted. CONSTANTS are numbers without variables attached, and those can be added and subtracted together as well. When simplifying an expression, like terms should be added or subtracted so that no individual group of variables occurs in more than one term. For example, the expression $5x + 6xy$ is in its simplest form, while $5x + 6xy - 11xy$ is not because the term xy appears more than once.

Example

Simplify the expression $5xy + 7y + 2yz + 11xy - 5yz$.

Start by grouping together like terms:

$(5xy + 11xy) + (2yz - 5yz) + 7y$

Now you can add together each set of like terms:

$16xy + 7y - 3yz$

Multiplying and Dividing Terms

To multiply a single term by another, simply multiply the coefficients and then multiply the variables. Remember that when multiplying variables with exponents, those exponents are added together. For example, $(x^5y)(x^3y^4) = x^8y^5$.

When multiplying a term by a set of terms inside parentheses, you need to DISTRIBUTE to each term inside the parentheses as shown below:

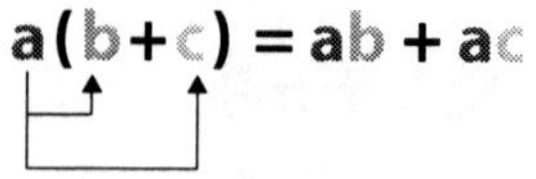

$$a(b+c) = ab + ac$$

Figure 4.1. Distribution

When variables occur in both the numerator and denominator of a fraction, they cancel each other out. So, a fraction with variables in its simplest form will not have the same variable on the top and bottom.

Examples

1. Simplify the expression $(3x^4y^2z)(2y^4z^5)$.

    Multiply the coefficients and variables together:

    $3 \times 2 = 6$

    $y^2 \times y^4 = y^6$

    $z \times z^5 = z^6$

    Now put all the terms back together:

    $6x^4y^6z^6$

2. Simplify the expression: $(2y^2)(y^3 + 2xy^2z + 4z)$

    Multiply each term inside the parentheses by the term $2y^2$:

    $(2y^2)(y^3 + 2xy^2z + 4z)$

    $(2y^2 \times y^3) + (2y^2 \times 2xy^2z) \times (2y^2 \times 4z)$

    $2y^5 + 4xy^4z + 8y^2z$

3. Simplify the expression: $(5x + 2)(3x + 3)$

    Use the acronym FOIL—First, Outer, Inner, Last—to multiply the terms:

    First: $5x \times 3x = 15x^2$

    Outer: $5x \times 3 = 15x$

Inner: $2 \times 3x = 6x$

Last: $2 \times 3 = 6$

Now combine like terms:

$15x^2 + 21x + 6$

4. Simplify the expression: $\dfrac{2x^4y^3z}{8x^2z^2}$

Simplify by looking at each variable and crossing out those that appear in the numerator and denominator:

$\dfrac{2}{8} = \dfrac{1}{4}$

$\dfrac{x^4}{x^2} = \dfrac{x^2}{1}$

$\dfrac{z}{z^2} = \dfrac{1}{z}$

$\dfrac{2x^4y^3z}{8x^2z^2} = \dfrac{x^2y^3}{4z}$

⚠️ When multiplying terms, add the exponents. When dividing, subtract the exponents.

Solving Equations

To solve an equation, you need to manipulate the terms on each side to isolate the variable, meaning if you want to find x, you have to get the x alone on one side of the equal sign. To do this, you'll need to use many of the tools discussed above: you might need to distribute, divide, add, or subtract like terms, or find common denominators.

Think of each side of the equation as the two sides of a see-saw. As long as the two people on each end weigh the same amount the see-saw will be balanced: if you have a 120 lb. person on each end, the see-saw is balanced. Giving each of them a 10 lb. rock to hold changes the weight on each end, but the see-saw itself stays balanced. Equations work the same way: you can add, subtract, multiply, or divide whatever you want as long as you do the same thing to both sides.

Most equations you'll see on the TEAS can be solved using the same basic steps:

1. Distribute to get rid of parentheses.
2. Use the least common denominator to get rid of fractions.
3. Add/subtract like terms on either side.
4. Add/subtract so that constants appear on only one side of the equation.
5. Multiply/divide to isolate the variable.

Examples

1. Solve for x: $25x + 12 = 62$

   This equation has no parentheses, fractions, or like terms on the same side, so you can start by subtracting 12 from both sides of the equation:

   $25x + 12 = 62$

$(25x + 12) - 12 = 62 - 12$

$25x = 50$

Now, divide by 25 to isolate the variable:

$\frac{25x}{25} = \frac{50}{25}$

$\boldsymbol{x = 2}$

2. Solve the following equation for x: $2x - 4(2x + 3) = 24$

   Start by distributing to get rid of the parentheses (don't forget to distribute the negative):

   $2x - 4(2x + 3) = 24 \rightarrow$

   $2x - 8x - 12 = 24$

   There are no fractions, so now you can join like terms:

   $2x - 8x - 12 = 24 \rightarrow$

   $-6x - 12 = 24$

   Now add 12 to both sides and divide by −6.

   $-6x - 12 = 24$

   $(-6x - 12) + 12 = 24 + 12 \rightarrow$

   $-6x = 36 \rightarrow$

   $\frac{-6x}{-6} = \frac{36}{-6}$

   $\boldsymbol{x = -6}$

3. Solve the following equation for x: $\frac{x}{3} + \frac{1}{2} = \frac{x}{6} - \frac{5}{12}$

   Start by multiplying by the least common denominator to get rid of the fractions:

   $\frac{x}{3} + \frac{1}{2} = \frac{x}{6} - \frac{5}{12} \rightarrow$

   $12\left(\frac{x}{3} + \frac{1}{2}\right) = 12\left(\frac{x}{6} - \frac{5}{12}\right) \rightarrow$

   $4x + 6 = 2x - 5$

   Now you can isolate x:

   $(4x + 6) - 6 = (2x - 5) - 6 \rightarrow$

   $4x = 2x - 11 \rightarrow$

   $(4x) - 2x = (2x - 11) - 2x \rightarrow$

   $2x = -11$

   $\boldsymbol{x = -\frac{11}{2}}$

4. Find the value of x: $2(x + y) - 7x = 14x + 3$

   This equation looks more difficult because it has 2 variables, but you can use the same steps to solve for x. First, distribute to get rid of the parentheses and combine like terms:

   $2(x + y) - 7x = 14x + 3 \rightarrow$

   $2x + 2y - 7x = 14x + 3 \rightarrow$

   $-5x + 2y = 14x + 3$

   Now you can move the x terms to one side and everything

else to the other, and then divide to isolate x:

$$-5x + 2y = 14x + 3 \rightarrow$$

$$-19x = -2y + 3 \rightarrow$$

$$x = \frac{2y - 3}{19}$$

INEQUALITIES

INEQUALITIES look like equations, except that instead of having an equal sign, they have one of the following symbols:

> Greater than: The expression left of the symbol is larger than the expression on the right.

< Less than: The expression left of the symbol is smaller than the expression on the right.

≥ Greater than or equal to: The expression left of the symbol is larger than or equal to the expression on the right.

≤ Less than or equal to: The expression left of the symbol is less than or equal to the expression on the right.

Inequalities are solved like linear and algebraic equations. The only difference is that the symbol must be reversed when both sides of the equation are multiplied by a negative number.

Example

Solve for x: $-7x + 2 < 6 - 5x$

Collect like terms on each side as you would for a regular equation:

$$-7x + 2 < 6 - 5x \rightarrow$$

$$-2x < 4$$

The direction of the sign switches when you divide by a negative number:

$$-2x < 4 \rightarrow$$

$$x > -2$$

See *Solving Equations* for step-by-step instructions on solving basic equations.

ABSOLUTE VALUE

The ABSOLUTE VALUE of a number (represented by the symbol $|x|$) is its distance from zero, not its value. For example, $|3| = 3$, and $|-3| = 3$ because both 3 and −3 are three units from zero. The absolute value of a number is always positive.

Equations with absolute values will have two answers, so you need to set up two equations. The first is simply the equation with the absolute value symbol removed. For the second equation, isolate the absolute value on one side of the equation and multiply the other side of the equation by −1.

Examples

1. Solve for x: $|2x - 3| = x + 1$

   Set up the first equation by removing the absolute value symbol, then solve for x:

   $|2x - 3| = x + 1$

   $2x - 3 = x + 1$

   $x = 4$

   For the second equation, remove the absolute value and multiply by -1:

   $|2x - 3| = x + 1 \rightarrow$

   $2x - 3 = -(x + 1) \rightarrow$

   $2x - 3 = -x - 1 \rightarrow$

   $3x = 2$

   $x = \frac{2}{3}$

   Both answers are correct, so the complete answer is **$x = 4$ or $\frac{2}{3}$.**

2. Solve for y: $2|y + 4| = 10$

   Set up the first equation:

   $2(y + 4) = 10 \rightarrow$

   $y + 4 = 5 \rightarrow$

   $y = 1$

   Set up the second equation. Remember to isolate the absolute value before multiplying by -1:

   $2|y + 4| = 10 \rightarrow$

   $|y + 4| = 5 \rightarrow$

   $y + 4 = -5$

   $y = -9$

   $y = 1$ or -9

SOLVING WORD PROBLEMS

Any of the math concepts discussed here can be turned into a word problem, and you'll likely see word problems in various forms throughout the test. (In fact, you may have noticed that several examples in the ratio and proportion sections were word problems.)

The most important step in solving any word problem is to read the entire problem before beginning to solve it: one of the most commonly made mistakes on word problems is providing an answer to a question that wasn't asked. Also, remember that not all of the information given in a problem is always needed to solve it.

When working multiple-choice word problems like those on the TEAS V, it's important to check your answer. Many of the incorrect choices will be answers that test takers arrive at by making common mistakes. So even if an answer you calculated is given as an answer choice, that doesn't necessarily mean you've worked the problem correctly—you have to check your own work to make sure.

General Steps for Word Problem Solving

Step 1: Read the entire problem and determine what the question is asking for.

Step 2: List all of the given data and define the variables.

Step 3: Determine the formula(s) needed or set up equations from the information in the problem.

Step 4: Solve.

Step 5: Check your answer. (Is the amount too large or small? Are the answers in the correct unit of measure?)

Key Words

Word problems generally contain key words that can help you determine what math processes may be required in order to solve them.

- Addition: added, combined, increased by, in all, total, perimeter, sum, and more than
- Subtraction: how much more, less than, fewer than, exceeds, difference, and decreased
- Multiplication: of, times, area, and product
- Division: distribute, share, average, per, out of, percent, and quotient
- Equals: is, was, are, amounts to, and were

Basic Word Problems

A word problem in algebra is just an equation or a set of equations described using words. Your task when solving these problems is to turn the "story" of the problem into mathematical equations.

Examples

1. A store owner bought a case of 48 backpacks for $476.00. He sold 17 of the backpacks in his store for $18 each, and the rest were sold to a school for $15 each. What was the salesman's profit?

   Start by listing all the data and defining the variable:

   total number of backpacks = 48

   cost of backpacks = $476.00

   backpacks sold in store at price of $18 = 17

   backpacks sold to school at a price of $15 = 48 − 17 = 31

   total profit = x

   Now set up an equation:

   total profit = *income* − *cost* = (306 + 465) − 476 = 295

   The store owner made a profit of **$295**.

⚠

Converting units can often help you avoid operations with fractions when dealing with time.

2. Thirty students in Mr. Joyce's room are working on projects over 2 days. The first day, he gave them $\frac{3}{5}$ hour to work. On the second day, he gave them half as much time as the first day. How much time did each student have to work on the project?

Start by listing all the data and defining your variables. Note that the number of students, while given in the problem, is not needed to find the answer:

time on 1st day = $\frac{3}{5}$ hr. = 36 min.

time on 2nd day = $\frac{1}{2}$(36) = 18 min.

total time = x

Now set up the equation and solve:

total time = time on 1st day + time on 2nd day

$x = 36 + 18 = 54$

The students had **54 minutes** to work on the projects.

Distance Word Problems

Distance word problems involve something traveling at a constant or average speed. Whenever you read a problem that involves *how fast*, *how far*, or *for how long*, you should think of the distance equation, $d = rt$, where d stands for distance, r for rate (speed), and t for time.

These problems can be solved by setting up a grid with d, r, and t along the top and each moving object on the left. When setting up the grid, make sure the units are consistent. For example, if the distance is in meters and the time is in seconds, the rate should be meters per second.

Examples

1. Will drove from his home to the airport at an average speed of 30 mph. He then boarded a helicopter and flew to the hospital with an average speed of 60 mph. The entire distance was 150 miles, and the trip took 3 hours. Find the distance from the airport to the hospital.

The first step is to set up a table and fill in a value for each variable:

Table 4.1. Drive Time

	d	r	t
driving	d	30	t
flying	$150 - d$	60	$3 - t$

You can now set up equations for driving and flying. The first row gives the equation $d = 30t$, and the second row gives the equation $150 - d = 60(3 - t)$.

Next, you can solve this system of equations. Start by substituting for d in the second equation:

$d = 30t$

$150 - d = 60(3 - t) \rightarrow 150 - 30t = 60(3 - t)$

Now solve for t:

$150 - 30t = 180 - 60t$

$-30 = -30t$

$1 = t$

Although you've solved for t, you're not done yet. Notice that the problem asks for distance. So, you need to solve for d: what the problem asked for. It does not ask for time, but the time is needed to solve the problem.

Driving: $30t = 30$ miles

Flying: $150 - d = 120$ miles

The distance from the airport to the hospital is **120 miles**.

2. Two cyclists start at the same time from opposite ends of a course that is 45 miles long. One cyclist is riding at 14 mph and the second cyclist is riding at 16 mph. How long after they begin will they meet?

First, set up the table. The variable for time will be the same for each, because they will have been on the road for the same amount of time when they meet:

Table 4.2. Cyclist Times

	d	r	t
Cyclist #1	d	14	t
Cyclist #2	$45 - d$	16	t

Next set up two equations:

Cyclist #1: $d = 14t$

Cyclist #2: $45 - d = 16t$

Now substitute and solve:

$d = 14t$

$45 - d = 16t \rightarrow 45 - 14t = 16t$

$45 = 30t$

$t = 1.5$

They will meet **1.5 hr.** after they begin.

Work Problems

WORK PROBLEMS involve situations where several people or machines are doing work at different rates. Your task is usually to figure out how long it will take these people or machines to complete a task while working together. The trick to doing work problems is to figure out how much of the project each person or machine completes in the same unit of time. For example, you might calculate how much of a wall a person can paint in 1 hour, or how many boxes an assembly line can pack in 1 minute.

Once you know that, you can set up an equation to solve for the total time. This equation usually has a form similar to the equation for distance, but here *work = rate × time*.

The TEAS will give you most formulas you need to work problems, but it won't give you the formulas for percent change or work problems.

Examples

⚠ See *Adding and Subtracting Fractions* for step-by-step instruction on operations with fractions.

1. Bridget can clean an entire house in 12 hours while her brother Tom takes 8 hours. How long would it take for Bridget and Tom to clean 2 houses together?

   Start by figuring out how much of a house each sibling can clean on his or her own. Bridget can clean the house in 12 hours, so she can clean $\frac{1}{12}$ of the house in an hour. Using the same logic, Tom can clean $\frac{1}{8}$ of a house in an hour.

   By adding these values together, you get the fraction of the house they can clean together in an hour:

   $$\frac{1}{12} + \frac{1}{8} = \frac{5}{24}$$

   They can do $\frac{5}{24}$ of the job per hour.

   Now set up variables and an equation to solve:

   t = time spent cleaning (in hours)

   h = number of houses cleaned = 2

   work = *rate* × *time*

   $$h = \frac{5}{24}t \rightarrow$$

   $$2 = \frac{5}{24}t \rightarrow$$

   $$t = \frac{48}{5} = \mathbf{9\frac{3}{5}} \textbf{ hours}$$

2. Farmer Dan needs to water his cornfield. One hose can water a field 1.25 times faster than a second hose. When both hoses are opened, they water the field in 5 hours. How long would it take to water the field if only the second hose is used?

   In this problem you don't know the exact time, but you can still find the hourly rate as a variable:

   The first hose completes the job in f hours, so it waters $\frac{1}{f}$ field per hour. The slower hose waters the field in 1.25f, so it waters the field in $\frac{1}{1.25f}$ hours. Together, they take 5 hours to water the field, so they water $\frac{1}{5}$ of the field per hour.

   Now you can set up the equations and solve:

   $$\frac{1}{f} + \frac{1}{1.25f} = \frac{1}{5} \rightarrow$$

   $$1.25f\left(\frac{1}{f} + \frac{1}{1.25f}\right) = 1.25f\left(\frac{1}{5}\right) \rightarrow$$

   $$1.25 + 1 = 0.25f$$

   $$2.25 = 0.25f$$

   $$f = 9$$

   The fast hose takes 9 hours to water the cornfield. The slower hose takes 1.25(9) = **11.25 hours.**

3. Alex takes 2 hours to shine 500 silver spoons, and Julian takes 3 hours to shine 450 silver spoons. How long will they take, working together, to shine 1000 silver spoons?

Calculate how many spoons each man can shine per hour:

Alex: $\dfrac{500 \text{ spoons}}{2 \text{ hours}} = \dfrac{250 \text{ spoons}}{\text{hour}}$

Julian: $\dfrac{450 \text{ spoons}}{3 \text{ hours}} = \dfrac{150 \text{ spoons}}{\text{hour}}$

Together: $\dfrac{(250 + 150) \text{ spoons}}{\text{hour}} = \dfrac{400 \text{ spoons}}{\text{hour}}$

Now set up an equation to find the time it takes to shine 1000 spoons:

total time $= \dfrac{1 \text{ hour}}{400 \text{ spoons}} \times 1000 \text{ spoons} = \dfrac{1000}{400} \text{ hours} =$

2.5 hours

5

STATISTICS AND GEOMETRY

GRAPHS AND CHARTS

These questions require you to interpret information from graphs and charts; they will be pretty straightforward as long as you pay careful attention to detail. There are several different graph and chart types that may appear on the TEAS.

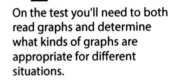

On the test you'll need to both read graphs and determine what kinds of graphs are appropriate for different situations.

Bar Graphs

BAR GRAPHS present the numbers of an item that exist in different categories. The categories are shown on the *x*-axis, and the number of items is shown on the *y*-axis. Bar graphs are usually used to easily compare amounts.

Examples

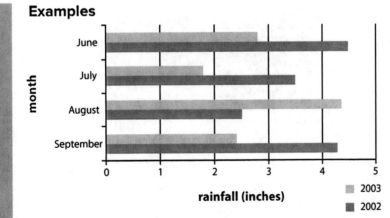

1. The graph above shows rainfall in inches per month. Which month had the least amount of rainfall? Which had the most?

   The shortest bar represents the month with the least rain, and the longest bar represents the month with the most rain: **July 2003 had the least**, and **June 2002 had the most**.

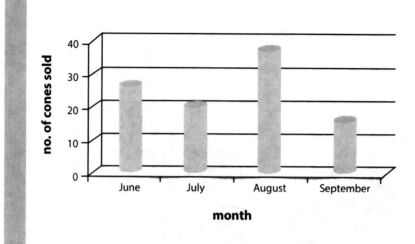

2. Using the graph above, how many more ice cream cones were sold in July than in September?

Tracing from the top of each bar to the scale on the left shows that sales in July were 20 and September sales were 15. So, **5 more cones were sold in July**.

Pie Charts

PIE CHARTS present parts of a whole, and are often used with percentages. Together, all the slices of the pie add up to the total number of items, or 100%.

Examples

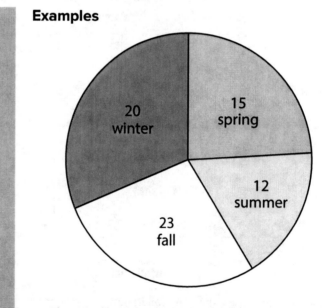

1. The pie chart above shows the distribution of birthdays in a class of students. How many students have birthdays in the spring or summer?

Fifteen students have birthdays in spring and 12 in winter, so there are **27 students** with birthdays in spring or summer.

2. Using the same Birthday Pie Chart in the example before, what percentage of students have birthdays in winter?

Use the equation for percent:

$$percent = \frac{part}{whole} = \frac{winter\ birthdays}{total\ birthdays} =$$

$$\frac{20}{20 + 15 + 23 + 12} = \frac{20}{70} = \frac{2}{7} = .286\ or\ \mathbf{28.6\%}$$

Line Graphs

LINE GRAPHS show trends over time. The number of each item represented by the graph will be on the y-axis, and time will be on the x-axis.

Examples

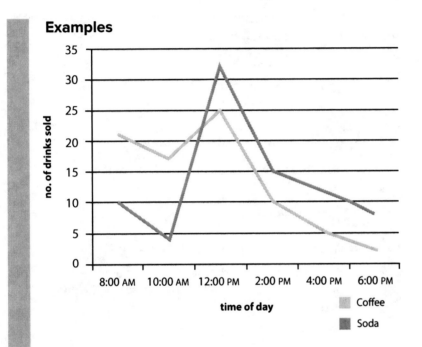

1. The line graph above shows beverage sales at an airport snack shop throughout the day. Which beverage sold more at 4:00 p.m.?

At 4:00 p.m., approximately 12 sodas and 5 coffees were sold, so more **soda** was sold.

2. At what time of day were the most beverages sold?

This question is asking for the time of day with the most sales of coffee and soda combined. It is not necessary to add up sales at each time of day to find the answer. Just from looking at the graph, you can see that sales for both beverages were highest at noon, so the answer must be **12:00 p.m.**

Mean, Median, and Mode

MEAN is a math term for average. To find the mean, total all the terms and divide by the number of terms. The MEDIAN is the middle number of a given set. To find the median, put the terms in numerical order; the middle number will be the median. In the case of a set of even numbers, the middle two numbers are averaged. Mode is the number which occurs most frequently within a given set.

Examples

1. Find the mean of 24, 27, and 18.

   Add the terms, then divide by the number of terms:

   $mean = \frac{24 + 27 + 18}{3} = \textbf{23}$

2. The mean of three numbers is 45. If two of the numbers are 38 and 43, what is the third number?

   Set up the equation for mean with x representing the third number, then solve:

   $mean = \frac{38 + 43 + x}{3} = 45$

   $38 + 43 + x = 135$

   $x = \textbf{54}$

3. What is the median of 24, 27, and 18?

   Place the terms in order, then pick the middle term:

   18, 24, 27

   The median is **24**.

4. What is the median of 24, 27, 18, and 19?

   Place the terms in order. Because there are an even number of terms, the median will be the average of the middle 2 terms:

   18, 19, 24, 27

   $median = \frac{19 + 24}{2} = \textbf{21.5}$

5. What is the mode of 2, 5, 4, 4, 3, 2, 8, 9, 2, 7, 2, and 2?

   The mode is 2 because it appears the most within the set.

AREA AND PERIMETER

Area and perimeter problems will require you to use the equations shown in the table below to find either the area inside a shape or the distance around it (the perimeter). These equations will not be given on the test, so you need to have them memorized on test day.

Table 5.1. Equations

SHAPE	AREA	PERIMETER
circle	$A = \pi r^2$	$C = 2\pi r = \pi d$
triangle	$A = \frac{b \times h}{2}$	$P = s^1 + s^2 + s^3$
square	$A = s^2$	$P = 4s$
rectangle	$A = l \times w$	$P = 2l + 2w$

Examples

1. A farmer has purchased 100 m of fencing to put around his rectangular garden. If one side of the garden is 20 m long and the other is 28 m, how much fencing will the farmer have left over?

   The perimeter of a rectangle is equal to twice its length plus twice its width:

   P = 2(20) + 2(28) = 96 m

   The farmer has 100 m of fencing, so he'll have
   100 − 96 = **4 m** left.

2. Taylor is going to paint a square wall that is 3.5 m tall. What is the total area that Taylor will be painting?

   Each side of the square wall is 3.5 m:

   $A = 3.5^2 = $ **12.25 m²**

Pythagorean Theorem

Shapes with 3 sides are known as TRIANGLES. In addition to knowing the formulas for their area and perimeter, you should also know the Pythagorean theorem, which describes the relationship between the three sides (*a*, *b*, and *c*) of a right triangle:

$$a^2 + b^2 = c^2$$

Example

Erica is going to run a race in which she'll run 3 miles due north and 4 miles due east. She'll then run back to the starting line. How far will she run during this race?

One leg of her route (the triangle) is missing, but you can find its length using the Pythagorean theorem:

$a^2 + b^2 = c^2$

$3^2 + 4^2 = c^2$

$25 = c^2$

$c = 5$

Adding all 3 sides gives the length of the whole race:

$3 + 4 + 5 = $ **12 miles**

PART III: SCIENCE

54 questions | 66 minutes

While the science sections of older versions of the TEAS were more balanced, the TEAS V focuses on human body science and life science. There will still be a significant number of chemistry problems, but the test will ask fewer questions about physics. The Science section of the TEAS covers four major areas:

- scientific reasoning (the scientific method and general scientific principles)
- human body science (anatomy and physiology)
- life science (biology)
- earth and physical science (chemistry and physics)

SCIENTIFIC REASONING

SYSTEMS

A **SYSTEM** is a set of interacting parts that work together to form an integrated whole. Many scientific disciplines study systems: doctors, for example, study organ systems like the respiratory system, which is made up of interacting parts that allow animals to breathe. Similarly, ecologists might look at all the plants and animals that interact in a specific area, and chemists might look at a set of chemicals interacting in a beaker.

While obviously different, all these systems share some common traits. We'll use the respiratory system to look at the important characteristics of systems.

- All systems have a structure. (The respiratory system is highly organized.)
- All systems perform an action. (The respiratory system allows animals to breathe.)
- All systems have interacting parts. (The respiratory system is made up of many interacting parts, including the lungs, blood vessels, and bronchial tubes.)
- All systems have boundaries. (We can separate structures that are part of the respiratory system from those that are not.)
- Systems may receive input and produce output. (The respiratory system brings oxygen into the body and gets rid of carbon dioxide.)
- The processes in a system may be controlled by feedback. (The action of breathing is controlled in part by how much oxygen and carbon dioxide are in the body.)

Sometimes larger systems are made of smaller, independent systems called SUBSYSTEMS. For example, a body cell is made of many organelles.

These organelles each perform their own tasks, which together support the system of the cell.

SCIENTIFIC INVESTIGATIONS

A theory and a hypothesis are both important aspects of science. There is a common misconception that they are one and the same, which is not true; however the two are very similar. A HYPOTHESIS is a proposed explanation for a phenomenon; it's usually based on observations or previous research. A THEORY is an explanation for a phenomenon that has been thoroughly tested and is generally accepted to be true by the scientific community.

Although science can never really prove something, it does provide a means to answering many questions about our natural world. Scientists use different types of investigations, each providing different types of results, based upon what they are trying to find. There are three main types of scientific investigations: descriptive, experimental, and comparative.

DESCRIPTIVE INVESTIGATIONS start with observations. A model is then constructed to provide a visual of what was seen: a description. Descriptive investigations do not generally require hypotheses, as they usually just attempt to find more information about a relatively unknown topic. EXPERIMENTAL INVESTIGATIONS, on the other hand, usually involve a hypothesis. These experiments are sometimes referred to as controlled experiments because they are performed in a controlled environment. During experimental investigations, all variables are controlled except for one: the dependent variable, which is part of the hypothesis being tested. Often, there are many tests involved in this process. Lastly, COMPARATIVE INVESTIGATIONS involve manipulating different groups in order to compare them with each other. There is no control during comparative investigations.

THE SCIENTIFIC METHOD

In order to ensure that experimental and comparative investigations are thorough and accurate, scientists use the scientific method, which has five main steps:

1. Observe and ask questions: look at the natural world to observe and ask questions about patterns and anomalies you see.

2. Gather information: look at what other scientists have done to see where your questions fit in with current research.

3. Construct a hypothesis: make a proposal that explains why or how something happens.

4. Experiment and test your hypothesis: set up an experimental investigation that allows you to test your hypothesis.

5. Analyze results and draw conclusions: examine your results and see whether they disprove your hypothesis. Note that you can't actually *prove* a hypothesis; you can only provide evidence to support it.

7

LIFE SCIENCE

BIOLOGICAL MOLECULES

ORGANIC compounds are those that contain carbon. These compounds, such as glucose, triacylglycerol, and guanine, are used in day-to-day metabolic processes. Many of these molecules are POLYMERS formed from repeated smaller units called MONOMERS. INORGANIC compounds are those that do not contain carbon. These make up a very small fraction of mass in living organisms, and are usually minerals such as potassium, sodium, and iron.

There are several classes of organic compounds commonly found in living organisms. These biological molecules include carbohydrates, proteins, lipids, and nucleic acids, which combined make up more than 95 percent of non-water material in living organisms.

Carbohydrates

CARBOHYDRATES, also called sugars, are molecules made of carbon, hydrogen, and oxygen. Sugars are primarily used in organisms as a source of energy: they can be catabolized (broken down) to create energy molecules such as adenosine triphosphate (ATP) or nicotinamide adenine dinucleotide (NAD+), providing a source of electrons to drive cellular processes.

The basic formula for a carbohydrate is CH_2O, and the majority of carbohydrates are multiples of this empirical formula. For example, GLUCOSE is $C_6H_{12}O_6$. Carbohydrates can also bond together to form polymeric compounds. Some polymers of glucose include starch, which is used to store excess sugar, and cellulose, which is a support fiber responsible in part for the strength of plants.

⚠

HYDROCARBONS AND CARBOHYDRATES
alkanes:
C_nH_{2n+2}

alkenes:
C_nH_{2n}

alkynes:
C_nH_{2n-2}

monosaccharides:
$(CH_2O)_n$

Lipids

LIPIDS are compounds primarily composed of carbon and hydrogen with only a small percentage of oxygen. Lipids contain a HEAD, usually formed of glycerol or phosphate, and a TAIL, which is a hydrocarbon chain. The composition of the head, whether it is a carboxylic acid functional group, a phosphate group, or some other functional group, is usually polar, meaning it is hydrophilic. The tail is composed of carbon and hydrogen, and is usually nonpolar, meaning it is hydrophobic.

The combined polarity of the lipid head and the non-polarity of the lipid tail is a unique feature of lipids critical to the formation of the phospholipid bilayer in the cell membrane. The fatty acid tails are all pointed inward, and the heads are pointed outward. This provides a semi-permeable membrane that allows a cell to separate its contents from the environment.

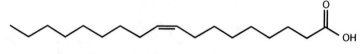

Figure 7.1. Free fatty acid lipid

The SATURATION of a lipid describes the number of double bonds in the tail of the lipid. The more double bonds a lipid tail has, the more unsaturated the molecule is, and the more bends there are in its structure. As a result, unsaturated fats (like oils) tend to be liquid at room temperature, whereas saturated fats (like lard or butter) are solid at room temperature.

Proteins

PROTEINS are large molecules composed of a chain of AMINO ACIDS. The sequence of amino acids in the chain determines the protein's structure and function. Each amino acid is composed of three parts:

- Amino group ($-NH_2$): The amino group is found on all amino acids.
- Carboxyl group ($-COOH$): The carboxyl group is found on all amino acids.
- R group: The R group is a unique functional group that is different for each amino acid. For example, in the histidine amino acid seen in Figure 7.2, the R group is a cyclic imidazole group.

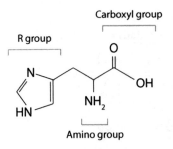

Figure 7.2. The amino acid histidine

The R group determines the amino acid's physiological function.

There are twenty-two amino acids used to produce proteins. It is not necessary to know each amino acid, but it is important to know that sequences of these amino acids form proteins, and that each amino acid has a unique R-functional group.

Nucleic Acids

NUCLEIC ACIDS, which include DNA and RNA, store all information necessary to produce proteins. These molecules are built using smaller molecules called NUCLEOTIDES, which are composed of a 5-carbon sugar, a phosphate group, and a nitrogenous base.

DNA is made from four nucleotides: adenine, guanine, cytosine, and thymine. Together, adenine and guanine are classified as PURINES while thymine and cytosine are classified as PYRIMIDINES. These nucleotides bond together in pairs; the pairs are then bonded together in a chain to create a double helix shape with the sugar as the outside and the nitrogenous base on the inside. In DNA, adenine and thymine always bond together as do guanine and cytosine. In RNA, thymine is replaced by a nucleotide called uracil, which bonds with adenine. RNA also differs from DNA in that it often exists as a single strand.

⚠
The major differences between DNA and RNA include:

- Uracil replaces thymine in RNA.

- RNA can exist as a single strand while DNA is double stranded.

- RNA contains ribose while DNA contains deoxyribose.

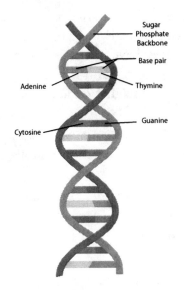

Figure 7.3. DNA

Examples

1. Match the polymer with the correct monomer.
   A) DNA; nucleic acid
   B) RNA; amino acid
   C) starch; lipid
   D) histidine; glucose

2. Which of the following is not found in DNA?
   A) adenine
   B) uracil
   C) thymine
   D) cytosine

3. Which of the following is not a compound created from sugar?
   A) glycogen
   B) starch
   C) cellulose
   D) guanine

4. An amino acid contains an R group, an amino group, and a:
   A) hydroxyl group
   B) carboxyl group
   C) phenyl group
   D) phosphate group

Answers: 1. A) 2. B) 3. D) 4. B)

THE HISTORY OF LIFE

Scientists believe life on Earth started around 3.8 billion years ago. The exact time when the first living cells appeared is unknown, but observations in geology have indicated the type of environment when living cells first appeared. It is hypothesized that life began due to a sequence of events that created biological molecules and cell-like structures:

1. synthesis of amino acid molecules and sugars, possibly from interaction of lightning and high temperatures near volcanic vents

2. joining and interaction of these molecules in something resembling modern-day proteins

3. assembly of these molecules within a membrane, which started to resemble a cell

The researchers STANLEY MILLER and HAROLD UREY had a hypothesis that the above three steps could have happened in a primordial environment in which there was no oxygen. Note that higher concentrations of oxygen did not appear until the evolution of plants, so life must have started without a significant oxygen presence.

Miller-Urey Experiment

In the **MILLER-UREY EXPERIMENT**, the researchers placed a mixture of ingredients that included water, methane, ammonia, and hydrogen into an enclosed reactor bulb. The conditions were modified to simulate those that were thought to exist on Earth several billion years ago. A pair of electrodes was placed into the reactor vessel, and sparks that simulated lightning were fired through the mixture every few minutes.

Miller and Urey found that their reaction mixture turned pink in color within a day, and after two weeks, the reactor vessel contained a thick solution that included a number of important molecules. Among the compounds that formed were with some amino acids, including glycine, as well as sugars. After full characterization, the scientists found that the experiment created eleven of the twenty-two known amino acids.

Fossil Record

The **FOSSIL RECORD** is a history of species that existed throughout time that has been unearthed by archaeologists. The fossils, if well preserved, are able to show us the bone structures and the forms of animals, plants, and even cells that existed billions of years ago. The fossils can be used to understand how species evolved through time and, in some cases, even to see what they ate and the environments in which they lived.

The age of fossils is determined through a method called **RADIOMETRIC DATING**, which examines the amount of radioactive carbon remaining in the sample. The radioactive carbon isotope carbon-14 has a half-life of 5,730 years, which means that this isotope can be used to reliably date fossils that are up to about ten half-lives, or 50,000 years in age. For fossils older than that, an isotope with a longer half-life is used. In some fossils, the presence of small amounts of uranium-238, with a half-life of 4.5 billion years, can aid in dating.

Timeline of Earth

- 4.6 billion years ago: formation of Earth
- 3.7 billion years ago: prokaryotes first came into existence
- 2.6 billion years ago: oxygen is believed to be present in the atmosphere
- 2.1 billion years ago: eukaryotic organisms have evolved

- 1.5 billion years ago: multicellular organisms have evolved
- 800 million years ago: the first animals exist
- 500 million years ago: Paleozoic Era
- 260 million years ago: Mesozoic Era
- 65 million years ago: Cenozoic Era
- 10,000 years ago: early humans

The three eras, the Paleozoic, Mesozoic, and Cenozoic, were each characterized by an explosion of different species. Each era was responsible for the formation of a number of different species.

PALEOZOIC: The Paleozoic era was characterized by the colonization of land, with many types of plants appearing, and the diversification of fish and reptile species.

MESOZOIC: The Mesozoic era saw the first flowering plants appearing, as well as many land animals, including the dinosaurs. However, at the end of the Mesozoic era, the extinction of the dinosaurs occurred, likely due to a catastrophic event such as a huge meteorite striking the earth.

CENOZOIC: In the Cenozoic era, many of the animals and plants that we see today started to evolve, including mammals, many different angiosperm plants, and the direct ancestors of humans.

Examples

1. A student is attempting to replicate the Miller-Urey experiment. Which of the following reagents does he *not* need?

   A) ammonia

   B) carbon dioxide

   C) oxygen

   D) water vapor

2. In the Miller-Urey experiment, which attempted to replicate conditions that were existent in early Earth, which of the following compounds was *not* created?

   A) amino acids

   B) methane

   C) lipid precursors

   D) chlorophyll

   Answers: 1. C) 2. D)

THE BASICS OF THE CELL

The CELL is the most basic unit of life; all higher organisms are composed of cells. Most cells range from 20 μm to 100 μm in size, although some can be even larger. Cells were first discovered by

---

⚠

THE BIOLOGICAL HIERARCHY
- atom
- molecule
- organelle
- cell
- tissue
- organ
- organ system
- organism
- population
- community
- ecosystem
- biome
- biosphere

the Englishman **Robert Hooke**, the inventor of the microscope, in the 1600s. However, cell theory truly began to develop when a Dutchman named **Antony van Leeuwenhoek** pioneered new developments in the field of microscopy, allowing scientists to view bacteria, protozoa, and other microorganisms.

Cell Subgroups

Cells are roughly divided into two large subgroups: prokaryotic cells and eukaryotic cells. The primary similarities and differences are listed in Table 7.1. below.

Table 7.1. Prokaryotic and eukaryotic cells

Traits unique to prokaryotic cells	Prokaryotic cells, such as bacteria, are the only types of cells which contain peptidoglycan, a sugar, and an amino acid layer that supports the cell membrane.	Prokaryotic cells do not have a nuclear membrane.	Many prokaryotic cells contain plasmids, which are circular rings of DNA that hold genetic information.
Traits shared by prokaryotic and eukaryotic cells	Both cells have cell membranes and often have cell walls.	Both types of cells contain DNA.	Both can have flagella and ribosomes.
Traits unique to eukaryotic cells	Eukaryotic cells have a nuclear membrane, and DNA is contained within the membrane.	Eukaryotic cells have a Golgi body, which is used for transport of proteins.	Some eukaryotic cells have lysosomes or peroxisomes, which are used in digestion.

Parts of the Cell

Although the cell is the smallest unit of life, there are many small bodies, called **organelles**, which exist in the cell. These organelles are required for the many process that takes place inside a cell.

- **Mitochondria:** The mitochondria are the organelles responsible for making ATP within the cell. A mitochondria has several layers of membranes used to assist the electron transport chain. This pathway uses energy provided by molecules such as glucose or fat (lipid) to generate ATP through the transfer of electrons.

- **Vacuole:** A vacuole is a small body used to transfer materials within and out of the cell. It has a membrane of its own and can carry things such as cell wastes, sugars, or proteins.

- **Nucleus:** The nucleus of a eukaryotic cell contains all of its genetic information in the form of DNA. In the nucleus, DNA replication and transcription occur. In the eukaryotic cell, after transcription, the mRNA is exported out of the nucleus into the cytosol for use.

- **Endoplasmic reticulum:** The ER, for short, is used for translation of mRNA into proteins, and for the transport of proteins out of the cell. The rough endoplasmic reticulum has many ribosomes attached to it, which function as the cell's machinery in transforming RNA into protein. The smooth endoplasmic reticulum is associated with the production of fats and steroid hormones.

- **RIBOSOME**: The ribosome is a small two-protein unit that reads mRNA and, with the assistance of transport proteins, creates an amino acid.

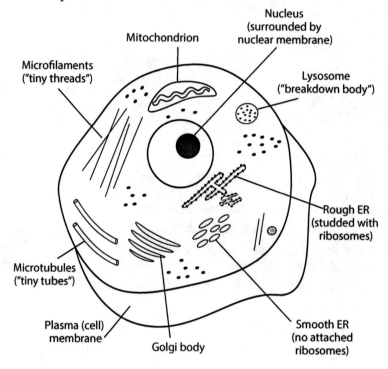

Figure 7.4. Animal cell

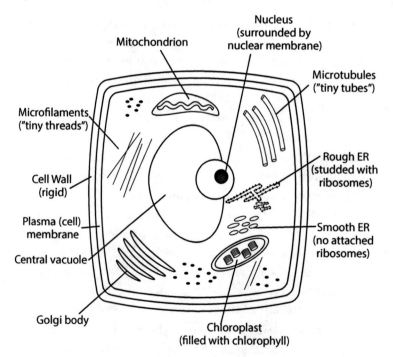

Figure 7.5. Plant cell

Cell Membrane

The CELL MEMBRANE is a unique layer that surrounds the cell and performs numerous functions. It is composed of compounds called PHOSPHOLIPIDS, which are amphipathic, and consist of an alkane tail and a phospho-group head. The alkane lipid tail is hydrophobic, meaning it will not allow water to pass through, and the phosphate group head is hydrophilic, which allows water to pass through. The arrangement of these molecules forms a bilayer, which has a hydrophobic middle layer. In this manner, the cell is able to control the import and export of various substances into the cell.

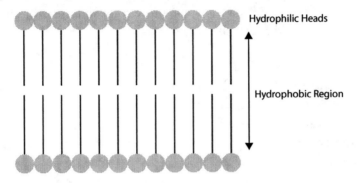

Figure 7.6. Cell membrane bilayer

In addition to the phospholipid bilayer, the cell membrane often includes proteins, which perform a variety of functions. Some proteins are used as receptors, which allow the cell to interact with its surroundings. Others are TRANSMEMBRANE PROTEINS, meaning that they cross the entire membrane. These types of proteins are usually channels which allow the transportation of molecules into and out of the cell.

Membrane proteins are also used in cell-to-cell interaction. This includes functions such as cell-cell joining or recognition, in which a cell membrane protein contacts a protein from another cell. A good example of this is the immune response in the human body. Due to the proteins found on the cell membrane of antigens, immune system cells can contact, recognize, and attempt to remove them.

Membrane Transport

A cell needs to be able to both import and export vital substances across the membrane while at the same time preventing harmful substances from entering the cell. Two major classes of transportation allow this process to occur: active transport and passive transport.

ACTIVE TRANSPORT uses ATP to accomplish one of two tasks: it can move a molecule against the concentration gradient (from low concentration to high), or it can be used to import or export a bulky molecule, such as a sugar or a protein, across the cell membrane. Active transport requires the use of proteins and energy in the form of ATP. The ATP produced by the cell binds to the proteins in the cell membrane and is hydrolyzed, producing the energy required to change the conformational structure of the protein. This change in the structure of the protein allows the protein to funnel molecules across the cell membrane.

PASSIVE TRANSPORT does not require energy and allows molecules such as water to passively diffuse across the cell membrane. Facilitated diffusion is a form of passive transport that does not require energy but does require the use of proteins located on the cell membrane. These transport proteins typically have a "channel" running through the core of a protein specific to a certain type of molecule. For example, a transport protein for sodium only allows sodium to flow through the channel.

Tonicity

The balance of water in the cell is one of the most important regulatory mechanisms for the cell. Water enters or exits the cell through a process called OSMOSIS. This movement of water does not usually require energy, and the movement is regulated by a factor called tonicity.

TONICITY is the concentration of solutes in the cell. Solutes can be salt ions, such as sodium or chlorine, or other molecules such as sugar, amino acids, or proteins. The difference in tonicity between the cell and its outside environment governs the transportation of water into and out of the cell. For example, if there is a higher tonicity inside the cell, then water will enter the cell. If there is a higher tonicity outside the cell, the water will leave the cell. This is due to a driving force called the CHEMIOSMOTIC POTENTIAL that attempts to make tonicity equal across a membrane.

There are three terms used to describe a cell's tonicity:

- An ISOTONIC cell has the same concentration of solutes inside and outside of the cell. There will be no transport of water in this case.

- A HYPERTONIC cell has a lower concentration of solutes inside than outside of the cell. The cell will lose water to the environment and shrivel. This is what happens if a cell is placed into a salty solution.

- A HYPOTONIC cell has a higher concentration of solutes inside than outside of the cell. The cell will absorb water from the environment and swell, becoming turgid.

Cell Interactions

With the vast number of cells in living organisms, (an estimated 100 trillion in the human body), how do they all interact and talk with one another? Cells are able to communicate with one other through cell signaling, which occurs via chemical signals excreted by the cell. It is also possible to have direct cell-to-cell communication through protein receptors located in the cell membrane. Important signaling molecules include CYCLIC AMP, which is best known for its function in the signaling cascade when epinephrine binds to a cell, and NEUROTRANSMITTERS such as glycine, aspartate, acetylcholine, dopamine, serotonin, and melatonin, among many others.

LOCAL or DIRECT SIGNALING is a signal that occurs between cells that are either right next to each other or within a few cells' distance. This communication can occur by two methods. First, GAP JUNCTIONS exist between the membranes of two cells that can allow signaling molecules to directly enter the cells. Second, the receptors on the membrane can bind with other cells that have membrane receptors to communicate.

The primary chemical used in long range signaling is called a HORMONE. In humans and animals, hormones are produced by organs and cells in the endocrine system such as the testes, hypo-thalamus, and pituitary glands. These hormones, once released, can travel throughout the organism through the circulatory system (blood). The hormones can then bind to other cells that have the appropriate receptor and cause a signal to start inside the cell.

One example of long range signaling in the human body is the production of insulin by the pancreas. Insulin spreads through the body via the blood, and when it binds to an insulin receptor on a cell, the cell begins to take in more glucose. This prcoess is called long range signaling because insulin is produced by cells in only one location (the pancreas) but is able to affect nearly all other cells in the body.

An example of long distance signaling in plants is the production of ethylene, a ripening chemical. It can be present in the air or diffuse through cell walls, and the production of ethylene by one plant can cause a chain reaction that causes nearby plants to also start ripening.

How do the hormones you studied in human body science act as long range signaling molecules?

Examples

1. The Golgi body is one of the largest organelles found in the cell, and is responsible for:

   A) protein synthesis

   B) intracellular and extracellular transport

   C) replication of DNA

   D) formation of ribosomes

2. In animal cell structure, the cell membrane is composed of a phospholipid bilayer that separates the cell from its surroundings. Which of the following is also present in the cell membrane?

   A) proteins

   B) ATP

   C) mitochondria

   D) vacuoles

3. A student places a cell with a 50 mM intracellular ion content into a solution containing 20 mM ion content. What will happen to the cell?

   A) The cell will shrink.

   B) The cell membrane will become porous.

   C) The cell will expand.

   D) The cell is isotonic, and nothing will occur.

4. Which of the following species cannot travel across a cell membrane without the use of energy?

   A) water

   B) potassium

   C) sodium

   D) glucose

5. Although plant cells and animal cells are roughly the same size, the volume of cytosol, or plasma, inside an animal cell is significantly larger than that seen in a plant cell. What is responsible for this difference?

   A) the presence of chlorophyll in plant cells

   B) the presence of an endoplasmic reticulum in plant cells

   C) the presence of a large storage vacuole in plant cells

   D) the presence of a cell wall in plant cells

6. The endoplasmic reticulum is broken up into the rough ER and the smooth ER. The rough ER is responsible for synthesis of proteins and some polysaccharides. What is the smooth ER responsible for?

   A) metabolism of carbohydrates and synthesis of lipids

   B) DNA replication and transcription

   C) modification of RNA after the transcription process

   D) degradation of residual amino acids and cell waste

7. Which of the following is not a type of cell connection or junction between cells?

A) tight junction

B) gap junction

C) desmosome

D) channel junction

Answers: 1. B) 2. A) 3. C) 4. D) 5. C) 6. D) 7. C)

ENZYMES

Enzymes are an important type of protein crucial for aiding various reactions in the cell. An **ENZYME** is a large protein that acts as a catalyst, which is a substance able to speed up a reaction by reducing the activation energy of a reaction or bringing reactants closer together.

All chemical reactions have something called an activation energy, which is the amount of energy required for a reaction to begin. For some reactions, this barrier is quite high, which is why enzymes are necessary. Enzymes can reduce the activation energy of a reaction through interaction with the bonds in the reactants. Many enzymes have something called an **ACTIVE SITE**, which is an area of the protein with certain functional groups that are able to bind with a reactant. This binding forms a stabilized intermediate that allows the reactant to more easily dissociate or react with another reagent.

Enzymes can also bring reactants closer together. Many reaction rates are limited by the concentration of reactants in the solution. For example, in a cell, the concentration of glucose is usually less than 0.5 mM. This means that the chance for a glucose molecule to contact another reactant is quite low. Enzymes can bind to a glucose molecule and then bind to the other reactant, forcing the reactants close enough together for the reaction to take place.

Some examples of important enzymes include:

- **DNA POLYMERASE:** the enzyme responsible for copying DNA. The enzyme binds to a single strand of DNA and assembles nucleotides to match the strand.

- **PYRUVATE KINASE:** the enzyme responsible for glycolysis, which is the initial breakdown of glucose in the human body (and other organisms).

- **ENDOGLUCANASE:** enzyme responsible for the breakdown of cellulose in fungi and bacteria. This enzyme breaks down the cellulose chain into smaller sugars.

CELLULAR METABOLISM

METABOLISM is the series of chemical reactions that produce the energy and molecules necessary for cellular activity. These processes can best be understood as a pathway. For example, a glucose molecule can be converted into an intermediate (pyruvate) which is then converted into a product (ATP). In a single cell, there are hundreds, if not thousands, of these metabolic pathways that all function to keep the cell alive.

Catabolism vs. Anabolism

A major function of metabolism is **CATABOLISM**, which is the breakdown of molecules. A catabolic pathway breaks down a larger molecule into smaller ones, often releasing energy. For example, the process of breaking down fat for energy is catabolic. **ANABOLISM** is the opposite of catabolism: in an anabolic pathway, energy and smaller molecules are used by the cell to build a more complicated molecule. A good example of an anabolic pathway is the synthesis of a protein.

⚠ _____

Under standard state conditions, the conversion of ATP to ADP releases 30.5 kilojoules per mole of energy. In a living cell, however, that value increases to 57 kilojoules per mole.

ATP: The Most Important Energy Molecule

ATP is short for **ADENOSINE TRIPHOSPHATE**, which is the most common molecule used for energy. The ATP molecule is formed from ribose, a sugar, and three phosphate groups (a phosphate group is written as Pi). ATP is primarily used for energy, but is also used to form adenine.

ATP is able to store energy through the formation of high-energy bonds between the phosphate groups in the "tail" of the molecule. When the last phosphate bond in the group is broken through a hydrolysis reaction, a phosphate molecule is released. This exothermic reaction releases energy that can then be used to drive another cellular reaction. The product of the reaction is a phosphate molecule and a lower energy adenosine diphosphate (ADP) molecule. When two phosphate groups are removed from ATP in a unit called a pyrophosphate (PPi), the molecule adenosine monophosphate (AMP) is produced.

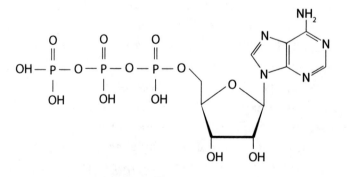

Figure 7.7. Adenosine triphosphate

Because ATP is highly reactive, it is not stored in the body in high quantities. Instead, ADP is recycled and converted to ATP by the addition of a phosphate group. This process of forming ATP is a catabolic pathway that largely occurs in the mitochondria. The energy for this process is stored in lipids, carbohydrates, and proteins.

Respiratory Pathways

ATP is produced through a catabolic process which can take place in one of two ways. The first method, in which oxygen is used, is called an **AEROBIC RESPIRATORY PATHWAY**. In a respiratory pathway, a food substance, such as glucose or amino acids, is broken down with the use of oxygen, and ATP is produced. The second method (addressed further below) is an anaerobic process called fermentation that does not use oxygen.

The basic overall process of aerobic cellular respiration is shown below:

$$\text{Organic compound + Oxygen} \rightarrow$$
$$\text{Carbon dioxide + Water + Energy}$$

Because the reaction requires oxygen, animals that use aerobic respiration require oxygen to live. For example, humans breathe in oxygen using our lungs for respiration, and produce carbon dioxide and water as a byproduct. (Note that while the act of breathing is often called respiration, it is a different process than cellular respiration.)

The energy obtained from the breakdown of organic compounds comes from the bonds of the compound. This energy can vary widely, from about four kilocalories of energy per gram in carbohydrates to nine kilocalories per gram in lipids. The transfer of energy from the bonds breaking in these molecules occurs through an oxidation-reduction reaction, which involves the transfer of electrons from one species to another.

In respiration, there are two primary pathways that are important to know. The first is glycolysis, which breaks down glucose into two molecules of pyruvate and produces a small amount of ATP. The second is the citric acid cycle, which takes pyruvate and produces much more ATP, as well as the byproduct carbon dioxide.

Glycolysis

GLYCOLYSIS is the first step in the breakdown of sugars. The overall reaction of glycolysis is as follows:

$$\text{Glucose + 2 [NAD]+ + 2 [ADP] + 2 [P]}_i \rightarrow$$
$$\text{2 Pyruvate + 2 [NADH] + 2H}^+ \text{ + 2 [ATP] + 2H}_2\text{O}$$

Overall, a glucose molecule is used to produce two pyruvate molecules (which are fed into the citric acid cycle), four energy

> Cellular respiration is the conversion of energy into a form that can be used by cells. Physiological respiration is the exchange of oxygen and carbon dioxide between cells and the environment.

molecules (two NADH and two ATP molecules), and two molecules of water.

The conversion of glucose into these products takes place over a ten-step pathway, which involves two phases. The first phase uses energy in order to break apart the glucose molecule. The second phase then recovers energy in the form of ATP and NADH, and results in the production of the pyruvate molecules.

As a result of these steps, there is a production of four molecules of ATP and two molecules of NADH; there is a corresponding use of two molecules of ATP. This results in the net production of two ATP, two NADH, and two pyruvate molecules.

Citric Acid Cycle

The majority of the energy in the glucose molecule has not been released by glycolysis. Under aerobic conditions, the citric acid cycle and electron transport chain, which follow glycolysis, will produce more ATP. The citric acid cycle is also known as the Krebs cycle or the tricarboxylic acid (TCA) cycle.

In eukaryotic cells, the CITRIC ACID CYCLE takes place in the matrix of the mitochondria of the cell. The same reaction can occur in the cytosol/cytoplasm of prokaryotic cells. The citric acid cycle gets its name from the production and re-absorption of citric acid during the process. During the course of the TCA cycle, a molecule of pyruvate derived from glycolysis is transformed into three molecules of CO_2 and two molecules of ATP. The TCA cycle needs to run twice for each molecule of glucose, due to the two molecules of pyruvate obtained from a molecule of glucose. Thus, at the end of two turns of the cycle, four ATP have been produced.

- In each turn of the citric acid cycle, which includes the oxidation of pyruvate (Step 1), four NADH, one $FADH_2$, one GTP, and two CO_2 are produced. NADH and $FADH_2$ are used to feed the electron transport chain, during which the bulk of ATP is produced.
- Each glucose molecule requires two turns of the citric acid cycle, yielding eight NADH, two $FADH_2$, two GTP, and four CO_2. The GTP can be converted to ATP.
- After glycolysis and the citric acid cycle have been completed, there is a net of four ATP, ten NADH, and two $FADH_2$.

The Electron Transport Chain

The ELECTRON TRANSPORT CHAIN is located in the inner membrane of the mitochondria in the eukaryotic cell. In the chain, a series of electron carriers couple the movment of electrons with the transportation of hydrogen ions (H+) across a membrane to create an electrochemical gradient. The source of these electrons is usually NADH and FADH$_2$ generated from the citric acid cycle.

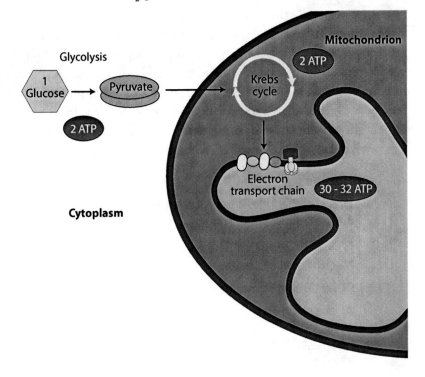

Figure 7.8. Cellular respiration

This electrochemical gradient is used by the molecule ATP synthase to create ATP from ADP: the flow of the hydrogen ions through the ATP synthase molecules provides the energy to generate ATP. Each NADH typically generates 2.5 ATP; each FADH$_2$ generates 1.5 ATP.

At the end of the Electron Transport Chain, 30 to 32 ATP have typically been produced. It is important to note, however, that this number can vary—up to 38 ATP are produced in plants—depending on what type of shuttles are used to transport the electrons from NADH across the membrane. (Plants don't spend an ATP to transport NADH into the mitochondria.)

Fermentation

Fermentation is an alternative process that can generate ATP in anaerobic conditions. Many organisms, such as yeast, can primarily use fermentation so they do not need oxygen to live. There are two primary forms of fermentation, alcohol and lactic acid fermentation.

ALCOHOL FERMENTATION is probably the most common type of fermentation. After glycolysis occurs, the pyruvate is converted into ethanol. 2-NADH is used in the process, but as acetaldehyde is converted into ethanol, 2-NADH is produced. Yeast are known to ferment sugars, producing ethanol and carbon dioxide, which is the source of the alcohol and carbonation in beer.

Lactic acid fermentation differs only slightly from alcohol fermentation. Instead of acetaldehyde being produced, the pyruvate is directly fermented into lactic acid. This takes place in some fungi and bacteria, and can occur in the human body. When you use up your excess stores of ATP during strenuous exercise, and the citric acid cycle is unable to provide more ATP quickly, lactic acid fermentation occurs in your muscles to produce additional energy. This is what causes the "burning" feeling during exercise.

✔

What are some other conditions under which cells might need to use anaerobic respiration?

Examples

1. Which of the following processes produces the most ATP during cellular respiration?

   A) glycolysis

   B) citric acid cycle

   C) lactic acid fermentation

   D) the electron transport chain

2. Which of the following statements about the cycling of ATP is NOT true?

   A) $ATP \rightarrow ADP + P_i$

   B) $ATP \rightarrow ADP + PP_i$

   C) $ATP \rightarrow AMP + PP_i$

   D) $ADP \rightarrow AMP + P_i$

3. In the citric acid cycle, how many runs of the cycle are required to process one molecule of glucose?

   A) 1

   B) 2

   C) 3

   D) 4

4. During the process of aerobic respiration, the movement of which of these ions is responsible for the generation of a large amount of ATP?

   A) potassium

   B) hydrogen

   C) sodium

   D) chlorine

5. Which of the following compounds is not produced by the citric acid cycle?

A) NADH

B) GTP

C) ATP

D) FADH

Answers: 1. D) 2. B) 3. B) 4. B) 5. D)

THE CELL CYCLE

The cell cycle is the process cells go through as they live, grow, and divide to produce new cells. The cell cycle can be divided into four primary phases:

1. G1 phase: growth phase one
2. S phase: DNA replication
3. G2 phase: growth phase two
4. Mitotic phase: The cell undergoes mitosis and splits into two cells.

Together, the G1, S, and G2 phases are known as INTERPHASE. During these phases, which usually take up 80 to 90 percent of the total time in a cell cycle, the cell is growing and conducting normal cell functions.

Mitosis

The process of cell division is called MITOSIS. When a cell divides, it needs to make sure that each copy of the cell has a roughly equal amount of the necessary elements, including DNA, proteins, and organelles.

A cell has a lot of DNA: even the smallest human cell contains a copy of the entire human genome. In human cells, this copy of the genome is nearly two meters in length—quite long when you consider that the average cell is only 100 μm in diameter.

In the nucleus, DNA is organized around proteins called HISTONES; together, this protein and DNA complex is known as CHROMATIN. During interphase, chromatin is usually arranged loosely to allow access to DNA. During mitosis, however, DNA is tightly packaged into units called CHROMOSOMES. When DNA has replicated, the chromosome is composed of two CHROMATIDS joined together at the CENTROMERE.

The mitotic phase is separated into five substages:

- Prophase: In prophase, the DNA in the cell winds into chromatin and each pair of duplicated chromosomes becomes joined. The mitotic spindle, which pulls apart the chromosomes later, forms and drifts to each end of the cell.

—▲————————————
THE CELL CYCLE
Go **S**ally **G**o, **M**ake **C**hildren!
- **g**rowth phase 1
- **D**NA synthesis
- **g**rowth phase 2
- **m**itosis
- **c**ytokinesis

- Prometaphase: In this phase, the nuclear membrane, which holds the DNA, dissolves, allowing the chromosomes to come free. The chromosomes now start to attach to microtubules linked to the centrioles.
- Metaphase: The centrioles, with microtubules attached to the chromosomes, are now on opposite sides of the cell. The chromosomes align in the middle of the cell, and the microtubules begin contracting.
- Anaphase: In anaphase, the chromosomes move to separate sides of the cell, and the cell structure begins to lengthen, pulling apart as it goes.
- Telophase: In this last part of the cell cycle, the cell membrane splits, and two new daughter cells are formed. The nucleolus, containing the DNA, reforms.

In this manner, cells are able to reproduce quite quickly. Many bacteria or yeast cells have a total cell cycle time of between twenty and thirty minutes, meaning they are able to double in number in that amount of time. This can lead to rapid proliferation of cells, assuming there is no food shortage. For example, a small colony of 200 *E.coli* cells can rapidly grow to more than 20 million cells in a matter of hours.

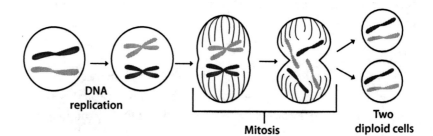

Figure 7.9. Mitosis

Meiosis

A somatic cell contains pairs of homologous chromosomes with one set of chromosomes coming from each parent. For example, humans have 23 pairs of chromosomes, for a total of 46 chromosomes. These cells are described as DIPLOID. Sex cells, on the other hand, have only one set of chromosomes (so, a human sex cell has 23 chromosomes), which is referred to as being HAPLOID. Meiosis is the process by which a diploid cell produces four haploid cells.

There are two consecutive stages of meiosis known as Meiosis I and Meiosis II. These two stages are further broken down into four stages each.

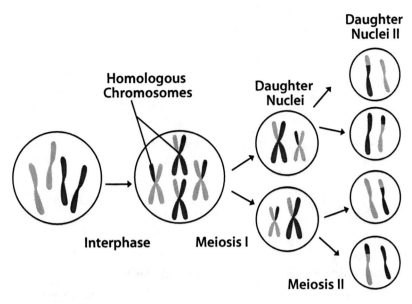

Figure 7.10. Meiosis

Meiosis I

1. Prophase I: In prophase, the chromosomes condense using histone proteins and become paired. The paired chromosomes will connect with each other via structures called the synaptonemal complexes. This is also known as synapsis. An important event called crossing-over occurs at this point. Genetic material is exchanged between sister chromatids, resulting in a random assembly of homologous chromosomes. After this is complete, microtubules attach to the chromosomes and centrioles and begin to align them in the middle of the cell.

2. Metaphase I: Similar to mitosis, the chromosomes align in the middle of the cell and begin to pull apart from one another.

3. Anaphase I: The sister chromatids separate and move toward opposite sides of the cell.

4. Telophase I: The cells separate, and each cell now has one copy each of a homologous chromosome.

Meiosis II

1. Prophase II: In prophase II, a spindle forms and aligns the chromosomes. No crossing-over occurs.

2. Metaphase II: In Metaphase II, the chromosomes again align at the metaphase plate. This time, however, when they are pulled apart, each daughter cell will not have the same copy of a sister chromatid. This is one of the causes of genetic variation among offspring.

3. Anaphase II: As in Anaphase I, the sister chromatids pull apart to opposite ends of the cell.

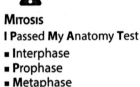

Mitosis
I Passed My Anatomy Test
- Interphase
- Prophase
- Metaphase
- Anaphase
- Telophase

4. Telophase II: The cell splits apart, resulting in four unique daughter cells.

Table 7.2. Mitosis vs. meiosis

EVENT	MITOSIS	MEIOSIS
DNA replication	Occurs in interphase	Occurs in interphase
Number of Divisions	1	2
Synapsis	Does not occur	Occurs in prophase I
Number of Daughter Cells	2	4
Role in Animals	Cell growth and repair	Production of gametes for reproduction

Introduction of Genetic Variation in Meiosis

One of meiosis' most important roles is the introduction of genetic variation. The INDEPENDENT ASSORTMENT of chromosomes in this process gives each gamete a unique subset of genes from the parent. When the haploid gamete combines with another to form a zygote, the result is a genetically unique organism that has a different gene composition than either of the parents.

The process of meiosis also introduces genetic variation during CROSSING OVER, which occurs in prophase I when homologous chromosomes pair along their lengths. Each gene on each chromosome becomes aligned with its sister gene. Then, when crossing over occurs, the DNA sequence is broken and crisscrossed, creating a new chromatid with pieces of each of the original homologous chromosomes.

Finally, meiosis allows for RANDOM FERTILIZATION. Although the gametes produced by each gender are unique, the fact that millions of sperm are produced by the human male (and quite a bit more in other species), means that there are many different possible combinations. For this reason, even though we might cross an animal pair together hundreds of times, it is next to impossible to get two children that have the same genotype (except identical twins).

Apoptosis

APOPTOSIS is an elaborate cellular signaling mechanism that determines when a cell dies. In normal animals and cells, apoptosis is a well-regulated occurrence that prevents the overgrowth of cells. In the process of apoptosis, enzymes and other cellular agents break down materials in the cell until the membrane dissociates and nothing remains.

Apoptosis has been observed in nearly all living organisms, and is an essential part of growth and regrowth. For example, humans' skin cells undergo apoptosis every day with dead skin cells shedding off and new skin cells replacing them.

The mechanism of apoptosis is one of the most studied in biology due to its link to many cancers. Cancerous tumors can develop due to a failure of the apoptosis pathway, leading to the growth of cells that never die. (Note, however, that cancer can be caused by many things, not just a lack of apoptosis.)

Examples

1. A scientist takes DNA samples from a cell culture at two different times, each sample having the same cell count. In the first sample, he finds that there is 6.5 pg of DNA, whereas in the second sample he finds that there is 13 pg of DNA. Which stage of the cell cycle is the second sample in?

   A) interphase G1

   B) interphase S

   C) interphase G2

   D) none of the above

2. Which of the following processes will take place in both mitosis and meiosis?

   A) separation of homologous chromatids

   B) formation of new nuclei that each have half the number of chromosomes that exist in the parent nuclei

   C) tightening of chromatin into chromosomes

   D) separation of duplicated sister chromatids

3. Meiosis creates genetic variation in all of the following ways except:

   A) creating haploid sex cells that will be randomly fertilized

   B) allowing for the exchange of genetic material between chromosomes

   C) increasing the probability of mutations in the nucleotide sequence of DNA

   D) sorting each set of homologous chromosomes independently

   Answers: 1. C) 2. D) 3. C)

DNA REPLICATION

DNA REPLICATION is the process by which a copy of DNA is created in a cell.

The Basics of DNA

Deoxyribonucleic acid, or DNA, has a double helix structure consisting of two complementary strands of DNA. Each DNA strand has a deoxyribose sugar backbone and one of four nucleic acid bases: guanine, adenine, thymine, and cytosine (G, A, T, and C, respectively). These bases bind together to create DNA's two strands: A and T form a pair, and G and C form a pair.

The individual strands of DNA are directional, meaning it matters in which direction the DNA is read. The two ends of a DNA strand are called the 3' end and the 5' end, and these names are included when describing a section of DNA, as shown below:

5'-ATGAATTGCCT-3'

For two complementary strands of DNA, one end starts at 5' and the other starts at 3':

5'-ATGAATTGCCT-3'

3'-TACTTAACGGA-5'

This naming convention is needed to understand the direction of DNA replication, and where the enzymes bind during the process.

The Process of Replication

During DNA replication, three steps will occur. The first step is INITIATION, in which an initiator protein binds to regions of DNA known as origin sites. Once the initiation protein has been bound, the DNA polymerase complex will be able to attach. At this point, the DNA will unwind into two separate single strands.

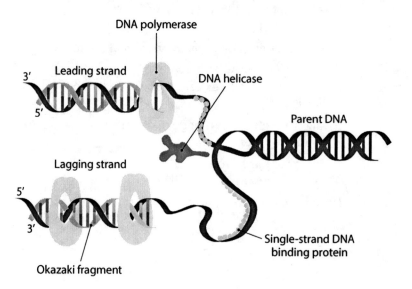

Figure 7.11. DNA replication

During the next step, ELONGATION, new strands of DNA are created. Single strand binding proteins (SSBs) will bind to each strand of the DNA. Then, DNA polymerase will attach and start replicating the strands by synthesizing a new, complementary strand. DNA polymerase reads the DNA in the 3' to 5' direction, meaning the new strand is synthesized in the 5' to 3' direction. This creates a problem, because the DNA can only be read in the 3' to 5' direction on one strand, known as the LEADING STRAND. The LAGGING STRAND, which runs from 5' to 3', has to be synthesized piece by piece in chunks called OKAZAKI FRAGMENTS. The breaks between these fragments are later filled in by DNA ligase.

The last step in the process of DNA replication is TERMINATION. After DNA polymerase completes the copying process, the replication forks meet and the process is terminated. There is one catch to this: because the DNA polymerase enzyme can never read or replicate the very end of a strand of DNA, every time a full chromosome is replicated, a small part of DNA is lost at the end. This piece of DNA is usually non-coding and is called a TELOMERE. The shortening of the telomeres is the reason why replication can only occur a limited number of times in somatic cells before DNA replication is no longer possible.

Table 7.3. Important enzymes in DNA replication

DNA HELICASE	Unwinds a section of DNA to create a segment with two single strands.
DNA POLYMERASE	DNA polymerase I is responsible for synthesizing Okasaki fragments. DNA polymerase III is responsible for the primary replication of the 5' to 3' strand.
DNA LIGASE	Ligase fixes small breaks in the DNA strand and is used to seal the finished DNA strands.
DNA TELOMERASE	In some cells, DNA telomerase lengthens the telomeres at the end of each strand of DNA, allowing it to be copied additional times.

Polymerase Chain Reaction (PCR)

PCR, which was developed in 1983, is a method used in biology to artificially replicate DNA. This can be useful when looking at the presence or size of a gene, or in order to get enough DNA to insert into a host organism. The PCR method uses primers, DNA polymerase, a template, and a machine called a thermocycler in order to replicate the DNA. The basic steps are as follows:

1. Denaturation: The DNA is heated to 90°C to denature it and cause it to form single strands.

2. Annealing: The reaction temperature is set to between 50 and 60°C, which allows the primers to anneal to the template.

3. Elongation: The reaction temperature is set between 70 and 80°C, which is an optimal temperature for a modified DNA polymerase called Taq polymerase. DNA replication occurs.

This set of steps is then repeated up to one hundred times in the thermocycler. As a result, one hundred copies of DNA can result in 1.1×10^{14} copies of DNA in forty cycles.

Examples

1. During DNA replication, the 3' strand and the 5' strand are simultaneously replicated. Which enzyme is responsible for replicated the 3' strand?

   A) DNA polymerase III

   B) DNA ligase

   C) DNA polymerase I

   D) DNA helicase

2. Small sections of DNA are lost during replication because

   A) the sections of DNA between Okazaki fragments cannot be recovered.

   B) DNA polymerase cannot replicate the end of the DNA strand.

   C) DNA cannot be read in the 5' to 3' direction.

   D) the initiator proteins bind to only one strand of DNA.

   Answers: 1. C) 2. B)

TRANSCRIPTION AND TRANSLATION

The processing of information stored in DNA to produce a protein takes place in two stages: transcription and translation. In transcription, an mRNA copy of the DNA is created. In translation, the mRNA strand is read by a ribosome to create an amino acid chain, which is folded into a protein.

Transcription

DNA TRANSCRIPTION is the process of making messenger RNA (mRNA) from a DNA strand. The steps for DNA transcription are similar to that of DNA replication, although different enzymes are used. The DNA strand provides a template for RNA polymerase: the DNA is first unwound, and then RNA polymerase makes a complementary transcript of the DNA sequence.

After the primary transcript has been made, the mRNA is sent to SPLICEOSOMES, which remove the non-coding regions of the RNA called INTRONS. The final RNA product is then available for translation into the actual protein.

Codons

The "message" contained in DNA and RNA is encoded in the nucleotides. Each amino acid is represented by a set of three base pairs in the nucleotide sequence called a CODON. There are 64 possible codons ($4 \times 4 \times 4$), which means many of the twenty-two amino acids are coded for with more than one codon. There is also a stop codon, which instructs the ribosome to stop processing the mRNA.

You will not need to memorize the codons, but you will need to identify corresponding codons and amino acids from a chart like the one shown here.

Table 7.4. Codons and amino acids

1st base	2nd base U		2nd base C		2nd base A		2nd base G		3rd base
U	UUU	(Phe/F) Phenylaline	UCU	(Ser/S) Serine	UAU	(Tyr/Y) Tyrosine	UGU	(Cys/C) Cysteine	U
	UUC		UCC		UAC		UGC		C
	UUA	(Leu/L) Leucine	UCA		UAA	Stop (Ochre)	UGA	Stop (Opal)	A
	UUG		UCG		UAG	Stop (Amber)	UGG	(Trp/W) Tryptophan	G
C	CUU		CCU	(Pro/P) Proline	CAU	(His/H) Histidine	CGU	(Arg/R) Arginine	U
	CUC		CCC		CAC		CGC		C
	CUA		CCA		CAA	(Gln/Q) Glutamine	CGA		A
	CUG		CCG		CAG		CGG		G
A	AUU	(Ile/I) Isoleucine	ACU	(Thr/T) Threon	AAU	(Asn/N) Asparagine	AGU	(Ser/Serine)	U
	AUC		ACC		AAC		AGC		C
	AUA		ACA		AAA	(Lys/K) Lysine	AGA	(Arg/R) Arginine	A
	AUG	(Met/M) Methionine	ACG		AAG		AGG		G
G	GUU	(Val/V) Valine	GCU	(Ala/A) Alanine	GAU	(Asp/D) Aspartic acid	GGU	(Gly/G) Glycine	U
	GUC		GCC		GAC		GGC		C
	GUA		GCA		GAA	(Glu/E) Glutamic acid	GGA		A
	GUG		GCG		GAG		GGG		G

Translation

The TRANSLATION process converts the mRNA transcript into a useable protein. This process occurs in a ribosome, which lines up the mRNA so it can bind to the appropriate tRNA (transfer RNA). Each tRNA includes an amino acid and an anti-codon, which matches to the complementary codon on the mRNA. When the tRNA is in place, the enzyme aminoacyl-tRNA synthetase uses a molecule of ATP to form a bond between the existing amino acid strand and the new amino acid brought in by the tRNA.

The translation process stops when a stop codon is reached in the sequence. These codons activate a protein called a release factor, which binds to the ribosome. The ribosome, which is made of two proteins, will split apart after the release factor binds. This releases the newly formed amino acid chain.

Protein Folding

After the amino acid chain has been produced, the process is still not complete: the amino acid chain needs to be folded into a protein. The polypeptide chain, now able to interact with itself due to hydrogen and disulfide bonds, will start to form a three-dimensional structure. A protein structure has four primary levels of structures:

1. The primary structure is the sequence of amino acids.
2. The secondary structure results from hydrogen bonds within the protein. These bonds create regular patterns called alpha helixes and beta sheets.
3. The tertiary structure is the overall three-dimensional structure and shape of the protein.
4. The quaternary structure results when multiple proteins interact. Not all proteins have a quarternary structure.

Mutations

The DNA or RNA sequence can sometimes undergo a MUTATION, which is a change in the base pair sequence of the DNA or RNA strand. A mutation can be benign or silent, meaning it has no effect, or it can cause a change in the protein structure.

An example of how a single POINT MUTATION can change the entire tertiary structure of a protein is sickle cell anemia. In sickle cell anemia, there is a single change in the base pair sequence from a T to an A. This results in an mRNA transcript codon change from GAA to GUA, which changes the amino acid from glutamate to valine. As a result, the protein is unable to fold properly, and the hemoglobin structure is longer than usual. When present in a red blood cell, this mutation causes the red blood cells to become elongated and sickle-like. As a result, oxygen is not carried as effectively in individuals who have sickle cell anemia.

On the other hand, many mutations will not result in any change in the protein sequence at all. For example, if the sequence CCG mutated to CCA, there would be no change, because the codon produced by both sequences corresponds to the amino acid glycine.

Gene Regulation

An important part of understanding metabolism is learning how genes are activated and deactivated. Studying gene expression and regulation is easier in bacteria due to their simple genomes and the simplicity of extracting their plasmids. Although human gene regulation is becoming more thoroughly understood, the vast complexity of the human metabolism and number of genes makes it difficult to get a full picture of all the interactions.

To understand gene regulation, it's necessary to understand the structure of the genetic code. Proteins are not produced from a single gene; instead, a set of genes, called an OPERON, is required. The operon includes a PROMOTER, which initiates transcription; an OPERATOR, to which an enzyme can bind to regulate transcription; and the protein coding sequence.

Either negative or positive regulation is used to control the operon. In negative regulation, a gene will be expressed unless a

How might mutations in DNA and RNA affect fitness and, consequently, natural selection?

repressor becomes attached. In positive regulation, genes are only expressed when an activator attaches to initiate expression.

In addition to interactions with the operon, the expression of DNA can be controlled by modifications to the chromatin. Because the location of the promoters in the chromatin sequence greatly affects access to the gene, expression can be regulated by managing how tightly bound the chromatin is in the nucleus. Modifications to histone proteins, small amino acid structures found only in eukaryotic cell nuclei, can also inhibit or allow access to DNA.

Lastly, gene expression can be controlled when DNA is methylated at the cytosine group. The methylation of DNA will prevent a DNA polymerase or RNA polymerase enzyme from attaching to the DNA, in effect preventing transcription.

Examples

1. A researcher has discovered a mutation in a sequence of mRNA, which changes a codon from AUG to AAG. What effect will this have on the sequence?

   A) There will be no effect.

   B) The codon sequence will start being translated at a different location than before.

   C) The codon sequence will stop being translated at a different location than before.

   D) The protein will no longer fold at all due to the mismatched codon.

2. Which of the following DNA sequences coding for an amino acid sequence does *not* include a stop codon?

   A) TTG-GTC-TAA-AAT

   B) TTT-GGC-AGA-CTC

   C) GTA-AUG-TAG-AGC

   D) TTC-CAT-CAC-TGA

3. Which of the following removes introns from mRNA?

   A) an operon

   B) an anti-codon

   C) a ribosome

   D) a spliceosome

4. Histone proteins can be found in which of these locations?

   A) eukaryotic cell nucleus

   B) prokaryotic cell nucleus

   C) mitochondria

   D) all of the above

5. Which of the following is not a method by which DNA expression can be controlled?

A) operon

B) methylation

C) promotion

D) sulfonation

Answers: 1. B) 2. B) 3. D) 4. A) 5. D)

GENETICS

GENETICS is the study of genes and how they are passed down to offspring. Before the discovery of genes, there were many theories about how traits are passed to offspring. One of the dominant theories in the 19th century was blending inheritance, which stated that the genetic material from the parents would mix to form that of the children in the same way that two colors might mix.

The idea was eventually displaced by the current theory, which is based on the concept of a GENE, which is a region of DNA that codes for a specific protein. Multiple versions of the same gene, called ALLELES, account for variation in a population.

During sexual reproduction, offspring receive a single copy of every gene from each parent. These two genes may be identical, making the individual HOMOZYGOUS, or they may be different, making the individual HETEROZYGOUS for that gene. In a heterozygous individual, the genes don't blend; instead they act separately, with one often being completely or partially suppressed.

Mendel's Laws

The idea that individual genes are passed down from parents to their children was conceived by **GREGOR MENDEL**. Mendel used various plants to test his ideas, but his best-known work is with pea plants.

Mendel became an Augustinian monk at the age of 21. He studied briefly at the University of Vienna, and after returning to the monastery, started work on breeding plants. During the course of his work, he discovered that the plants had heritable features, meaning features that were passed from parent to offspring. Because of the short generation time of peas, Mendel started working on identifying the traits that could be passed on in the pea plant. He tracked two characteristics: pea flower color and pea shape. From this, he found that the traits were independent of one another, meaning that the pea's flower color in no way affected the pea shape.

During the course of his work, Mendel came up with three laws to describe genetic inheritance: the laws of segregation, independent assortment, and dominance. The LAW OF SEGREGATION states that genes come in allele pairs (if the organism is diploid, which most

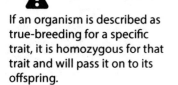

If an organism is described as true-breeding for a specific trait, it is homozygous for that trait and will pass it on to its offspring.

are), and that each parent can only pass a single allele down to its child. Thus, for a pair of alleles in a gene, one comes from the father and one comes from the mother in sexual reproduction. The law of segregation also states that the alleles must separate during the course of meiosis so that only one is given to each gamete.

The **LAW OF INDEPENDENT ASSORTMENT** states that genes responsible for different traits are passed on independently. Thus, there is not necessarily a correlation between two genes. For example, if a mother is tall and has brown hair, she might pass on her genes for tallness to her child, but perhaps not the ones for brown hair. This law can be seen in the use of the Punnett square, in which gene alleles are separated to determine inheritance.

Lastly, the **LAW OF DOMINANCE** states that some alleles are dominant and some are recessive. Dominant alleles will mask the behavior of recessive ones. For example, in a rose red might be dominant, and white recessive. Thus, if a homozygous red rose mates with a homozygous white rose, all of their offspring will be red. Although the white gene allele will be present, it will not be expressed.

Punnett Square

A **PUNNETT SQUARE** is a table-based diagram that can be used to predict the offspring outcome from the mating of a set of parents; it was developed by Reginald Punnett. In the square, the alleles from each parent (the P generation) are placed on the X and Y axes of the square, and the boxes are then filled in to represent the possible offspring gene combinations (F_1 for the first generation). Note that dominant genes are described with capital letters, and recessive genes with lower case letters.

Examples

1. Potatoes can be either round or oval. The dominant gene is oval. A heterozygous oval potato plant (Oo) is mated with a homozygous round potato plant (oo). What will be the distribution of this trait in the first generation of offspring?

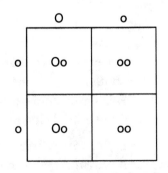

In the Punnett Square above, we have placed the parents on each side of the box. The heterozygous parent is seen on the X-axis as Oo, and the homozygous is on the Y-axis as oo. By separating the alleles (the law of segregation)

and then recombining the possible combinations from the parents, we can predict what the genotype, and thus phenotype, of the offspring will be. **In this case, half of the offspring will be round (oo), and the other half will be oval (Oo).**

2. In the same plant described in problem #1, purple flowers are dominant, and pink flowers are recessive. If an OoPP parent is crossed with an ooPp parent, what would the resulting offspring look like?

	OP	OP	oP	oP
oP	OoPP	OoPP	ooPP	ooPP
oP	OoPP	OoPP	ooPP	ooPP
op	OoPp	OoPp	ooPp	ooPp
op	OoPp	OoPp	ooPp	ooPp

In this case, we separate out the alleles so that each one is matched with the other allele in all the possible combinations:

The four possible combinations for OoPP are OP, OP, oP, and oP. The four combinations for ooPp are oP, oP, op, and op. Filling in the squares gives all possible outcomes for the offspring.

Half will be oval and purple, and half will be round and purple.

Phenotype vs. Genotype

A PHENOTYPE is an organism's observable characteristics, such as height, eye color, skin color, and hair color. GENOTYPE is an organism's genetic code. Although the genotype of two different people might be different, they could have the same phenotype, depending on which alleles are dominant or recessive. For example, the two types of roses Rr and RR are both red, meaning they have the same phenotype. However, they have a different genotype, with one rose type being heterozygous and the other being homozygous.

Individuals with the same genotype may also have different phenotypes. For example, the environment can have a large effect on phenotypic traits. Someone with light brown skin will tan in the sunlight, for instance, and a malnourished child may grow up to be shorter than expected.

Examples

1. In a type of plant newly discovered in South America, the seed color is controlled by the gene R. In these plants, those having the dominant allele R have bright red seeds, and those that have the homozygous recessive allele pair rr have pale pink seeds. In the first generation, a scientist crosses a true-breeding RR plant with a recessive rr plant. The F1 plant is then crossed with itself, resulting in the F2 generation. In the F2 generation, what percentage of the plants will have bright red seeds?

   A) 25%

   B) 50%

   C) 75%

   D) 100%

2. If a recessive trait is linked to the X-chromosome, it will most likely be seen in:

   A) males

   B) females

   C) both genders

   D) neither gender

3. A sex-linked trait primarily seen in males but sometimes seen in females is passed along on the:

   A) 22nd chromosome

   B) 18th chromosome

   C) X chromosome

   D) Y chromosome

4. Below are four statements regarding mutations. Which of these statements are true?

   I.   Mutations are always harmful to the individual or species.

   II. Mutations can be beneficial.

   III. Mutations can occur randomly, without the aid of radiation or chemicals.

   IV. Mutations play an important role in evolution.

   A) I and II are true.

   B) Only II is true.

   C) II and III are true.

   D) II, III, and IV are true.

   Answers: 1. C) 2. A) 3. C) 4. D)

EVOLUTION

Evolution is best defined as descent from previous species with modification. That is, each generation changes slightly from the last until the difference is so great that a new species is formed. Evolution is why there is a diversity of life on Earth; it's the reason there are different species of animals and plants. This was what Charles Darwin meant by the title of his book *On the Origin of Species*.

Charles Darwin

CHARLES DARWIN was an Englishman with an intense interest in nature. Darwin enrolled at several universities, including Cambridge. He became interested in botany there, and had a chance to accompany the HMS *Beagle* on a voyage around the world. It was during this trip that he came across numerous species and started to form the theory of evolution.

Upon his return, Darwin published a book called *On the Origin of Species*. It is worth noting that Darwin did not coin the term evolution at this time, but rather called it "descent with modification." He stated that all organisms were inter-related, and could be traced to a distant ancestor. He was also one of the first to describe evolution as a tree, with different species branching off at different parts of the "tree."

Based on his observations, Darwin proposed the theory of NATURAL SELECTION. Charles Darwin noticed that birds on the Galapagos Islands, while mostly similar, had unique beak shapes that allowed them to eat particular foods. Some beaks were small, some were wide and blunt, and some were needle like. Darwin hypothesized that these different beak shapes arose due to a selection process.

A selection process, whether natural or artificial, refers to the removal of inferior organisms that cannot survive in an environment. For example, farmers use artificial selection when they plant only seeds from plants that have produced a large yield in the past. This practice creates a field of plants that only produces large yields. Natural selection works in a similar fashion, except it is the conditions in nature that determine whether a particular individual will thrive and reproduce.

Darwin proposed the theory of natural selections based on specific observations. These were:

1. The members of a population of species have varied traits. For example, one species of monkey might have fur color varying from white to brown.
2. All species produce excess offspring. For example, if left uncontrolled, rabbit populations will more than double

> **⚠** Natural selection acts on an organism's phenotype, not its genotype. Only alleles that affect an organism's fitness will be selected for or against.

in size every year. Secondly, not all offspring are able to survive.

3. The traits in an individual of a population that give it a higher chance of surviving also allow it to produce more offspring.

4. As a result, "more fit" individuals are more likely to pass on their traits; this will result in a change in the species over time.

This difference in reproduction is the basis of natural selection. Essentially, the traits of an individual determine whether it is "selected" by the environment. Individuals with superior traits are more likely to survive and reproduce, and thus pass on their genes. Individuals with inferior traits will not survive, and their genes will be lost. Over many generations, natural selection will lead to a species being driven toward a certain set of characteristics, which is how evolution occurs.

Speciation

SPECIATION is the process by which organisms evolve and become new species. A SPECIES is generally defined as a group of organisms in which two hybrids are able to produce fertile offspring. However, there is often debate and uncertainty about how species are defined and identified.

Speciation can occur under a number of different conditions. In ALLOPATRIC SPECIATION, a population becomes geographically separated, and the separated populations evolve to the point that they can no longer interbreed. In PERAPATRIC EVOLUTION, a new species is formed when a small portion of the population becomes isolated. PARAPATRIC SPECIATION occurs when populations are mostly separated but share a small area of overlap; selection pressures prevent interbreeding and eventually result in the development of new species.

Patterns of Evolution

Evolution can follow a number of different patterns depending on environmental factors. In DIVERGENT EVOLUTION, two species descended from the same ancestor develop different traits. In CONVERGENT EVOLUTION, two unrelated species develop similar traits, usually to meet the same basic need. For example, flight developed independently in a number of groups of organisms, including insects, birds, and bats. Finally, PARALLEL EVOLUTION occurs when two related species independently develop the same traits.

Case Study: Drug-Resistant Bacteria

Antibiotics and other chemicals are commonly used to treat infections. This has, over the course of the last twenty to thirty years, acted as a selection pressure on bacteria.

Staphylococcus aureus is a dangerous bacteria that resides on the skin of many people. It is ordinarily harmless, but if the individual has a weakened immune system, or the bacteria are allowed to enter the body in large amounts, *S. aureus* will eat away at the flesh of that person. This is the reason it is called the flesh-eating disease, or necrotizing fasciitis.

The best drug to treat *S. aureus* infections is methicillin, which was developed in 1959. However, just several years after the use of methicillin was introduced, methicillin-resistant *S. aureus* bacteria (called MRSA) began to appear. How did this happen?

The use of antibiotics will usually kill 99.9 percent of the bacteria, but some bacteria will manage to survive, through either genetic resistance or an insufficient dose. These bacteria have been artificially selected and will reproduce. Over time, as more and more people use the antibiotic, the small proportion of bacteria able to survive will thrive and multiply, eventually creating a population of methicillin-resistant bacteria.

Today, more than half of *S. aureus* infections are methicillin-resistant, causing doctors to have to look elsewhere for an effective method of treatment. This is a present-day study of evolution in progress.

Examples

1. In order for genetic drift to occur, in which a gene allele drops out of the population, which of the following must be true of the population?

   A) The population is large.

   B) The population is small.

   C) The population has many food sources.

   D) The population is able to survive in many niches.

2. Charles Darwin based his theory of natural selection on a number of logical observations and premises. Which of the following is *not* one of them?

   A) Organisms have many more offspring that the environment could be expected to support.

   B) Many species are able to mutate or alter their genes in order to adapt to the environment.

   C) Organisms are unique, and their offspring inherit traits from their parents.

   D) In a given environment, populations of species typically remain about the same throughout time.

3. Which of the following is an example of convergent evolution?

A) The evolution of tails in both whales and sharks

B) The evolution of pine cones in both southern pine and spruce trees

C) The evolution of pincers in both ants and termites

D) The evolution of feathers in both the sparrow and finch

Answers: 1. B) 2. B) 3. A)

PHYLOGENY AND SPECIES CLASSIFICATION

PHYLOGENY is the understanding of how species evolved through time. The study of phylogeny creates charts called phylogeny trees, which show the inter-relatedness of different species. For example, humans are quite closely related to many mammals, with our DNA being 90 percent similar to that of cats.

The Phylogenetic Tree

A PHYLOGENETIC TREE, shown in the diagram below, shows how groups of organisms are related to each other. The branches represent the relative point in time when each group of species, or family, diversified. For example, we can say according to the tree below that animals and fungi are more closely related than animals and flagellates, due to their relative distances on the tree.

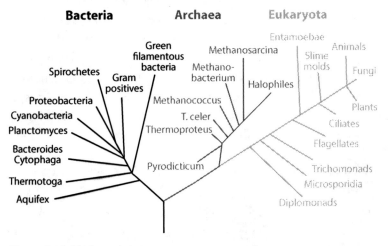

Figure 7.12. Phylogenetic tree

This type of diagram is useful for showing relationships in genetics, but not necessarily actual physical similarity. It should be easy to see that although animals and fungi might share their genotype, they definitely have almost no similar phenotypic characteristics.

The diagram is also relative in nature, meaning that no absolute geologic time scale can be assigned to the branches. We know from the fossil record and DNA evidence which species are more closely related than others are; this allows us to construct the tree. However, other than a rough estimation on when the branching actually occurred, we cannot put exact numbers on the ages of the species.

Taxonomy

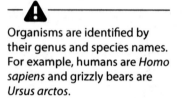

Organisms are identified by their genus and species names. For example, humans are *Homo sapiens* and grizzly bears are *Ursus arctos*.

TAXONOMY is the science of grouping species into correct taxa, or related groups. Groups descend in nature of similarity. For example, the kingdom group is less similar than the genus group. The current classification of species is:

- domain
- kingdom
- phylum
- class
- order
- family
- genus
- species

According to this organization, two species from the same phylum are more related than two species from the same order. A good mnemonic to remember this organization scheme is: *Dear King Phillip Cried Out For Good Soup!*

Morphological Similarities Between Species

Many organisms share phenotypic similarities; these may or may not be due to shared ancestry. A **HOMOLOGOUS STRUCTURE** is a phenotype structure that is similar due to genetic relatedness, as in one species evolved from another, or two species both evolved from a common ancestor. A good example of a homologous structure is the thumb. In the fossil record and from present day analysis, the thumb bone is seen in nearly all mammalian species. This is because they were all derived from a common ancestor.

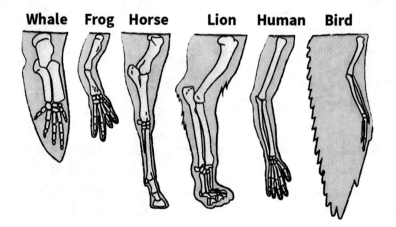

Figure 7.13. Homologous structures

An ANALOGOUS STRUCTURE is one not based on DNA similarity or shared ancestry. A good example of an analogous structure is the comparison between a bird wing and a bat wing. Upon looking at the bone structure, there are some similarities, but the two species have a completely different genetic history, having evolved independently by convergent evolution. As a result, it would be incorrect to conclude that birds and bats are closely related.

Examples

1. Which of the following is an example of an analogous structure?

    A) the fact that salmon and tuna both have gills

    B) the ability of multiple types of plants to grow in a rainforest

    C) the ability of both birds and butterflies to fly

    D) the many different species of elephants that exist

2. Which two species will likely share the greatest percentage of their genomes?

    A) those in the same family

    B) those in the same order

    C) those in the same kingdom

    D) those in the same class

3. A student proposes the idea that the modern day sparrow is a descent of the genus Archaeopteryx, an ancient bird. Which of the following findings would help support this hypothesis?

    A) The finding that Archaeopteryx and sparrows had the same diet.

    B) The finding that Archaeopteryx and sparrows lived in the same region.

    C) The finding that Archaeopteryx and sparrows were both able to fly.

    D) The finding that Archaeopteryx and sparrows share bone structure homology.

    Answers: 1. C) 2. A) 3. D)

BACTERIA

BACTERIA and **ARCHAEA** are a large subset of species that are mostly unicellular. Unlike the kingdoms Plantae and Animalia, nearly all of these species are single-celled prokaryotes, which are unicellular organisms that are quite small, usually less than 10 μm in diameter. (The smallest eukaryotic cells are usually larger than 10μm.)

Like plants, prokaryotes have a cell wall. However, unlike plants, the cell wall structural material is peptidoglycan, which is a polymer created by a mixture of cross-linked proteins and sugar. The cell wall supporting material in plants is called cellulose, which is made entirely from glucose, a sugar. The presence of the cell wall allows prokaryotes to be separated into two classes: gram-positive and gram-negative.

GRAM-POSITIVE bacteria contain peptidoglycan in their cell walls, and they turn purple-red when dyed with gram stain (a solution of crystal violet and iodine). Archaea cell walls contain a cross-linked polysaccharide, but do not have any peptidoglycan. As a result, they are GRAM-NEGATIVE.

As prokaryotes, none of the bacteria or Archaea species contain nuclear membranes. All of the DNA is freely arranged within the cytosol in a structure called the NUCLEOID. In addition to the chromosomal DNA contained inside the nucleoid, the cells also contain plasmids, which are ring-shaped DNA sequences that contain an active gene.

Example

Which of the following is a key difference between organisms in the domains Archaea and Bacteria?

A) Archaea cells do not contain peptidoglycan in their cell wall.

B) Archaea cells do not contain phospholipids in their cell membrane.

C) Archaea cells do not use RNA.

D) Archaea cells do not use ribosomes to produce amino acid chains.

Answer: A)

VIRUSES

A VIRUS is a special form of organism designed to be infectious. Its name is derived from the Latin word for poison. Viruses are interesting organisms that do not contain organelles or other structures usually found in living creatures. For this reason, the question of whether viruses are alive has been a subject of serious debate.

What is the Definition of Life?

Scientists debate many different definitions of life, but in general, there is agreement on the following characteristics:

1. Growth: A living organism must be able to grow, usually by converting some external material into its own mass.

2. Stimulus response: A living organism must be able to react to stimuli in its environment, such as light, other organisms, or toxins.

3. Energy use: A living organism must be able to use energy and convert energy into different forms, either as heat or as a stored energy compound.

4. Homeostasis: A living organism must be able to maintain its own organism conditions within a certain level.

5. Reproduction: Living organisms must be able to reproduce.

6. Mutation: The genetic code of living organisms must be able to change between generations.

7. Autonomous motion: Living organisms must be able to move, even if it is just a short distance.

Under these requirements, the majority of scientists do not consider viruses to be alive. This is because they do not have a metabolism of their own and cannot reproduce by themselves: they require a host.

Virus Structure and Lifecycle

A virus' structure is simple: it consists of a protein coat, known as a CAPSID, which surrounds a nucleic acid, which can be either DNA or RNA. The capsid is a tough layer of protein that is resistant to heat, moisture, and other environmental variables. It protects the genetic information inside the virus, and usually has some sort of receptor or protein that allows the virus to inject its DNA to a host organism.

Viruses can infect many types of cells, including animal somatic cells, plant cells, and bacteria. Because the capsid of a virus reacts with particular receptors on the cell's membrane, viruses usually require a specific type of host cell. For example, HIV infects human immune cells, and the cauliflower mosaic virus mostly infects members of the Brassicaceae family. A virus that infects bacteria is called a BACTERIOPHAGE.

Viruses are obligate parasites (meaning they cannot complete their life cycle outside a host) and inject their DNA or RNA into other organisms in order to reproduce. In most cases, a virus will enter a host and use the host cell's energy and resources to reproduce, and then lyse the host cell, releasing more virus cells. This is known as the LYTIC CYCLE. The lytic cycle of a typical virus is detailed below:

1. Attachment: the virus bonds to the host cell using proteins on the capsid.

2. Entry: the proteins inject DNA into the host cell.

3. Synthesis and reproduction: the DNA is replicated using the host cell's machinery.

4. Assembly: new viruses are assembled from the reproduced parts in the cell.

5. Lysis and release: the virus destroys the host cell, lysing the cell membrane and releasing the newly created virus cells.

Some viruses contain RNA genomes rather than DNA. Among these viruses is the human immunodeficiency virus, or HIV. These viruses inject RNA, and the RNA can be translated into proteins or enzymes directly after infection. In order for this method of transmission to work, the virus must carry some RNA reverse transcriptase. This protein is able to translate RNA back into DNA, so that the host organism can utilize it.

Although viruses are not "alive" per se, they are capable of evolving very quickly due to their short life cycle and their ability to use a host genome. Many viruses are capable of assimilating other pieces of DNA into their own genome, often creating a new virus. For example, what people refer to as influenza, or the flu, is actually a group of viruses that continue to change and evolve; this is why new vaccines are introduced each year.

⚠️
Vaccines contain harmless versions of infectious agents that activate the body's immune system without causing illness.

Examples

1. Viruses and prokaryotes both differ from eukaryotes in that they do not have a nuclear membrane. What is one manner in which viruses are distinguished from prokaryotes?

   A) Viruses contain RNA, and prokaryotes do not.

   B) Prokaryotes have ribosomes, whereas viruses do not.

   C) Prokaryotes can form a protein shell, whereas viruses cannot.

   D) Viruses are harmful to humans, whereas prokaryotes are not.

2. Which of the following statements about viruses is not true?

   A) Viruses are only able to reproduce after infecting a host cell.

   B) Because they are obligate parasites, viruses do not evolve.

   C) Some viruses contain RNA instead of DNA inside their capsid.

   D) Bacteriophages are viruses that infect bacteria.

Answers: 1. B) 2. B)

PLANTS

Plants make up the largest percentage of organic matter on the planet. Without plants, which are autotrophs, the majority of other living organisms could not exist. Plants act as a necessary source of both oxygen and nutrients for the organisms that consume them.

A plant is composed of three basic units: the roots, stems, and leaves. The ROOTS of plants usually reside in the soil and are responsible for absorbing water and minerals from the soil. There are two types of roots: a taproot, which is a central, thick root (think of a carrot), and lateral roots, which are smaller roots that branch out from the main root. Some root tubers, such as potatoes and carrots, are able to elongate and store significant amounts of nutrients.

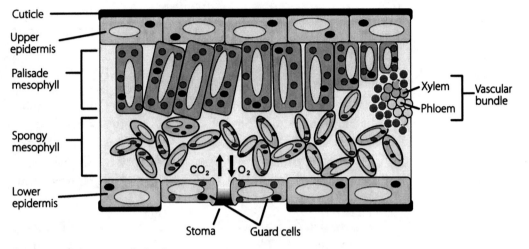

Figure 7.14. Structure of a leaf

The STEM of the plant provides structural stability and also moves water and nutrients from the roots to the other parts of the plant. The LEAVES of the plant are high in surface area and contain the majority of the plant's chlorophyll. They absorb sunlight and perform photosynthesis.

Plants are composed of three main types of cells:

- The PARENCHYMA cells have thin, flexible cell walls and have a large vacuole in the middle of the cell used for storage. These types of cells perform many functions, including many metabolic reactions. Root tissue, the interior of leaves, and most fruit tissue is made from parenchyma cells.
- The COLLENCHYMA cells are seen in parts of the stem and support the plant as it is growing. These cells remain flexible even as they get older.
- The SCLERENCHYMA cells are the most rigid of the cells. These cell types contain high amounts of lignin and cellulose in the secondary cell wall, making it an indigestible structural component of the plant.

The Vascular Tissue System

VASCULAR TISSUE is able to transport sugar and water to other parts of the plant. Plants contain two types of vascular tissue: xylem and phloem. XYLEM is commonly known as woody tissue, and is very stiff. It consists of a series of hollow cell structures that move water from the roots up to the leaves or flowers. PHLOEM is a living tissue near the outside of the stem of the plant which transports sugars.

In plants, the movement of water from the roots to the top of the plant is an important and difficult process. Diffusion is effective over short distances, but in order to move water to the top of a twenty-meter tall tree, additional forces are needed. In plants, the bulk flow of water from the roots is regulated by several mechanisms. These include the capillary action of water moving up the xylem, the transpiration of water from the leaves at the top of the tree, osmotic pressure in the roots, and active transport in the plant.

Plant Growth

Plant growth takes place at MERISTEMS, which are groups of undifferentiated, quickly dividing cells. The roots grow starting at the ROOT APICAL MERISTEM, where new root cells are created and capped by a harder layer of tissue known as the ROOT CAP. Shoot growth occurs at the SHOOT APICAL MERISTEM, and flowers grow from FLORAL MERISTEMS.

The growth at these meristems elongates the plants and is known as PRIMARY GROWTH. Plant stems will also expand outward in a process called SECONDARY GROWTH. The majority of this growth occurs in the CAMBIUM, a layer of high growth cells on the outer edge of the stem. These cells increase the diameter of the stem, and create the wood and bark in woody plants.

Leaves

The EPIDERMIS is the outer layer of leaf cells, and is surrounded by the CUTICLE, a waxy layer that aids the plant in retaining moisture and preventing evaporation from the leaf. The epidermis also contains structures called STOMATA (singular: stoma). These openings in the leaf structure allow carbon dioxide and oxygen to be exchanged for photosynthesis.

The MESOPHYLL consists of parenchyma cells that contain large amounts of chlorophyll and are specialized for photosynthesis. In the middle of the leaf are the two types of mesophyll: the palisade and spongy mesophyll. The PALISADE MESOPHYLL has layers of parallel cells and is located on the upper portion of the leaf. The SPONGY MESOPHYLL is a collection of loosely organized cells that have many spaces in which carbon dioxide and oxygen are able to penetrate.

Plant Reproduction

Plants have a wide variety of reproductive strategies and life cycles. Some plants are able to reproduce asexually by producing genetically identical clones, but the majority of plants reproduce sexually. These plants produce seeds from female and male gametes, known respectively as eggs and pollen.

Seed-producing plants are broken down into two groups: gymniosperms and angiosperms. GYMNOSPERMS, which include conifers, Ginkgos, and cycads, produce "naked" seeds that grow in cones or on the surface of leaves. ANGIOSPERMS, or flowering plants, produce seeds that are surrounded by a fruit which provides protection and can help with seed dispersal.

The reproductive organs of angiosperms are contained in flowers. The PETALS of the flowers are usually colorful appendages that attract pollinators and protect the reproductive organs. At the base of the flower are the SEPALS, protective leaf-like structures. The male and/or female reproductive organs are contained within the petals.

The female organs include the OVARY, which contains egg-producing ovules. The STYLE is a long, slender stalk that connects the ovary to the STIGMA, which collects pollen. Together the ovary, style, and stigma are called the PISTOL (and sometimes the carpel).

The male organs include the ANTHER, which contains the pollen, and the FILAMENT, which holds the anther. Together, the anther and filament comprise the STAMEN. The male gametophytes are known as POLLEN, and are housed inside the anther. Inside each anther are microsporangia, which contain the cells that undergo meiosis to produce pollen.

> ⚠ Flowers often have colors, scents, or shapes that have evolved to attract a specific pollinator. For example, bees can see ultraviolet (UV) light, so many flowers have UV patterns in their petals that humans cannot see.

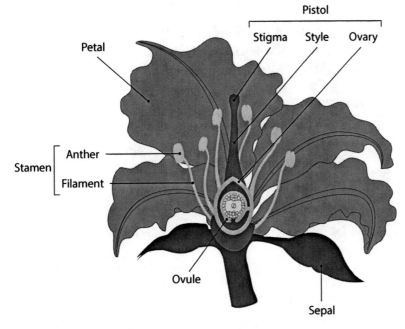

Figure 7.15. Parts of a flower

POLLINATION occurs when there is a transfer of pollen from the anther of one flower to the ovaries of another flower. Pollination can occur through many means, including wind, water, or animals.

After pollination occurs, a pollen tube starts to grow down from the stigma to the ovaries. Upon reaching the ovaries, the pollen tube will discharge two sperm cells into the embryo sac. One sperm cell will be able to fertilize the egg, creating the zygote. The other sperm is involved in the formation of the **ENDOSPERM**, which grows into a nutritious layer that surrounds the zygote. Examples of the endosperm include the grain of wheat and the white meat of a coconut.

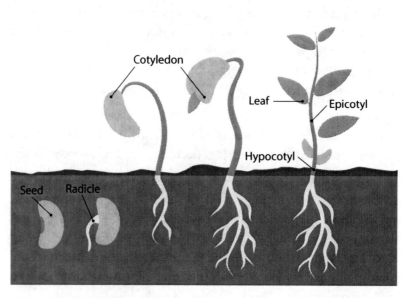

Figure 7.16. Seed germination

The embryo develops a short while after the endosperm. After it has matured, the seed will have several parts, including the epicotyl, the hypocotyl, the radicle, and the cotyledon.

Examples

1. Stomata allow for the passage of all of the following except

    A) carbohydrates

    B) carbon dioxide

    C) oxygen

    D) water

2. In plants, the formation of a seed includes the creation of an endosperm. Which of the following is not true about the endosperm?

    A) It can have a triploid (3n) chromosome number.

    B) The endosperm in many plants contains fats and nutrients for the growing embryo.

    C) The endosperm is created solely from maternal tissue.

    D) The endosperm begins formation after a pollen grain contacts the maternal cell.

3. Which of the following phenomena is not a mechanism by which trees move water from the roots to the leaves?

   A) transpiration

   B) osmotic pressure

   C) capillary action

   D) sublimation

4. Both gymnosperms and angiosperms produce which of the following?

   A) seeds

   B) fruits

   C) petals

   D) endosperm

   Answers: 1. A) 2. C) 3. D) 4. A)

PHOTOSYNTHESIS

DURING PHOTOSYNTHESIS, light energy is absorbed by plants and converted via photosynthesis into sugars. This process is the energy source for nearly all the biomass on Earth. The term is derived from *photo*, meaning light, and *synthesis*, meaning construction. Organisms that are able to produce their own sustenance in this manner are known as AUTOTROPHS.

Photosynthesis takes place in CHLOROPLASTS, which are small organelles in plant tissue that contain CHLOROPHYLL, a green pigment that allows plants to capture the energy from light. Chloroplasts are contained inside the mesophyll of the plant leaf (the section sandwiched between the top and bottom layers of the leaf). Inside the chloroplast are two primary structures: the STROMA, which is the envelope of the chloroplast, and the THYLAKOIDS, which are stacks of sacs that contain the chlorophyll.

The Chemistry of Photosynthesis

The overall chemical reaction of photosynthesis is as follows:

$$6\ CO_2 + 6\ H_2O + \text{Light energy} \rightarrow C_6H_{12}O_6\ \text{(Glucose)} + 6\ O_2$$

The photosynthesis reaction uses carbon dioxide and water, in addition to energy from sunlight, to produce glucose and oxygen. In this reaction, the carbon from carbon dioxide ends up in the glucose molecule. Half of the oxygen from carbon dioxide ends up in the glucose, and the other half ends up in the produced water. All of the oxygen from the water molecules on the reactant side of the equation ends up in the oxygen produced.

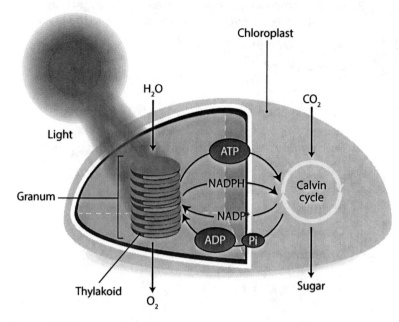

Figure 7.17. Photosynthesis

Similar to aerobic respiration, photosynthesis is an oxidation-reduction process, and relies on the transfer of electrons to be effective. These reactions take place in two phases. The first is the light reactions, in which the energy from the sun is captured and translated into high-energy electrons. The second is in the Calvin cycle, where this energy is used in conjunction with carbon dioxide and water to produce a glucose molecule.

Light Reactions

The **LIGHT REACTIONS** occur in the chloroplast. They take light from the sun, which is best absorbed by chlorophyll between the wavelengths of 420 nanometers to 460 nanometers, and convert it into active electrons.

The movement of electrons in chlorophyll occurs in two systems: **PHOTOSYSTEM I** and **PHOTOSYSTEM II**. These systems work together to funnel high-energy electrons down to a terminal electron acceptor. The passage of electrons along the system is aided by molecules called quinones. At the end of the chain, the enzyme NADP+ reductase adds an electron to an NADP+ molecule, creating the energy storage molecule NADPH. The basic steps of the light reactions are as follows:

1. Light strikes PS II, energizing an electron.
2. The electron is transferred to a primary electron acceptor in P680, a compound in the chlorophyll.
3. An enzyme splits water, supplying two H+ ions and an oxygen atom. The H+ ions form a gradient across the lumen layer in the thylakoid membrane.

4. The energized electrons pass to PSI via a chain of quinone structures.

5. The transport of electrons helps to drive the gradient of H+ ions even further onto one side of the thylakoid membrane.

6. The enzyme NADP+ reductase takes the active electrons and catalyzes the formation of NADPH. Two electrons are needed for one molecule of NADPH.

The Calvin Cycle

Now that the energy molecules of NADPH have been produced by the light-fixing reactions, they can be used to fix carbon dioxide and turn it into glucose. The **CALVIN CYCLE** is somewhat similar to the citric acid cycle, in that there is an intermediate compound (oxalo-acetate in the TCA cycle) recycled after every round of synthesis. The Calvin cycle produces a sugar precursor, known as glyceralde-hyde 3-phosphate (G3P). This 3-carbon molecule requires three cycles of the Calvin cycle for construction with each cycle fixing one molecule of carbon dioxide. Two molecules of G3P are required to create one 6-carbon glucose molecule.

The steps of the Calvin cycle are as follows:
1. Three CO_2 molecules are used by RuBisCo (Ribulose-1, 5-bisphosphate carboxylase/oxygenase), an enzyme, to produce six molecules of 3-phosphoglycerate.

2. 6-ATP is then used to convert the 3-phosphoglycerate into six molecules of 1, 3-bisphosphoglycerate, an activated compound.

3. 6-NADPH is then used to convert the 1, 3-bisphos-phoglycerate into six molecules of glyceraldehyde 3-phosphate. At this point, one molecule of the G3P is exported for conversion to glucose or other materials, and five molecules of G3P continue in the cycle.

4. The five molecules of G3P, in addition to three ATP, are used to regenerate the three molecules of ribulose bisphosphate that catalyze the CO_2 fixation reaction.

Note that this is a energy-intensive process. In order to make one G3P molecule, a plant has to expend nine units of ATP and six units of NADPH. These energy molecules are generated from light reactions that occur in the chloroplast.

C3 vs. C4 Plants

There are two types of carbon fixing plants, referred to as C3 or C4 plants because of the number of carbons that the fixed molecule contains. The majority of plants are C3 and fix carbon into G3P.

C4 plants are rarer, and are seen in only about 20 different plant families. Instead of fixing carbon into glyceraldehyde 3-phosphate, these plants fix carbon into a 4-carbon molecule known as oxaloacetate, which becomes malate that is then transformed into pyruvate for the production of sugar or ATP.

The major difference between these plants is the manner in which they PHOTORESPIRATE. In order to get an adequate amount of carbon dioxide, plants need to have stomata open, which allows air to enter the leaf. This is typical in most C3 plants. However, in hot environments, such as the desert, having stomata open during the day, when the light fixing reactions take place, can be lethal. Thus, C4 plants use a different enzyme, called PEP carboxylase, that can fix carbon dioxide even in very low concentrations. This eliminates the need to have stomata open during the day and reduces the amount of water lost due to photorespiration.

Examples

1. Which of the following is the primary feature distinguishing C3 from C4 plants?

    A) C3 plants use the Krebs cycle and C4 plants use the Citric Acid cycle.

    B) C3 plants produce a 3-carbon glucose precursor whereas C4 plants produce a 4-carbon glucose precursor.

    C) C4 plants are able to tolerate extreme cold temperatures but C3 plants cannot.

    D) C4 plants produce four molecules of ATP per round of the citric acid cycle whereas C3 plants only produce three molecules of ATP per round of the citric acid cycle.

2. The thylakoid membrane structures, found only in organisms with chlorophyll, are the sites that

    A) produce ATP from sugar, much like mitochondria.

    B) trap energy from the sun in the form of NADH and ATP.

    C) provide an active site for the enzyme RuBisCo to fix carbon dioxide.

    D) act as a structural platform from which the plant cell wall is generated.

3. Which of the following is correct regarding the relationship between photosystem I and II?

    A) Electrons are trapped by photosystem I, and proceed to photosystem II.

    B) Photosystem I and II both trap electrons, but only photosystem II produces ATP.

    C) Photosystem II traps energy from the sun to excite electrons, which are then provided to photosystem I.

    D) Photosystem I is located in the cytosol, whereas photosystem II is located in the chloroplasts.

4. A scientist provides a growing sunflower plant with CO_2 that has been made with heavy oxygen, an isotope of normal oxygen that has a weight of 18 AMUs, rather than 16. After the carbon dioxide has been metabolized, where will the heavy oxygen show up?

A) in water secreted by the plant

B) in glucose created by the plant

C) in pyruvate created by the plant

D) in oxygen produced by the plant

Answers: 1. B) 2. B) 3. C) 4. B)

ECOLOGY

Ecology is the study of the relationships between organisms and their environment, including both the BIOTIC components, which are alive, and the ABIOTIC components, which are not alive.

Population Ecology

A POPULATION is a group of individuals of the same species. (As discussed above, a species is any group of organisms who can interbreed and produce fertile hybrids.) This field of study focuses on how populations grow and interact with the enviornment.

Ecologists have developed a number of mathemeatical models that describe how populations may grow. In theory, a population would show geometric (generational) or logarithmic (continuous) growth. In practice, population size is constrained by the enviroment and the resources available. A population's CARRYING CAPACITY (K) is the number of individuals the environment can support.

Species can be placed into two broad categories based on their life histories. Species that produce large amounts of offspring with low parental investment and high mortality rates are known as R-SELECTED species. Examples of such species include rodents and insects. Conversely, some species produce fewer offspring but invest more in each, resulting in a lower mortality rate among the young. These species, which includes humans, are K-SELECTED.

Community Ecology

A COMMUNITY is comprised of populations of many species occupying the same geographic area. Much of community ecology focuses on the many types of interactions between species.

- **COMPETITION** occurs when species compete for the same resources.
- **PREDATION** occurs when one individual (the predator) consumes another (the prey) for sustenance.
- **MUTUALISM** is an interaction between species in which both benefit.

✓

Would the following species be described as r-selected or K-selected?
- mice
- elephants
- whales
- mosquitos
- wheat

The species within a community consume each other for energy and nutrients; these interactions are mapped out in a **FOOD WEB**. In a food web, it's possibly to see which **TROPHIC LEVEL** a particular species occupies. Primary producers (plants) occupy the first trophic level, herbivores make up the second level, and predators comprise the remaining trophic levels.

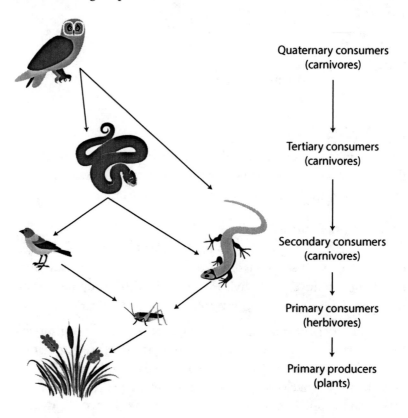

Quaternary consumers
(carnivores)

Tertiary consumers
(carnivores)

Secondary consumers
(carnivores)

Primary consumers
(herbivores)

Primary producers
(plants)

Figure 7.18. Food web

Ecosystems

An **ECOSYSTEM** includes all the biotic and abiotic components in a particular geographic area. Ecosystems are typically defined by their climate, which is the average temperature and precipitation in the area.

- A **TROPICAL RAINFOREST** is typically moist and warm, with average temperatures year round of 25° – 29° Celsius, and receiving 150 – 200 centimeters of precipitation every year. Tropical forests have a large number of species and are the most species-dense of all the ecosystems.

- **DESERTS** are characterized by extreme temperatures and low rainfall. Daytime temperatures can exceed 45° Celsius, and nighttime temperatures can fall below 30° Celsius. Average precipitation is less than 30 centimeters per year.

- The SAVANNA is best characterized as grassland with moderate precipitation. Rainfall is usually between 30 – 50 centimeters every year, and temperatures range between 24° – 29° Celsius.

- CHAPARRAL is an ecosystem characterized by shrubs and low trees. A temperate ecosystem, it features rocky soil and low, rolling hills.

- TEMPERATE GRASSLANDS typically receive 40 – 60 centimeters of seasonal precipitation every year. There are well-defined seasons, with temperatures in the summer rising above 30° Celsius, and temperatures in the winter falling below 0° Celsius.

- CONIFEROUS FORESTS are the most common type of forest. They are characterized by moderately cold temperatures, with an average year-round temperature around 15° Celsius. They feature plentiful coniferous trees, such as pine, hemlock, and spruce.

- BROADLEAF FORESTS, containing many deciduous trees, are characterized by moderate temperatures. They receive 70 – 150 centimeters of precipitation annually.

- The TUNDRA is one of the world's largest land area ecosystems, covering 20% of the world's existing land mass. It is quite cold, with temperatures usually no higher than 10° Celsius, even in the summer.

- WETLANDS, or swamps, are areas of land permeated with shallow water. They are among the most productive habitats in the world and support a high level of biodiversity.

- ESTUARIES are regions that flow from the river into the sea. They are characterized by low beds of silt and sand. Many invertebrate crustaceans live in this zone.

- FRESHWATER ECOSYSTEMS include lakes, streams, and rivers. These bodies of water have a low salt concentration and support a wide variety of wildlife.

- MARINE ECOSYSTEMS, which include oceans, coral reefs, and tidal zones are bodies of water characterized by their high salt content. They cover 71 percent of the Earth's surface.

8

HUMAN BODY SCIENCE

Anatomy and physiology are the studies of body parts and body systems. This section will cover all necessary medical terms, prefixes, suffixes, and terminology as well as the anatomy and physiology of each body system.

TERMINOLOGY

Table 8.1. Directional terms

TERM	DEFINITION
superior	toward the head, or toward the upper body region
inferior	toward the lower body region
anterior (ventral)	on the belly or front side of the body
posterior (dorsal)	on the buttocks or back side of the body
proximal	near the trunk or middle part of the body
distal	furthest away from the point of reference
medial	close to the midline of the body
lateral	away from the midline of the body

Table 8.2. Prefixes and suffixes

PREFIX	DEFINITION	SUFFIX	DEFINITION
epi–	on/upon	–coccus	spherical bacterium
hyper–	over	–ia	condition
hypo–	under	–ectomy	removal
intra–	within	–malacia	softening
para–	beside	–tomy	to cut
per–	through	–rrhea	discharge
peri–	surrounding	–plasty	surgical repair
sub–	under	–opsy	view of

These prefixes can help you on the Reading and English Language Usage portions of the test.

Table 8.3. Cavities

CAVITY	CONTAINS
cranial	the brain
spinal	contains the spinal cord, and extends from the brainstem in the cranial cavity to the end of the spinal cord
thoracic	contains the lungs, heart, and large blood vessels, and is separated from the abdomen by the diaphragm
abdominal	contains the stomach, intestines, liver, gallbladder, pancreas, spleen, and kidneys, and is separated from the thoracic cavity by the diaphragm
pelvic	contains the urinary bladder, urinary structures, and reproductive organs

THE CIRCULATORY SYSTEM

The CIRCULATORY SYSTEM circulates nutrients, gases, wastes, and other substances throughout the body. This system includes the blood, which carries these substances; the heart, which powers the movement of blood; and the blood vessels, which carry the blood.

The Heart

The whole system relies on the HEART, a cone-shaped muscular organ that is no bigger than a closed fist. The heart must pump the blood low in oxygen to the lungs; once the blood is in the lungs, it is oxygenated and returned to the heart. The heart then pumps the oxygenated blood through the whole body.

The heart is located inside the rib cage. It can be found approximately between the second and the sixth rib from the bottom of the rib cage. The heart does not sit on the body's midline. Rather, two-thirds of it is located on the left side of the body. The narrower part of the heart is called the apex, and it points downwards and to the left of the body; the broader part of the heart is called the base, and it points upwards.

The cavity that holds the heart is called the PERICARDIAL CAVITY. It is filled with serous fluid produced by the pericardium, which is the lining of the pericardial cavity. The serous fluid acts as a lubricant for the heart. It also keeps the heart in place and empties the space around the heart.

The heart wall has three layers:

- EPICARDIUM: the outermost layer of the heart, and is one of the two layers of the pericardium.
- MYOCARDIUM: the middle layer of the heart that contains the cardiac muscular tissue. It performs the function of pumping what is necessary for the

circulation of blood. It is the most massive part of the heart.

- **ENDOCARDIUM:** the smooth innermost layer that keeps the blood from sticking to the inside of the heart.

The heart wall is uneven because some parts of the heart—like the atria—don't need a lot of muscle power to perform their duties. Other parts, like the ventricles, require a thicker muscle to pump the blood.

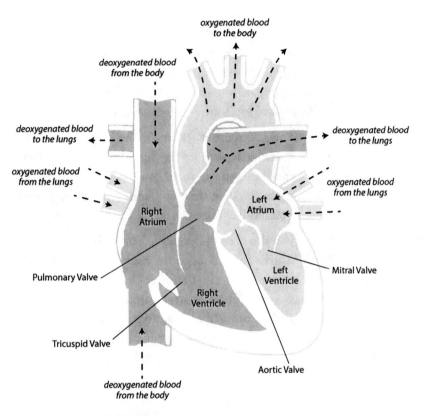

Figure 8.1. Heart diagram

There are four **CHAMBERS** in the heart: the right and left atria, and the right and left ventricles. The **ATRIA** (plural for atrium) are smaller than the ventricles, and they have thin walls, as their function is to receive blood from the lungs and the body and pump it to the ventricles. The **VENTRICLES** have to pump the blood to the lungs and the rest of the body, so they are larger and have a thicker wall. The left half of the heart, which is responsible for pumping the blood through the body, has a thicker wall than the right half which pumps the deoxygenated blood to the lungs.

The heart has one-way valves allowing the blood to flow in only one direction. The valves that keep the blood from going back into the atria from the ventricles are called the **ATRIOVENTRICULAR VALVES**, and the valves that keep the blood from going back into the ventricles from the arteries are called the **SEMILUNAR VALVES**.

The pumping function of the heart is made possible by two groups of cells that set the heart's pace and keep it well-coordinated: the sinoatrial and the atrioventricular node. The SINOATRIAL NODE sets the pace and signals the atria to contract; the ATRIOVENTRICULAR NODE picks up the signal from the sinoatrial node, and this signal tells the ventricles to contract.

The Blood Vessels

The BLOOD VESSELS carry the blood from the heart throughout the body and then back. They vary in size depending on the amount of the blood that needs to flow through them. The hollow part in the middle, called the LUMEN, is where the blood actually flows. The vessels are lined with endothelium, which is made out of the same type of cells as the endocardium and serves the same purpose—to keep the blood from sticking to the walls and clotting.

ARTERIES are blood vessels that transport the blood away from the heart. They work under a lot more pressure than the other types of blood vessels; hence, they have a thicker, more muscular wall, which is also highly elastic. The smaller arteries are usually more muscular, while the larger are more elastic.

The largest artery in the body is called the AORTA. It ascends from the left ventricle of the heart, arches to the back left, and descends behind the heart. Narrower arteries that branch off of main arteries and carry blood to the capillaries are called ARTERIOLES. The descending part of the aorta carries blood to the lower parts of the body, except for the lungs. The lungs get blood through the PULMONARY ARTERY that comes out of the right ventricle.

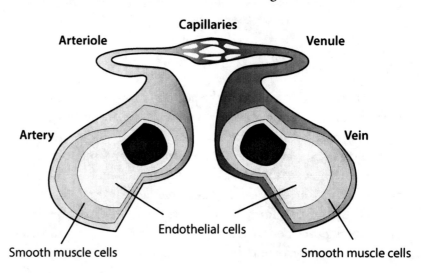

Figure 8.2. Artery and vein diagram

The arching part of the aorta (called the AORTIC ARCH) branches into three arteries: the brachiocephalic artery, the left common artery, and the left subclavian artery. The BRACHIOCEPHALIC ARTERY carries blood to the brain and head. The brachiocephalic artery divides into the right subclavian artery, which brings the blood to the right arm. The LEFT COMMON CAROTID ARTERY carries blood to the brain; the LEFT SUBCLAVIAN ARTERY carries blood to the left arm.

VEINS are blood vessels that bring the blood from the body back to the heart. As they don't work under the same pressure as the arteries, they are much thinner and not as muscular or elastic. The veins also have a number of one-way valves that stop the blood from going back through them.

Veins use inertia, muscle work, and gravity to get the blood to the heart. Thin veins that connect to the capillaries are called VENULES. The lungs have their own set of veins: the LEFT and RIGHT SUPERIOR and INFERIOR PULMONARY VEINS. These vessels enter the heart through the left atrium.

The two main veins are called the superior vena cava and the inferior vena cava. The SUPERIOR VENA CAVA ascends from the right atrium and connects to the head and neck, delivering the blood supply to these structures. The superior vena cava also connects to the arms via both subclavian and brachiocephalic veins. The INFERIOR VENA CAVA descends from the right atrium, carrying the blood from the lumbar veins, gonadal veins, hepatic veins, phrenic veins, and renal veins.

CAPILLARIES are the smallest blood vessels, and the most populous in the body. They can be found in almost every tissue. They connect to arterioles on one end and the venules on the other end. Also, capillaries carry the blood very close to the cells and thus enable cells to exchange gases, nutrients, and cellular waste. The walls of capillaries have to be very thin for this exchange to happen.

The Blood

BLOOD is the medium for the transport of substances throughout the body. There are four to five liters of this liquid connective tissue in the human body. Blood is comprised of red blood cells, hemoglobin, white blood cells, platelets, and plasma.

CONTINUE

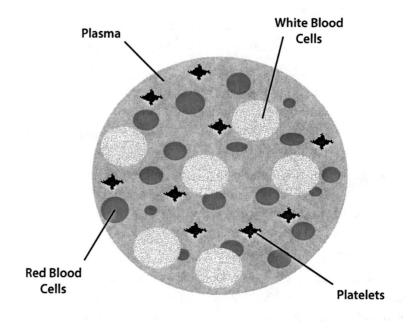

Plasma

White Blood
Cells

Red Blood
Cells

Platelets

Figure 8.3. Blood

Also called ERYTHROCYTES, RED BLOOD CELLS (RBCs) are produced inside the red bone marrow and transport oxygen. HEMO-GLOBIN (HGB) is a red pigment found in the red blood cells, and it is rich in iron and proteins, which both allow these cells to transport the oxygen. RBCs also have a biconcave shape, which means they are round and thinner in the middle. This shape gives them a larger surface area, making them more effective.

WHITE BLOOD CELLS (WBCs), also called LEUKOCYTES, are important for the human immune system. There are two classes of white blood cells: granular and agranular leukocytes. GRANULAR LEUKOCYTES are divided into three types: the neutrophils that digest bacteria, the eosinophils that digest viruses, and the basophils that release histamine. AGRANULAR LEUKOCYTES are divided into two classes: the lymphocytes, which fight off viral infections and produce antibodies for fighting pathogen-induced infection, and the monocytes, which play a role in removing pathogens and dead cells from wounds.

PLATELETS, also called THROMBOCYTES, are vital for blood clotting. They are formed in the red bone marrow and serve many functions in the body. Finally, PLASMA is the liquid part of blood, and it forms 55 percent of the total blood volume. Plasma consists of up to 90 percent water, as well as proteins, including antibodies and albumins. Other substances circulating in the blood plasma include glucose, nutrients, cell waste, and various gases.

The Cardiac Cycle

The heart works by shifting between two states: systole and diastole. In SYSTOLE, the cardiac muscles are contracting and moving blood from any given chamber. During DIASTOLE, the muscles are relaxing and the chamber is expanding to fill with blood. The systole and diastole are responsible for the pressure in the major arteries. This is the BLOOD PRESSURE that is measured in a regular exam. The two values are systolic and diastolic pressures respectively, with the former being larger than the latter.

A CARDIAC CYCLE is the series of events that occur during one heartbeat. These events include:

- Atrial systole: The first phase of the cardiac cycle is atrial systole. With this, the blood is pushed by the atria through the valves into ventricles, which are in diastole during that event.

- Ventricular systole: After atrial systole, ventricular systole occurs. This pushes the blood from the ventricles to the organs, which occurs while the atria are in diastole.

- Relaxation phase: After ventricular systole, there is a pause called the relaxation phase. During this, all the chambers are in diastole, and the blood enters the atria through the veins.

- Refilling phase: When atria are at about 75 percent of their capacity, the cycle starts again. With the refilling phase, the atria are fully filled before atrial systole occurs again.

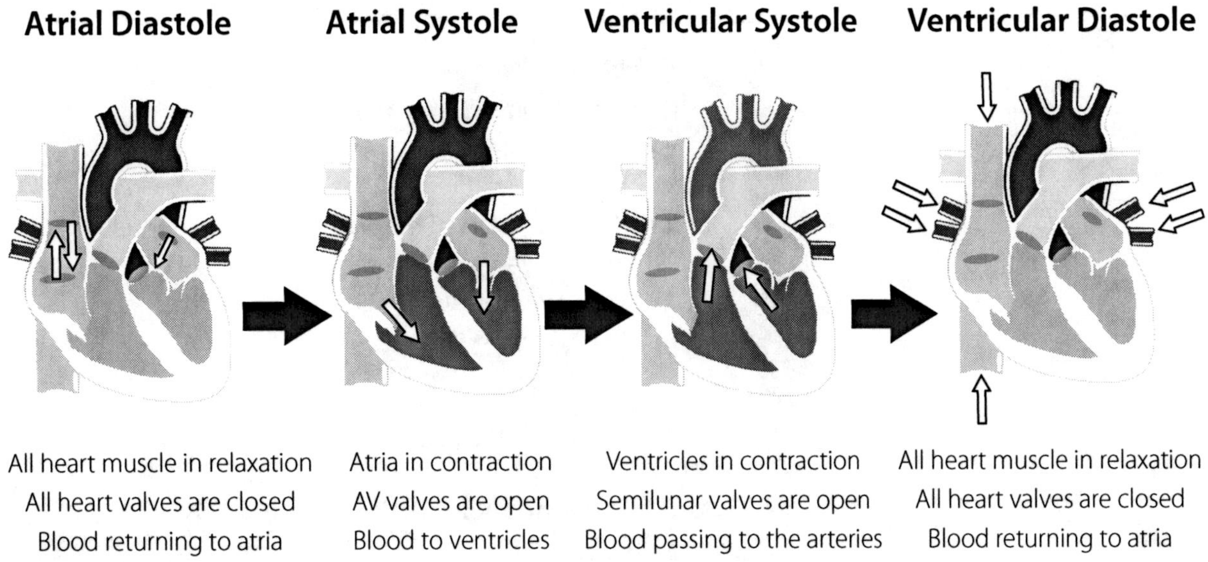

THE HEART VALVES
Try Pulling My Aorta
- Tricuspid
- Pulmonary
- Mitral
- Aorta

Atrial Diastole   **Atrial Systole**   **Ventricular Systole**   **Ventricular Diastole**

All heart muscle in relaxation | Atria in contraction | Ventricles in contraction | All heart muscle in relaxation
All heart valves are closed | AV valves are open | Semilunar valves are open | All heart valves are closed
Blood returning to atria | Blood to ventricles | Blood passing to the arteries | Blood returning to atria

Figure 8.4. Cardiac cycle

Oxygenating the Blood

There are four steps to blood cell oxygenation:

1. The poorly oxygenated blood comes into the right atrium through the superior and inferior vena cava.

2. The blood is then passed to the right ventricle, which sends it through the pulmonary artery into the lungs where oxygenation occurs.

3. The oxygen-rich blood then comes to the left atrium through the pulmonary veins, and gets moved from the left atrium to the left ventricle.

4. By way of blood pressure, the blood is then sent from the left ventricle through the aorta and the aortic arch into the arteries in the whole body.

After leaving the left ventricle, the blood passes from the arteries to the arterioles and on to the capillaries, where the exchange of gases, nutrients, wastes, and hormones occur. The blood then passes into venules, and gets back to the heart through the veins. A healthy resting heart can pump around five liters per minute through this cycle.

The veins of the stomach and intestines don't carry the blood directly to the heart. Rather, they divert it to the liver first, through the hepatic portal vein, so that the liver can store sugar, remove toxins, and process the products of digestion. The blood then goes to the heart through the inferior vena cava.

Examples

1. At what rate does a healthy heart pump blood while resting?

   A) around 3 liters per minute

   B) around 5 liters per minute

   C) around 8 liters per minute

   D) around 10 liters per minute

2. Which of the layers of the wall of the heart contains cardiac muscles?

   A) myocardium

   B) epicardium

   C) endocardium

   D) all layers of the heart

3. The heart chamber with the thickest wall is:

   A) the left atrium

   B) the right ventricle

   C) the right atrium

   D) the left ventricle

4. The blood from the left ventricle goes to:

   A) the right ventricle

   B) the vena cava

   C) the aorta and aortic arch

   D) the lungs

5. The blood vessels that carry the blood from the heart are called:

   A) veins

   B) venules

   C) capillaries

   D) arteries

Answers: 1. B) 2. A) 3. D) 4. C) 5. D)

THE RESPIRATORY SYSTEM

The human body needs oxygen in order to function. The system that is responsible for intake of this gas is called the **RESPIRATORY SYSTEM**. It's also in charge of removing carbon dioxide from the body, which is equally important. The respiratory system can be divided into two sections: the upper respiratory tract and the lower respiratory tract.

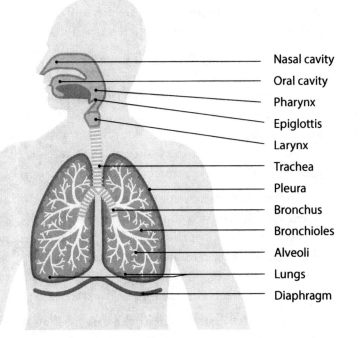

Figure 8.5. Respiratory tract

→

CONTINUE

The Upper Respiratory Tract

The UPPER RESPIRATORY TRACT consists of the nose, nasal cavity, olfactory membranes, mouth, pharynx, epiglottis, and the larynx.

The NOSE is the primary body part for air intake and removing carbon dioxide. The nose itself is made out of bone, cartilage, muscle, and skin, and it serves as a protector of the hollow space behind it called the NASAL CAVITY. The nasal cavity is covered with hair and mucus, which together serve an important function—they stop contaminants from the outside. Common contaminants include dust, mold, and other particles. The nasal cavity prevents the contaminants from entering further into the respiratory system; it also warms and moisturizes air.

The nose and the nasal cavity also contain OLFACTORY MEMBRANES, which are small organs responsible for our sense of smell. They are located on the top of the nasal cavity, just under the bridge of the nose.

We can also breathe through the MOUTH, although it is not the primary breathing opening. The mouth doesn't perform as well when it comes to the three functions of the primary opening (filtering, moisturizing, and warming of air). However, the mouth does have advantages over the nose when it comes to breathing, including its larger size and proximity to the lungs.

The next part of the respiratory system is the THROAT, which is also called the PHARYNX. The pharynx is a smooth, muscular structure lined with mucus and divided into three regions: the naso-pharynx, the oropharynx, and the laryngopharynx.

Air comes in through the nose and then passes through the NASOPHARYNX, which is also where the Eustachian tubes from the middle ears connect with the pharynx. The air then enters the ORO-PHARYNX, which is where air from the mouth enters the pharynx; this is the same passageway used for transporting food when eating. Both air and food also pass through the LARYNGOPHARYNX, where these substances are diverted into different systems.

The EPIGLOTTIS is responsible for ensuring that air enters the trachea and food enters the esophagus. The epiglottis is a flap made of elastic cartilage, which covers the opening of one passageway to allow the air or food to go into the other one. When you breathe, the epiglottis covers the opening of the esophagus, and when you swallow, it protects the opening of the trachea.

The LARYNX is the part of the airway that sits between the pharynx and the trachea. It is also called the voice box, because it contains mucus membrane folds (vocal folds) that vibrate when air passes through them to produce sounds. The larynx is made out of three cartilage structures: the epiglottis, the thyroid cartilage (also called the Adam's apple), and the cricoid cartilage, a ring-shaped structure that keeps the larynx open.

The Lower Respiratory Tract

The LOWER RESPIRATORY TRACT consists of the trachea, bronchi, lungs, and the muscles that help with breathing.

The lower respiratory tract begins with the TRACHEA, also known as the windpipe. The trachea is the part of the respiratory system between the larynx and the bronchi. As its name suggests, the windpipe resembles a pipe, and it's really flexible so it can follow various head and neck movements. The trachea is made out of fibrous and elastic tissues, smooth muscle, and about twenty cartilage rings.

The interior of the windpipe is lined with mucus-producing cells called GOBLET CELLS, as well as cells that have small fringes that resemble hair. These hair-like structures, called CILIA, allow air to pass through the windpipe, where it is further filtered by the mucus. The fringes also help to move mucus up the airways and out, keeping the air passage free.

Connecting to the trachea are the BRONCHI. The PRIMARY BRONCHI, consisting of many C-shaped cartilage rings, branch into the secondary bronchi. Two extend from the left primary bronchi, and three branch from the right, corresponding to the number of lobes in the lungs.

The SECONDARY BRONCHI contain less cartilage and have more space between the rings. The same goes for the TERTIARY BRONCHI, which are extensions of the secondary bronchi as they divide throughout the lobes of the lungs. Like the trachea, the bronchi are lined with epithelium that contains goblet cells and cilia.

BRONCHIOLES branch from the tertiary bronchi. They contain no cartilage at all; rather, they are made of smooth muscle and elastic fiber tissue, which allows them to be quite small yet still able to change their diameter. For example, when the body needs more oxygen, they expand, and when there is a danger of pollutants entering the lungs, they constrict.

Bronchioles end with TERMINAL BRONCHIOLES, which connect them with ALVEOLI, which is where the gas exchange happens. Alveoli are small cavities located in alveolar sacs and surrounded by capillaries. The inner surface of alveoli is coated with ALVEOLAR FLUID, which plays a vital role in keeping the alveoli moist, the lungs elastic, and the thin wall of the alveoli stable. The wall of the alveoli is made out of alveolar cells and the connective tissue that forms the respiratory membrane where it comes into contact with the wall of the capillaries.

The LUNGS themselves are two spongy organs that contain the bronchi, bronchioles, alveoli, and blood vessels. The lungs are contained in the rib cage, and are surrounded by the pleura, a double-layered membrane consisting of the outer PARIETAL PLEURA and the inner VISCERAL PLEURA. Between the layers of the pleura is a hollow space called the PLEURAL CAVITY, which allows the lungs to expand.

The lungs are wider at the bottom, which is referred to as the BASE, and they are narrower at the top part, which is called the APEX. The lungs are divided into LOBES, with the larger lung (the right one) consisting of three lobes, and the smaller lung (the left lung) consisting of two lobes.

Respiration

The muscles that play a major role in respiration are the diaphragm and the intercostal muscles. The DIAPHRAGM is a structure made of skeletal muscle, and it is located under the lungs, forming the floor of the thorax. The INTERCOSTAL MUSCLES are located between the ribs. The INTERNAL INTERCOSTAL MUSCLES help with breathing out (expiration) by depressing the ribs and compressing the thoracic cavity; the EXTERNAL INTERCOSTAL MUSCLES help with breathing in (inspiration).

Breathing in and out is also called PULMONARY VENTILATION. The two types of pulmonary ventilation are inhalation and exhalation.

During INHALATION (also called inspiration), the diaphragm contracts and moves a few inches towards the stomach, making more space for the lungs to expand, and this movement pulls the air into the lungs. The external intercostal muscles also contract to expand the rib cage, and pull more air into the lungs. The lungs are now at a lower pressure than the atmosphere, (called negative pressure), which causes air to come into the lungs until the pressure inside the lungs and the atmospheric pressure are the same.

During EXHALATION (in expiration), the diaphragm and the external intercostal muscles relax, and the internal intercostal muscles contract. This causes the thoracic cavity to become smaller, and the pressure in the lungs to climb higher than the atmospheric pressure, which moves air out of the lungs.

Types of Breathing

In shallow breathing, around 0.5 liters of air is circulated, a capacity called TIDAL VOLUME. During deep breathing, a larger amount of air is moved, usually three to five liters, a volume known as VITAL CAPACITY. The abdominal, as well as other muscles, are also involved in breathing in and out during deep breathing.

EUPNEA is a term for the breathing our body does when resting, which consists of mostly shallow breaths with an occasional deep breath. The lungs are never completely without air—around a liter of air is always present in the lungs.

Examples

1. The primary opening for breathing in and out is:
   A) the nose
   B) the mouth
   C) the skin pores
   D) the pharynx

2. The air that we breathe in through the mouth enters the throat at the:
   A) nasopharynx
   B) oropharynx
   C) laryngopharynx
   D) larynx

3. For air to go to the lungs, the epiglottis needs to close the:
   A) bronchi
   B) pharynx
   C) larynx
   D) esophagus

4. How many lobes does the left lung have?
   A) 1
   B) 2
   C) 3
   D) 4

5. Bronchioles branch from the:
   A) primary bronchi
   B) secondary bronchi
   C) tertiary bronchi
   D) quaternary bronchi

Answers: 1. A) 2. B) 3. D) 4. B) 5. C)

THE SKELETAL SYSTEM

There are a number of roles the skeletal system plays in the body. The bones and joints that make up the skeletal system are responsible for:

- providing support and protection
- allowing movement

- blood cell genesis
- storing fat, iron, and calcium
- guiding the growth of the entire body

Generally, the skeleton can be divided into two parts: the axial skeleton and the appendicular skeleton. The AXIAL SKELETON consists of eighty bones placed along the body's midline axis and grouped into the skull, ribs, sternum, and vertebral column. The APPENDICULAR SKELETON consists of 126 bones grouped into the upper and lower limbs and the pelvic and pectoral girdles. These bones anchor muscles and allow for movement.

Bone Components

On the cellular level, the bone consists of two distinctively different parts: the matrix and living bone cells. The BONE MATRIX is the non-living part of the bone, which is made out of water, collagen, protein, calcium phosphate, and calcium carbonate crystals. The LIVING BONE CELLS (OSTEOCYTES) are found at the edges of the bones and throughout the bone matrix in small cavities. Bone cells play a vital part in the growth, development, and repair of bones, and can be used for the minerals they store.

Looking at a cross section of a bone, you can see that it is made out of layers. These include the PERIOSTEUM, which is the topmost layer of the bone, acting as a layer of connective tissue. The periosteum contains collagen fibers that anchor the tendons and the muscles; it also holds the stem and the osteoblast cells that are necessary for growth and repair of the bones. Nervous tissue, nerve endings, and blood vessels are also present in the periosteum.

Under the periosteum is a layer of COMPACT BONE, which gives the bone its strength. Made out of mineral salts and collagen fibers, it also contains many cavities where osteocytes can be found. Under the compact bone is a layer where the bone tissue grows in columns called TRABECULAE. The bone tissue forms space that contains the red bone marrow. The trabeculae provide structural strength, even while keeping the bones light.

Hematopoiesis and Calcification

Inside the red bone marrow, which is located in the medullar cavity of the bones, a process called HEMATOPOIESIS occurs. In the process, white and red blood cells are made from stem cells. The amount of the red bone marrow declines at the end of puberty, as a significant part of it is replaced by the yellow bone marrow.

When we are born, we have 300 bones. As we grow, the structure of the bones changes. In CALCIFICATION, bones transform from mostly hyaline cartilage and connective tissue to osseous tissue. They also fuse together, which is why adults have 206 instead of 300 bones.

The Five Types of Bones

The LONG BONES make up the major bones of the limbs. They are longer than they are wide, and they are responsible for most of our height. The long bones can be divided in two regions: the EPIPHYSES, located at the ends of the bone, and DIAPHYSIS, located in the middle. The middle of the diaphysis contains a hollow medullary cavity, which serves as a storage for bone marrow.

The SHORT BONES are roughly as long as they are wide, and are generally cube-shaped or round. Short bones in the body include the carpal bones of the wrist and tarsal bones of the foot. The FLAT BONES do not have the medullary cavity because they are thin and usually thinner on one end region. Flat bones in the body include the ribs, the hip bones, as well as the frontal, the parietal, and the occipital bones of the skull. The IRREGULAR BONES are those bones that do not fit the criteria to be the long, the short, or the flat bones. The vertebrae and the sacrum, among others, are irregular bones.

There are only two SESAMOID BONES that are actually counted as proper bones: the patella and the pisiform bone. Sesamoid bones are formed inside the tendons located across the joints, and apart from the two mentioned, they are not present in all people.

The Skull

Made out of twenty-two bones, the SKULL protects the brain and the sense organs for vision, hearing, smell, taste and balance. The skull has only one movable joint that connects it with the mandible—the jaw bone, which is the only movable bone of the skull. The other twenty-one are fused together.

The upper part of the skull is known as the CRANIUM, which is the part that protects the brain, while the lower and frontal parts of the skull form the facial bones. Located just under the mandible, and not a part of the skull, is the HYOID BONE. The hyoid is the only bone in the body that is not attached to any other bone. It helps keep the trachea open and is where the tongue muscles are anchored.

Other bones closely connected to, but not part of the skull, are the AUDITORY OSSICLES: the malleus, incus, and stapes. These bones play an important role in hearing.

The Vertebral Column

The VERTEBRAL COLUMN, or the spine, begins at the base of the skull and stretches through the trunk down the middle of the back to the coccyx; it provides support for the weight of the upper body and protects the spinal cord. It is made up of twenty-four vertebrae, plus the SACRUM and the COCCYX (the tailbone). These twenty-four vertebrae are divided into three groups:

- the CERVICAL, or the neck vertebrae (seven bones)
- the THORACIC, or the chest vertebrae (twelve bones)
- the LUMBAR, or the lower back vertebrae (five bones)

Furthermore, each vertebra has its own name, which is derived from the first letter of the group to which it belongs (for example, *L* for lumbar vertebrae). The letter is placed first, followed by a number (the first of the lumbar vertebrae is thus called *L1*).

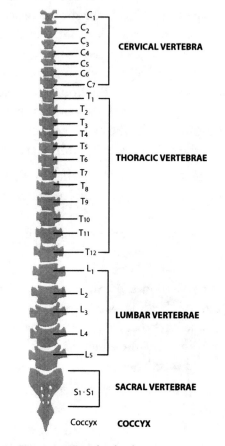

Figure 8.6 Vertebral column

The Ribs and the Sternum

The ribs and the sternum are the bones that form the rib cage of the thoracic region. The STERNUM, also known as the breastbone, is a thin bone that goes along the midline of the thoracic region. Most of the ribs are connected to this bone via the COSTAL CARTILAGE, a thin band of cartilage.

The human skeleton has twelve RIBS. On the back side, they are attached to the thoracic vertebrae. On the front, the first seven of them attach directly to the sternum, the next three attach to the cartilage between the seventh rib and the sternum, and the remaining two do not attach to the sternum at all. Rather, they protect the kidneys, not the lungs and heart. The first seven ribs are known as the true ribs, and the rest are known as false ribs. Together, these bones form the THORACIC CAGE, which supports and protects the heart and lungs.

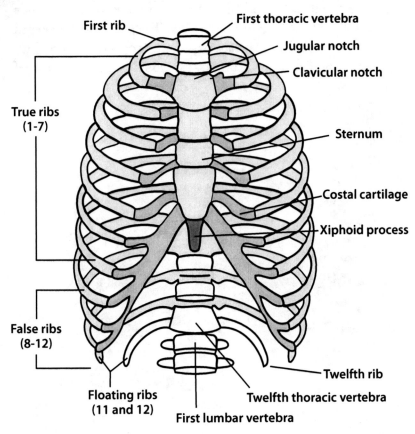

First rib

First thoracic vertebra

Jugular notch

Clavicular notch

True ribs
(1-7)

Sternum

Costal cartilage

Xiphoid process

False ribs
(8-12)

Twelfth rib

Floating ribs
(11 and 12)

Twelfth thoracic vertebra

First lumbar vertebra

Figure 8.7. Ribs

The Appendicular Skeleton

The upper limbs, which belong to the APPENDICULAR SKELETON, are connected with the axial skeleton by the PECTORAL GIRDLE. The pectoral girdle is formed from the left and right CLAVICLE and SCAPULA. The scapula and the HUMERUS, the bones of the upper arm, form the ball and socket of the shoulder joint. The upper limbs also include the ULNA, which forms the elbow joint with the humerus, and the RADIUS, which allows the turning movement at the wrist.

The WRIST JOINT is formed out of the forearm bones and the eight CARPAL bones, which themselves are connected with the five METACARPALS. Together, these structures form the bones of the hand. The metacarpals connect with the fingers, each made out of three bones called PHALANGES, except the thumb which only has two phalanges.

The lower limbs are connected to the axial skeleton by the PELVIC GIRDLE, which includes the left and right hip bones. The hip joint is formed by the hip bone and the FEMUR, which is the largest bone in the body. On its other end, the femur forms the knee joint with the PATELLA (the kneecap) and the TIBIA, which is one of the bones of the lower leg.

Of the two lower leg bones, the TIBIA is the larger, and it carries the weight of the body. The FIBULA, the other leg bone, serves mostly to anchor the muscle. Together, these two bones form the ankle joint with a foot bone called the TALUS. The talus is one of seven tarsal bones which form the back part of the foot and the heel. They connect to the five long METATARSALS, which form the foot itself and connect to the toes. Each toe is made out of three phalanges, except the big toe, which has only two phalanges.

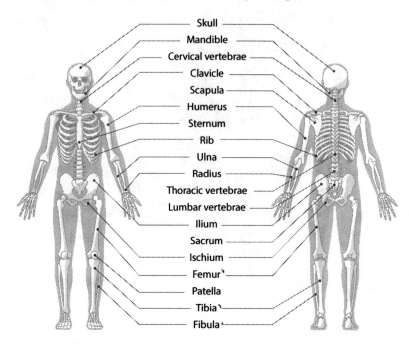

Figure 8.8. Skeletal system

The Joints

The JOINTS, also known as articulations, are where the bones come into contact with each other, with cartilage, or with teeth. There are three types of joints: synovial, fibrous, and cartilaginous joints.

The SYNOVIAL JOINTS feature a small gap between the bones that is filled with synovial fluid, which lubricates the joint. They are the most common joints in the body, and they allow the most movement. FIBROUS JOINTS, found where bones fit tightly together, permit little to no movement. These joints also hold teeth in their sockets. In a CARTILAGINOUS JOINT, two bones are held together by cartilage; these joints allow more movement than fibrous joints but less than synovial ones.

Examples

1. How many bones do adults have?
   A) 201
   B) 206
   C) 222
   D) 300

2. Stem cells can be found in the:

A) red bone marrow

B) periosteum

C) compact bones

D) cartilaginous joints

3. The long bones are the main bones of the:

A) limbs

B) thoracic cage

C) scull

D) vertebral column

4. The jawbone is called the:

A) mandible

B) cranium

C) hyoid

D) ulna

5. The second vertebra in the chest region is called:

A) L2

B) L3

C) T2

D) T3

Answers: 1. B) 2. A) 3. A) 4. A) 5. C)

THE MUSCULAR SYSTEM

Movement is the main function of the MUSCULAR SYSTEM; muscles are found attached to the bones in our bodies and allow us to move our limbs. They also work in the heart, blood vessels, and digestive organs, where they facilitate movement of substances through the body. In addition to movement, muscles also help support the body's posture and create heat. There are three types of muscle: visceral, cardiac, and skeletal.

Visceral Muscle

VISCERAL MUSCLE is the weakest type of muscle. It can be found in the stomach, intestines, and blood vessels, where it helps contract and move substances through them. We cannot consciously control visceral muscle—it is controlled by the unconscious part of the brain. That's why it's sometimes referred to as *involuntary muscle*.

Visceral muscle is also called SMOOTH MUSCLE because of its appearance under the microscope. The cells of the visceral muscle form a smooth surface, unlike the other two types of muscle.

Cardiac Muscle

CARDIAC MUSCLE is only found in the heart; it makes the heart contract and pump blood through the body. Like visceral muscle, cardiac muscle cannot be voluntarily controlled. Unlike visceral muscle, however, the cardiac muscle is quite strong.

Cardiac muscle is composed of individual muscle cells called CARDIOMYOCYTES that are joined together by INTERCALATED DISCS. These discs allow the cells in cardiac muscle to contract in sync. When observed under a microscope, light and dark stripes are visible in the muscle: this pattern is caused by the arrangement of proteins.

Skeletal Muscle

The last type of muscle is SKELETAL MUSCLE, which is the only type of muscle that contracts and relaxes by voluntary action. Skeletal muscle is attached to the bone by tendons. Tendons are formed out of connective tissue rich in collagen fibers.

Skeletal muscle is made out of cells that are lumped together to form fiber structures. These fibers are covered by a cell membrane called the SARCOLEMMA, which serves as a conductor for electrochemical signals that tell the muscle to contract or expand. The TRANSVERSE TUBES, which are connected to the sarcolemma, transfer the signals deeper into the middle of the muscle fiber.

CALCIUM IONS, which are necessary for muscle contraction, are stored in the SARCOPLASMIC RETICULUM. The fibers are also rich in MITOCHONDRIA, which act as power stations fueled by sugars and providing the energy necessary for the muscle to work. Muscle fibers are mostly made out of MYOFIBRILS, which do the actual contracting. Myofibrils are made out of protein fibers arranged into small subunits called SARCOMERES.

Skeletal muscle can be divided into two types, according to the way it produces and uses energy. TYPE I fibers contract slowly and are used for stamina and posture. They produce energy from sugar using aerobic respiration, making them resistant to fatigue. TYPE II muscle fibers contract more quickly. Type IIA fibers are found in the legs, and are weaker and show more endurance than Type IIB fibers, which are found mostly in the arms.

Skeletal muscles work by contracting. This shortens the length in their middle part, called the muscle belly, which in turn pulls one bone closer to another. The bone that remains stationary is called the ORIGIN. The other bone, the one that is actually moving towards the other, is called the INSERTION.

Skeletal muscles usually work in groups. The muscle mainly responsible for the action is called the AGONIST, and it's always paired with another muscle that does the opposite action, called the ANTAGONIST. If the two were to contract together at the same time, they would cancel each other out and produce no movement. Other muscles that support the agonist include SYNERGISTS, which are found near the agonist, attach to the same bones, stabilize the movement, and reduce unnecessary movement. FIXATORS are other support muscles that keep the origin stable.

There are several different ways to name the more than 600 skeletal muscles found in the human body. Muscles can be named according to:

- the region of the body in which they're located (e.g., transverse abdominis)
- number of origins (e.g., biceps)
- bones to which they are attached (e.g., occipitofrontalis)
- function (e.g., flexor)
- relative size (e.g., gluteus maximus)

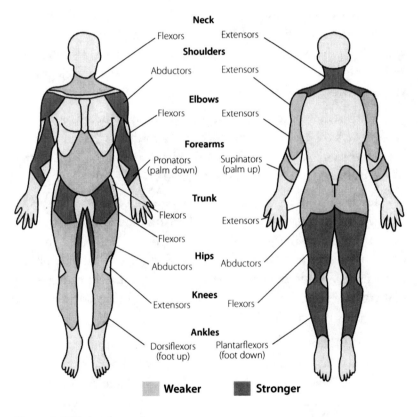

Figure 8.9. Skeletal muscles

Motor Neurons and Contractions

The neurons that control muscles are called MOTOR NEURONS. Motor neurons control a number of muscle cells that together are called the MOTOR UNIT. The number of cells in the motor unit is larger in big muscles that need more strength, like those in the arms and legs. In small muscles where precision is more important than strength, like the muscles in fingers and around the eyes, the number of cells in motor units is smaller.

When signaled by motor neurons, muscles can contract in several different ways:

- Isotonic muscle contractions produce movement.
- Isometric muscle contractions maintain posture and stillness.
- Muscle tone is naturally occurring constant semi-contraction of the muscle.
- Twitch contraction is a short contraction caused by a single, short nerve impulse.
- Temporal summation is a phenomenon in which a few short impulses delivered over time build up the muscle contraction in strength and duration.
- Tetanus is a state of constant contraction caused by many rapid short impulses.

Muscle Metabolism

There are two ways muscles get energy: through aerobic respiration, which is most effective, and through LACTIC ACID FERMENTATION, which is a type of anaerobic respiration. The latter is less effective and it only happens when blood cannot get into the muscle due to very strong or prolonged contraction.

In both these methods, the goal is to produce ADENOSINE TRI-PHOSPHATE (ATP) from glucose. ATP is the most important energy molecule for our bodies. During its conversion to ADENOSINE DI-PHOSPHATE (ADP), energy is released.

Muscles also use other molecules to help in the production of energy. MYOGLOBIN stores oxygen, allowing muscles to use aerobic respiration even when there is no blood coming into the muscles. CREATINE PHOSPHATE creates ATP by giving its phosphate group to the energy-depleted adenosine di-phosphate. Lastly, muscles use GLYCOGEN, a large molecule made out of several glucose molecules, which helps muscles make ATP.

When it runs out of energy, a muscle goes into a state called MUSCLE FATIGUE. This means it contains little to no oxygen, ATP, or glucose, and that it has high levels of lactic acid and ADP. When a muscle is fatigued, it needs more oxygen to replace the oxygen used up from myoglobin sources, and to rebuild its other energy supplies.

Examples

1. Which type of muscle is found in the blood vessels?
   A) cardiac muscle
   B) skeletal muscle
   C) visceral muscle
   D) Type IIA

2. Cardiac muscle is:

A) involuntary muscle

B) voluntary muscle

C) both

D) neither

3. Tendons always attach skeletal muscle to bone:

A) along the entire length of the bone

B) at one end only

C) at both ends

D) on at least one end

4. Myofibrils:

A) store sugars

B) are found only in smooth muscle

C) make up the sarcolemma

D) cause muscle contractions

5. Which is the strongest type of skeletal muscle?

A) Type I

B) Type II A

C) Type II B

D) Type III

Answers: 1. C) 2. A) 3. D) 4. D) 5. C)

THE NERVOUS SYSTEM

The NERVOUS SYSTEM consists of the brain, the spinal cord, the nerves, and the sensory organs. This system is responsible for gathering, processing, and reacting to information from both inside and outside of the body. It is divided into two parts: the central nervous system and the peripheral nervous system. The CENTRAL NERVOUS SYSTEM (CNS) is made of the brain and spinal cord and is responsible for processing and storing information, as well as deciding on the appropriate action and issuing commands.

The PERIPHERAL NERVOUS SYSTEM (PNS) is responsible for gathering information, transporting it to the CNS, and then transporting commands from the CNS to the appropriate organs. Sensory organs and nerves do the gathering and transporting of information, while the efferent nerves transport the commands.

Nervous System Cells

The nervous system is mostly made out of nervous tissue, which in turn consists of two classes of cells: neurons and neuralgia. NEURONS are the nerve cells. They can be divided into several distinct parts.

The SOMA is the body of the neuron; it contains most of the cellular organelles. DENDRITES are small, treelike structures that extend from the soma. Their main responsibility is to carry information to the soma, and sometimes away from it. Also extending from the soma is the long, thin AXON. There is usually one axon per soma, but the axon can branch out farther. It is responsible for sending information from the soma, rarely to it. Lastly, the places where two neurons meet, or where they meet other types of cells, are called SYNAPSES.

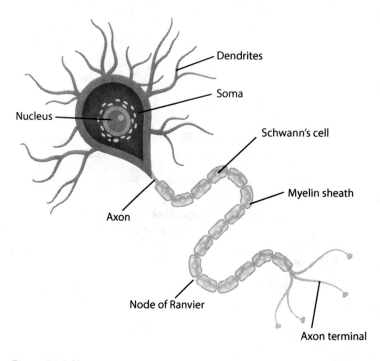

Figure 8.10. Neuron

Neurons can be divided into three classes. EFFERENT NEURONS are motor neurons responsible for transmitting signals from the CNS to the effectors in the body, while AFFERENT NEURONS transmit signals from receptors in the body to the CNS. The third type of neuron—INTERNEURONS—form complex networks in the CNS. They integrate the signals received from the afferent neurons, and control the body by sending signals through the efferent neurons.

Together, these three types of neurons perform the three main tasks of the nervous system:

1. Efferent neurons (also called motor neurons) signal effector cells in muscles and glands to react to stimuli.

2. Afferent neurons (also called sensory neurons) take in information from inside and outside the body through the sensory organs and receptors.

3. Interneurons transmit information to the CNS where it is evaluated, compared to previously stored information, stored or discarded, and used to make a decision (a process called integration).

NEUROGLIA are the maintenance cells for neurons. Neurons are so specialized that they almost never reproduce. Therefore, they need the neuroglial cells, a number of which surround every neuron, to protect and feed them. Neuroglia are also called the GLIAL CELLS.

Protecting the Central Nervous System (CNS)

The **CNS** consists of the brain and spinal cord. Both are placed within cavities in protective skeletal structures: the brain is housed in the cranial cavity of the skull, and the spinal cord is enclosed in the vertebral cavity in the spine.

Since the organs that form the CNS are vital to our survival, they are also protected by two other important structures: the meninges and the cerebrospinal fluid. The MENINGES are a protective covering of the CNS made up of three distinct layers. The first is the DURA MATER, which, as its name suggests, is the most durable, outer part of the meninges. It is made out of collagen fibers—rich and thick connective tissue, and it forms a space for the cerebrospinal fluid around the CNS.

Next is the ARACHNOID MATER, which is the thin lining on the inner side of the dura mater. It forms many tiny fibers that connect the dura mater with the next layer, the PIA MATER, which is separated from the arachnoid mater by the SUBARACHNOID SPACE. The pia mater directly covers the surface of the brain and spinal cord, and it provides sustenance to the nervous tissue through its many blood vessels.

The subarachnoid space is filled with CEREBROSPINAL FLUID (**CSF**), a clear fluid formed from blood plasma. CSF can also be found in the ventricles (the hollow spaces in the brain) and in the central canal (a cavity found in the middle of the spinal cord).

As the CNS floats in the cerebrospinal fluid, it appears lighter than it really is. This is especially important for the brain, because the fluid keeps it from being crushed by its own weight. The floating also protects the brain and the spinal cord from shock—like sudden movements and trauma. Additionally, the CSF contains the necessary chemical substance for the normal functioning of the nervous tissue, and it serves to remove the cellular waste from the neurons.

The Brain

The nervous tissue that makes up the brain is divided into two classes. The GRAY MATTER, which consists mostly of interneurons that are unmyelinated, is the tissue where the actual processing of signals happens. It is also where the connections between neurons are made. The WHITE MATTER, which consists mostly of myelinated neurons, is the tissue that conducts signals to, from, and between the gray matter regions.

The brain can be divided into three distinct parts: the prosencephalon (forebrain), the mesencephalon (midbrain), and the rhombencephalon (hindbrain).

The PROSENCEPHALON is further broken down into two more regions: the cerebrum and the diencephalon. The outermost and the largest part of the brain, the CEREBRUM is divided through the middle by the longitudinal fissure into the left and the right hemisphere, each of which is further divided into four lobes: the frontal, parietal, temporal, and occipital.

The surface of the cerebrum, called the CEREBRAL CORTEX, is made out of gray matter with characteristic grooves (SULCI) and bulges (GYRI). The cerebral cortex is where the actual processing happens in the cerebrum: it's responsible for the higher brain functions like thinking and using language. Under the cerebral cortex, there is a layer of white matter, which connects the regions of the cerebrum with one another, and the cerebrum itself with the rest of the body. It contains a special band of white matter that connects the two hemispheres, which is called the CORPUS CALLOSUM. The regions located under the white matter are divided into two groups: the basal nuclei, which help control and regulate the movement of muscles, and the limbic system, which plays a role in memory, emotions, and survival.

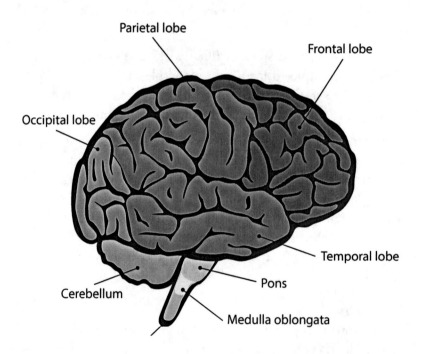

Figure 8.11. The brain

The DIENCEPHALON is a structure formed by the thalamus, hypothalamus, and the pineal gland. Made out of two gray matter masses, the THALAMUS is located around the third ventricle of the brain. Its role is to route the sensory signals to the correct parts of the cerebral cortex. Under the thalamus is the HYPOTHALAMUS, which plays a role in regulating hunger, thirst, blood pressure and body temperature changes, as well as heart rate and the production of hormones. The PINEAL GLAND is located beneath the hypothalamus (and is directly controlled by it) and produces the hormone melatonin, which plays a vital role in sleep.

The MESENCEPHALON is the topmost part of the brain stem. It is divided into two regions. The first is the TECTUM, which plays a role in reflex reactions to visual and auditory information. Second is the CEREBRAL PEDUNCLES, which connect the cerebrum and thalamus with the lower parts of the brain stem and the spinal cord. It also contains the SUBSTANTIA NIGRA, which is involved in muscle movement, reward-seeking, and learning.

The RHOMBENCEPHALON consists of the brain stem and the cerebellum. The brain stem is further broken down into the medulla oblongata and the pons. The MEDULLA OBLONGATA connects the spinal cord with the pons. It is mostly made out of white matter, but it also contains gray matter that processes involuntary body functions like blood pressure, level of oxygen in the blood, and reflexes like sneezing, coughing, vomiting, and swallowing. The PONS is located between the medulla oblongata and the midbrain, and in front of the cerebellum. It is in charge of transporting signals to and from the cerebellum, and between the upper regions of the brain, the medulla, and the spinal cord.

The CEREBELLUM looks like a smaller version of the cerebrum—it has two spheres and is wrinkled. Its outer layer, called the CEREBELLAR CORTEX, consists of gray matter, while the inner part, called the ARBOR VITAE, consists of white matter which transports signals between the cerebellum and the rest of the body. The cerebellum's role is to control and coordinate complex muscle activities. It also helps us maintain posture and keep balance.

The Spinal Cord
The SPINAL CORD, located inside the vertebral cavity, is made out of both white and gray matter. It carries signals and processes some reflexes to stimuli. The spinal nerves stretch out from it.

Peripheral Nervous System (PNS)
The nerves that form the **PNS** are made of bundled axons whose role is to carry signals to and from the spinal cord and the brain. A single axon, covered with a layer of connective tissue called the ENDONEURIUM, bundles with other axons to form FASCICLES. These are covered with another sheath of connective tissue called the PERINEURIUM. Groups of fascicles wrapped together in another layer of connective tissue, the EPINEURIUM, form a whole nerve.

There are five types of peripheral nerves. The AFFERENT, EFFERENT and MIXED nerves are formed out of the neurons that share the same name and perform the same roles. The SPINAL NERVES—thirty-one pairs in total—extend from the side of the spinal cord. They exit the spinal cord between the vertebrae, and they carry information to and from the spinal cord and the neck, the arms, the legs, and the trunk. They are grouped and named according to the region they originate from: eight pairs of cervical, twelve pairs of thoracic, five pairs of lumbar, five pairs of sacral, and one pair of coccygeal nerves. Lastly, the CRANIAL NERVES—twelve pairs in total—extend from the lower side of the brain. They are identified by their number, and they connect the brain with the sensory organs, head muscles, neck and shoulder muscles, the heart, and the gastrointestinal track.

The Sense Organs

The sense organs include the specialized sense organs, which are responsible for the specialized senses: hearing, sight, balance, smell, and taste. Sense organs also have sensory receptors for the general senses, which include touch, pain, and temperature. These senses are part of the PNS, and their role is to detect the stimuli and send the signal to the CNS when the detection occurs.

The Divisions of the Peripheral Nervous System

The PNS is divided into two parts based on our ability to exert conscious control. The part of the PNS we can consciously control is the SOMATIC NERVOUS SYSTEM (SNS), which stimulates the skeletal muscles. The AUTONOMIC NERVOUS SYSTEM (ANS) cannot be consciously controlled; it stimulates the visceral and cardiac muscle, as well as the glandular tissue.

The ANS itself is further divided into the sympathetic, parasympathetic, and enteric nervous systems. The SYMPATHETIC NERVOUS SYSTEM forms the fight or flight reaction to stimuli like emotion, danger, and exercise. It increases respiration and heart rate, decreases digestion, and releases stress hormones. The PARASYMPATHETIC NERVOUS SYSTEM is responsible for stimulating activities that occur when the body is at rest, including digestion and sexual arousal.

Lastly, the ENTERIC NERVOUS SYSTEM is responsible for the digestive system and its processes. This system works mostly independently from the CNS, although it can be regulated through the sympathetic and parasympathetic systems.

Examples

1. Which of the following forms the CNS with the brain?
   A) the peripheral nerves
   B) the sensory organs
   C) the spinal cord
   D) the cerebral cortex

2. The part of the neuron that is mainly responsible for transporting information from the cell is called the:

A) soma

B) axon

C) dendrites

D) sulci

3. The neurons that signal muscles to contract are called:

A) neuroglia

B) afferent neurons

C) interneurons

D) efferent neurons

4. Cerebrospinal fluid can be found in all of the following except:

A) arachnoid mater

B) the central canal

C) the ventricles

D) the subarachnoid space

5. The hypothalamus is located in the:

A) mesencephalon

B) rhombencephalon

C) prosencephalon

D) pineal gland

Answers: 1. C) 2. B) 3. D) 4. A) 5. C)

THE DIGESTIVE SYSTEM

The **DIGESTIVE SYSTEM** is a system of organs in the body that is responsible for the intake and processing of food and the removal of food waste products. The digestive system ensures that the body has the necessary nutrients and the energy it needs to function.

The digestive system includes the **GASTROINTESTINAL (GI) TRACT**, which is formed by the organs through which the food passes on its way through the body:

1. oral cavity
2. pharynx
3. esophagus
4. stomach
5. small intestines
6. large intestines

Throughout the digestive system there are also organs that have a role in processing food, even though food doesn't pass through them directly. These include the teeth, tongue, salivary glands, liver, gallbladder, and pancreas.

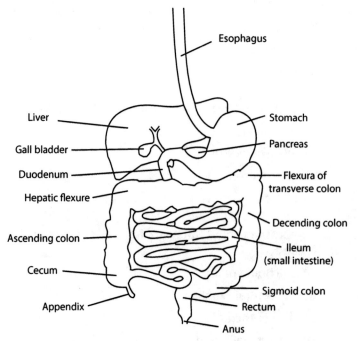

Figure 8.12. Digestive system

Questions about the order of the organs in the digestive tract are common on the TEAS.

The Mouth

The digestive system begins with the MOUTH. Also known as the oral cavity, the mouth contains other organs that play a role in digestion. The TEETH are small organs that cut and grind food. They are located on the edges of the mouth, are made out of dentin, which is a substance that resembles bone, and are covered by enamel. The teeth are very hard organs, and each of them has its own blood vessels and nerves, which are located in the matter that fills the tooth, called the pulp.

Also in the mouth is the TONGUE, which is a muscle located behind the teeth. The tongue contains the taste buds and moves food around the mouth as it is being processed by the teeth. It then moves food towards the pharynx when it's time to swallow. The SALIVARY GLANDS, located around the mouth, produce saliva. There are three pairs of salivary glands, and the saliva they produce lubricates and digests carbohydrates.

The Pharynx

The PHARYNX is a tube that enables the passage of food and air further into the body. This structure performs two functions. The pharynx needs the help of the epiglottis, which allows food to pass to the esophagus by covering the opening of the larynx, a structure that carries air into the lungs. When you need to breathe in, the esophagus is closed, so the air passes only into the larynx.

The Esophagus

The ESOPHAGUS begins at the pharynx and continues to carry food all the way to the stomach. The esophagus is a muscular tube, and the muscles in its wall help to push food down. During vomiting, it pushes food up.

The esophagus has two rings of muscle, called SPHINCTERS. These sphincters close at the top and the bottom ends of the esophagus when food is not passing through it. Heartburn occurs when the bottom sphincter cannot close entirely and allows the contents of the stomach to enter the esophagus.

The Stomach

The stomach is a round organ located on the left side of the body just beneath the diaphragm. It is divided into four different regions. The CARDIA connects the stomach to the esophagus, transitioning from the tube-like shape of the esophagus into the sack shape of the rest of the stomach. The cardia is also where the lower sphincter of the esophagus is located.

The BODY of the stomach is its largest part, and the FUNDUS is located above the body. The last part of the stomach is the PYLORUS, a funnel-shaped region located beneath the body of the stomach. It controls the passage of partially digested food further down the GI tract through the PYLORIC SPHINCTER.

The stomach is made out of four layers of tissue. The innermost layer, the MUCOSA, contains a smooth muscle and the mucus membrane that secretes digestive enzymes and hydrochloric acid. The cells that secrete these products are located within the small pores called the GASTRIC PITS. The mucus membrane also secretes mucus to protect the stomach from its own digestive enzymes.

The SUBMUCOSA is located around the mucosa and is made of connective tissue; it contains nerves and blood vessels. The MUSCULARIS layer enables the movement of the stomach; it's made up of three layers of smooth muscle. This layer enables the movement of the stomach. The outermost layer of the stomach is the serosa. It secretes SEROUS FLUID that keeps the stomach wet and reduces friction between the stomach and the surrounding organs.

The Small Intestine

The SMALL INTESTINE continues from the stomach and takes up most of the space in the abdomen. It's attached to the wall of the abdomen and measures around twenty-two feet long.

The small intestine can be divided into three parts. The DUODENUM is the part of the small intestine that receives the food and chemicals from the stomach. The JEJUNUM, which continues from the duodenum, is where most of the nutrients are absorbed

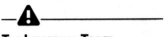

THE INTESTINAL TRACT
Dow Jones Industrial Climbing Average Closing Stock Report
- Duodenum
- Jejunum
- Ileum
- Cecum
- Appendix
- Colon
- Sigmoid colon
- Rectum

into the blood. Lastly, the ILEUM, which continues from the jejunum, is where the rest of the nutrients are absorbed.

Absorption in the small intestine is helped by the VILLI, which are small protrusions that increase the surface area available for absorption. The villi are made out of smaller microvilli.

The Liver and Gallbladder

The LIVER is not a part of the GI tract. However, it performs roles that are vital for digestion and life itself. The liver is located just beneath the diaphragm and is the largest organ in the body after the skin. It's triangular in shape, and extends across the whole width of the abdomen.

The liver is divided into four lobes: the left lobe, the right lobe, the caudate lobe (which wraps around the inferior vena cava), and the quadrate lobe (which wraps around the gallbladder). The liver is connected to the peritoneum by the coronary, left, right, and falciform ligaments.

The liver is responsible for a number of functions, including detoxification of the blood, storage of nutrients, and production of components of blood plasma. Its role in digestion is to produce BILE, a fluid that aids in the digestion of fats. After its production, bile is carried through the bile ducts to the GALLBLADDER, a small, muscular, pear-shaped organ that stores and releases bile.

The Pancreas

The PANCREAS is another organ that is not part of the GI tract but which plays a role in digestion. It's located below and to the left of the stomach. The pancreas secretes both the enzymes that digest food and the hormones insulin and glucagon, which control blood sugar levels.

The pancreas is what is known as a HETEROCRINE GLAND, which means it contains both endocrine tissue, which produces insulin and glucagon that move directly into the bloodstream, and exocrine tissue, which produces digestive enzymes that pass into the small intestine. These enzymes include:

- pancreatic amylase that breaks large polysaccharides into smaller sugars
- trypsin, chymotrypsin, and carboxypeptidase that break down proteins into amino acid subunits
- pancreatic lipase that breaks down large fat molecules into fatty acids and monoglycerides
- ribonuclease and deoxyribonuclease that digest nucleic acids

The Large Intestine

The LARGE INTESTINE continues from the small intestine and loops around it. No digestion actually takes place in the large intestine. Rather, it absorbs water and some leftover vitamins. The large intestine carries waste (feces) to the RECTUM, where it's stored until it's expelled through the ANUS.

Examples

1. Food passes through all of the following organs except:

   A) stomach

   B) large intestine

   C) esophagus

   D) liver

2. How many pair(s) of salivary glands are in the human body?

   A) 1

   B) 2

   C) 3

   D) 4

3. The esophagus performs all of the following functions except:

   A) connecting the pharynx to the stomach

   B) preventing stomach acid from reaching the pharynx

   C) pushing food into the stomach

   D) moving food from the stomach to the small intestine

4. Which layer of the stomach contains blood vessels and nerves?

   A) the mucosa

   B) the submucosa

   C) the serosa

   D) the cardia

5. Bile is stored in the:

   A) liver

   B) duodenum

   C) gallbladder

   D) pancreas

Answers: 1. D) 2. C) 3. D) 4. B) 5. C)

CONTINUE

THE ENDOCRINE SYSTEM

The **ENDOCRINE SYSTEM** consists of many **GLANDS** that produce and secrete hormones, which send signals to molecules that are traveling through the bloodstream. **HORMONES** allow cells, tissues, and organs to communicate with each other, and they play a role in almost all bodily functions, including growth, sleeping, digestion, response to stress, and sexual functioning. The glands of the endocrine system are scattered throughout the body, and each has a specific role to play.

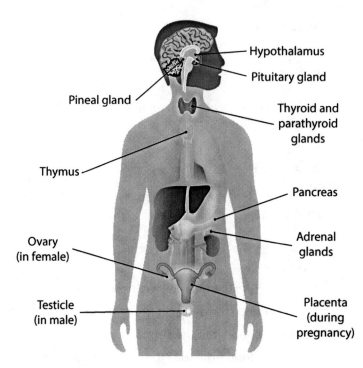

Figure 8.13. Endocrine system

- The **PITUITARY GLAND** hangs from the base of your brain and produces the hormone which controls growth and some aspects of sexual functioning (hormones: growth hormone, thyroid-stimulating hormone, oxytocin, follicle-stimulating hormone).

- The **HYPOTHALAMUS** is also located in the brain. Its main function is to control the pituitary gland, and many of the hormones it releases stimulate the pituitary gland to in turn release hormones itself (hormones: dopamine, thyrotropin-releasing hormone, growth-hormone-releasing hormone).

- The **PINEAL GLAND**, located in the brain, releases melatonin, a hormone that induces drowsiness and lowers body temperature (hormone: melatonin).

- The **THYROID GLAND** is found in the neck just below the Adam's apple. It controls protein production and the body's use of energy (hormones: T_3 and thyroxine).

The thyroid is regulated by the thyroid-stimulating hormone, which is released by the pituitary gland.

- The PARATHYROID GLANDS are located behind the thyroid. They produce parathyroid hormone, which regulates calcium and phosphate levels in the body (hormones: parathyroid hormone).

- The PANCREAS, discussed above, is located behind the stomach and releases hormones that regulate digestion and blood-sugar levels (hormones: insulin, glucagon, somatostatin).

- The ADRENAL GLANDS sit atop the kidneys. The adrenal glands have two regions that produce two sets of hormones: the adrenal cortex releases corticosteroids and androgens while the adrenal medulla regulates the fight-or-flight response (hormones: cortisol, testosterone, adrenaline, noradrenaline, dopamine).

- The TESTES are glands found in males; they regulate maturation of sex organs and the development of secondary sex characteristics like muscle mass and growth of axillary hair (hormones: testosterone, estradiol).

- The OVARIES are glands found in females; they regulate the menstrual cycle, pregnancy, and secondary sex characteristics like enlargement of breasts and the widening of the hips (hormones: progesterone, estrogen).

Examples

1. Which gland(s) indirectly controls growth by acting on the pituitary?

   A) hypothalamus

   B) thyroid

   C) adrenal glands

   D) parathyroid glands

2. Which hormone is primarily responsible for the development of male secondary sexual characteristics?

   A) melatonin

   B) follicle-stimulating hormone

   C) estrogen

   D) testosterone

CONTINUE

3. A patient experiencing symptoms such as kidney stones and arthritis due to a calcium imbalance probably has a disorder of which gland?

A) hypothalamus

B) thyroid

C) parathyroid

D) adrenal glands

Answers: 1. A) 2. D) 3. C)

THE REPRODUCTIVE SYSTEM

Reproductive systems are the groups of organs that enable the successful reproduction of a species. In humans, fertilization is internal, with sperm being transferred from the male to the female during copulation.

The Male Reproductive System

The male reproductive system consists of the organs that produce and ejaculate SPERM, the male gamete. Sperm are produced in the TESTES, which are housed in the SCROTUM, which is located under the penis. During sexual arousal, the VAS DEFERENS carry sperm to the URETHRA, the tube which runs through the PENIS and carries semen (and urine) out of the body. Also emptying into the urethra is the PROSTATE GLAND, which produces a nutrient-filled fluid that protects sperm and makes up the majority of SEMEN. Before ejaculation, the COWPER'S GLAND produces a thin, alkaline fluid that flushes any remaining urine from the urethra and makes up a small portion of the semen.

The Female Reproductive System

Sexual reproduction in animals occurs in cycles that depend on the production of an OVULE, or egg, by the female of the species. In humans, the reproductive cycle occurs approximately once a month, when an egg is released from the female's ovaries.

The female reproductive organs, or gonads, are called OVARIES. Each ovary has a follicle that contains OOCYTES, or undeveloped eggs. The surrounding cells in the ovary help to protect and nourish the oocyte until it is needed. During the menstrual cycle, one or more oocytes will mature into an egg with help from the CORPUS LUTEUM, a mass of follicular tissue that provides nutrients to the egg and secretes estradiol and progesterone.

Once it has matured, the egg will be released into the FALLOPIAN TUBE where fertilization will take place if sperm are present. The egg will then travel into the UTERUS. Unfertilized eggs are shed along with the uterine lining during MENSTRUATION. Fertilized eggs,

THE PATH OF SPERM
SEVEn UP
- Seminiferous tubes
- Epididymis
- Vas deferens
- Ejaculatory duct
- Urethra
- Penis

known as **ZYGOTES**, implant in the lining of the uterus where they continue to develop.

Embryo Fertilization and Development

After fertilization, the cell will start to divide and, after four to five days, become a ball of cells known as a **BLASTOCYST**. The blastocyst is then implanted into the **ENDOMETRIUM** of the uterus. After the blastocyst has been implanted into the endometrium, the placenta develops. The **PLACENTA** is a temporary organ that attaches the embryo to the mother; it provides nutrients to the fetus, carries waste away from the fetus, protects the fetus from infection, and produces hormones that support pregnancy. The placenta develops from cells called the **TROPHOBLAST**, which come from the outer layer of the blastocyst.

In humans, the gestation period of the **EMBRYO** (also called the **FETUS**), is 266 days or roughly 8.8 months. The human development cycle in the womb is divided into three trimesters. In the first trimester, the organs responsible for the embryo's growth develop. This includes the placenta and umbilical cord. During this time, **ORGANOGENESIS** occurs, and the various stem cells from the blastocyst differentiate into the organs of the body. The organs are not fully developed at this point, but they do exist.

In the second trimester, the fetus experiences rapid growth, up to about twenty-five to thirty centimeters in length. At this point, it is usually apparent that the woman is pregnant, as the uterus grows and extends, and the woman's belly becomes slightly distended. In the third trimester, the fetus finishes developing. The baby exits the uterus through the **CERVIX** and leaves the body through the **VAGINA**.

Examples

1. All of the following contribute material to semen except:

   A) the prostate

   B) Cowper's gland

   C) the penis

   D) the testes

2. Fertilization typically takes place in the:

   A) fallopian tubes

   B) ovaries

   C) uterus

   D) cervix

→

CONTINUE

3. Which of the following statements about the placenta is not true?

A) The placenta serves as part of the endocrine system because it releases hormones.

B) The placenta provides nutrients to the fetus.

C) The placenta develops from the outer layer of cells on the blastocyst.

D) The placenta is expelled during the menstrual cycle if fertilization does not take place.

Answers: 1. C) 2. A) 3. D)

9

CHEMISTRY

THE ATOM

The ATOM is the basic building block of all physical matter. It is composed of three subatomic particles: protons, electrons, and neutrons. A PROTON is a positively charged subatomic particle with a mass of approximately 1.007 atomic mass units. The number of protons in an atom determines which ELEMENT it is. For example, an atom with 1 proton is hydrogen, and an atom with 12 protons is carbon.

A NEUTRON is a non-charged subatomic particle with a mass of approximately 1.008 atomic mass units. The number of neutrons in an atom does not affect its chemical properties, but will influence its rate of radioactivity. Both protons and neutrons are found in the center, or NUCLEUS, of the atom.

Lastly, an ELECTRON is a negatively charged subatomic particle with a mass of approximately 0.00055 atomic mass units. The number of electrons in an atom, in conjunction with the protons, determines the atom's charge. In addition, the number of electrons in the valence shell of an atom affects its reactivity. Electrons move in a cloud that surrounds the nucleus.

The modern concept of the atom, which provided the basis for all of chemistry, was first laid out in John Dalton's ATOMIC THEORY, which was developed in 1808. Atomic theory states that:

1. An element is composed of atoms, which are extremely small, indivisible particles. Although we now know that atoms are composed of smaller units such as protons, electrons, and neutrons, it is still recognized that atoms are the basic building block of matter.

2. Each individual element has a set of properties that are distinct and different from that of other elements.

3. Atoms cannot be created, destroyed, or transformed through physical changes. We now know that atoms can be created or destroyed, although this requires a massive amount of energy. Furthermore, radioactive elements can be transformed into other elements.

4. Compounds are defined by a specific ratio of atoms that are combined with one another, and the relative numbers and types of atoms are constant in any given compound.

Previous Models of the Atom

When the field of chemistry was young, people proposed many different models of the structure of an atom.

DALTON'S MODEL (EARLY 1800'S)

Dalton was the first to propose some aspects of atomic theory, including atomic weights and a general shape. According to Dalton's model of the atom, each atom was a single, indivisible unit that was solid. Simply put, an atom was something like a very small marble, and a solid was something composed of many of these marbles.

Dalton's model was disproved in the early twentieth century when the proton and neutron were discovered by Ernest Rutherford. Rutherford found that a hydrogen atom could be extracted from a nitrogen atom by collision, and that it had a positive charge. This showed that an atom was composed of smaller, positively charged pieces, and was not a unified whole.

RUTHERFORD'S MODEL (1911)

Rutherford proposed that an atom was a core of heavier particles (protons and neutrons) surrounded by a layer of electrons. In this model, the electrons were evenly dispersed around the core of the atom.

In Rutherford's model, physics would predict that the evenly dispersed electrons would slowly lose energy while orbiting the nucleus. As a result, if Rutherford's model were true, all electrons would eventually collapse into the nucleus.

BOHR'S THEORY

To fix this problem with the model, Niels Bohr proposed that electrons can only orbit the nucleus in certain energy stages, or orbits, that are a set distance from the nucleus. The electrons orbiting closer to the nucleus have the highest energy, and shells have lower energy moving away from the nucleus. He further proposed that it is possible to change the energy state of electrons through the emission or addition of electromagnetic waves. The idea of electron shells was thus introduced by Bohr's theory, and Bohr's model is still used today, (with some modifications).

Atomic Structure

The atom consists of a nucleus of protons and neutrons surrounded by a shell, or multiple shells, of electrons. The nucleus is very dense and contains the majority of mass in the atom. The actual size of the atom, due to the large electron shell, is much larger than the nucleus.

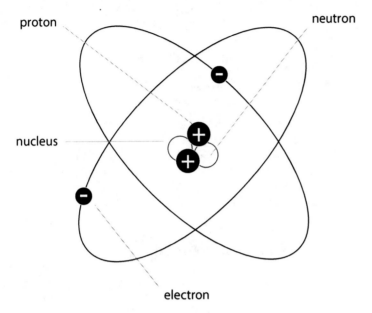

Figure 9.1. Atomic structure

Electrons surround the nucleus in clouds called **ORBITALS**; each orbital has a particular shape and holds a particular number of electrons. There are four orbital shapes: *s* orbitals hold 2 electrons, *p* orbitals hold 6 electrons, *d* orbitals hold 10 electrons, and *f* orbitals hold 14 electrons. The size and distance of the orbital from the nucleus is described by an integer value (1, 2, ...).

The location of an electron can be described with an integer number and orbital letter, for example the single electron in hydrogen is in orbital 1s. The number of electrons in each orbital is written as a superscript. For example, the two electrons in helium are described as $2s^2$. With some exceptions, electrons fill orbitals in a specific order (see Fig. 9.2). This order can also be found using the periodic table (more on this on the following page).

CONTINUE

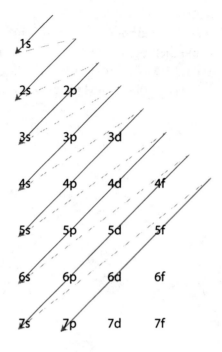

$$1s^2 2s^2 2p^6 3s^2 3p^6 4s^2 3d^{10} 4p^6 5s^2 \ldots$$

Figure 9.2. Electron orbitals

Valence Shell Reactivity

The reactivity of each individual atom is determined by the number of electrons in its electron shells, of which the most important is the outermost, or VALENCE, shell. Typically, the closer an atom is to reaching a full valence shell, the more reactive it is. Elements that have a single electron in a shell (such as sodium: last orbital $3s^1$) or need only a single electron to fill a shell (such as chlorine: last orbital $2p^5$) are the most reactive.

There are some elements that are not reactive at all. These are the noble gases, which possess a full valence shell. Thus, they have no free electrons with which to react. In chemistry, there are no common reactions that occur with a noble gas.

Examples

1. Which of these is the correct electron configuration for gold?
   A) $[Xe]\ 6s^2\ 5d^9$
   B) $[Xe]\ 5d^9\ 6s^2$
   C) $[Xe]\ 4f^{14}\ 5d^{10}\ 6s^1$
   D) $[Xe]\ 6s^2\ 5d^{10}\ 4f^{13}$

2. The electron configuration for phosphorus is:

A) $1s^2 2s^2 2p^6 3s^2 3p^3$

B) $1s^2 2s^2 2p^6 3s^2 3p^6$

C) $1s^2 2p^6 3s^2 3p^3$

D) $1s^2 2s^2 2p^2 3s^2 3p^3 4s^2 4p^3$

3. Which subatomic particles are found in the nucleus of an atom?

I.	protons
II.	electrons
III.	neutrons

A) I only

B) II only

C) I and III

D) I, II, and III

Answers: 1. C) 2. C) 3. C)

THE PERIODIC TABLE OF ELEMENTS

The **PERIODIC TABLE** is a table used to organize and characterize the various elements. The table was first proposed by Dimitri Mendeleev in 1869, and a similar organization system is still used today. In the table, each column is called a **GROUP** and each row is called a **PERIOD**. Elements in the same column have similar electron configurations and the same number of electrons in their valence shells.

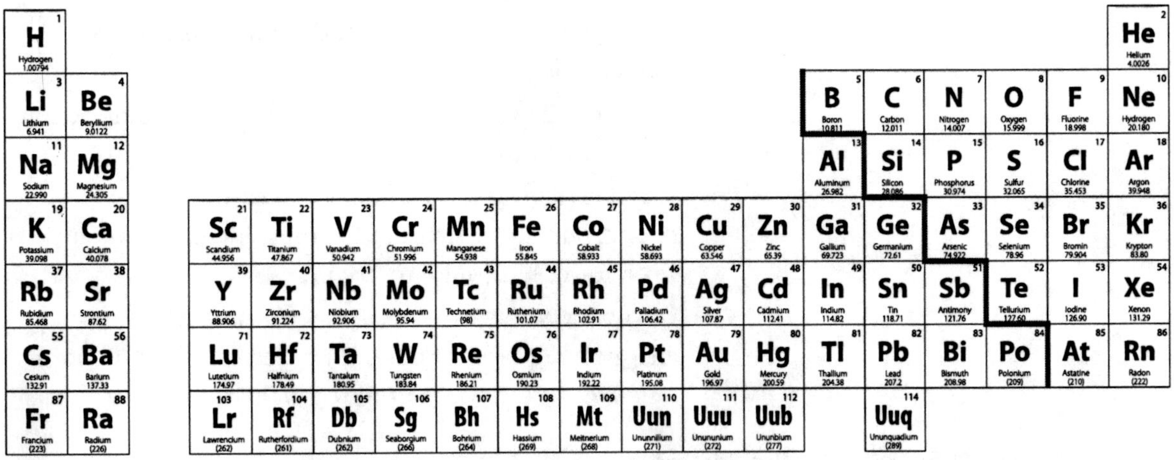

Figure 9.3. Periodic table

Reading the Periodic Table

Each cell in the table includes the symbol for the element, which is a letter or set of letters. For example, C for carbon and Fe for iron. The number at the top of each cell in the table is the ATOMIC NUMBER. This represents the number of protons in the element. The number below the element symbol is the ATOMIC MASS, which represents the total mass of the element (atomic mass – atomic number = # of neutrons).

Because atoms of the same element can have different numbers of neutrons, elements have no single standard atomic mass. Instead, the atomic mass is the weighted average of all commonly found species of the element. For this reason, it is almost never a whole number. For example, a small amount of carbon actually has an atomic mass of 13, possessing 7 neutrons instead of the usual 6, giving carbon an atomic mass of 12.011. Atoms of the same element with different numbers of neutrons are called ISOTOPES.

Trends in the Periodic Table

Some element properties can be predicted based on the placement of the element on the periodic table.

- Elements in groups 1 and 2 are the alkali and the alkali earth metals, which are very reactive.
- Elements in group 17 are the halogens, which are very reactive.
- Elements in group 18 are the noble gases, which are very unreactive.
- Elements along the "staircase" (marked in gray in the periodic table in Figure 9.3) consisting of boron, silicon, etc., are semi-metallic. They have some properties of metals, and some properties of non-metals.
- The atomic radius of an element increases from the top left to the bottom right.
- ELECTRONEGATIVITY, which is a measure of how strongly an atom attracts electrons, increases roughly from lower left to the top right.
- IONIZATION ENERGY, which is a measure of how much energy is required to remove an electron from an atom, increases from lower left to top right.

Properties of Elements

Below are the important properties of various groups of elements.

GROUP 1 (THE ALKALI METALS)

The elements in group 1 are all silvery metals that are soft and can be easily crushed or cut. They all possess a single valence electron, which makes them very reactive. The presence of just a single valence

Many elemental symbols are derived from the Latin names for elements. For example, gold's symbol is Au from its Latin name Aurum.

You don't need to memorize all of these properties, but be able to recognize the general similarities of a group's chemical properties.

electron means that there is a high likelihood of losing the electron, resulting in a +1 cation. Because these metals are so reactive, they are not usually found in their pure form. Bonds that involve Group 1 metals are always bonds that have high ionic character.

GROUP 2 (THE ALKALI EARTH METALS)

The elements in group 2 are also silvery metals that are soft. These metals contain two valence electrons, which fill the S-shell, so these elements are not as reactive as those in group 1. However, they still have a high tendency to lose these electrons, and form a +2 cation. Normally, group 2 elements are found in this +2 oxidation state. Bonds that involve group 2 metals are almost always bonds that have high ionic character.

GROUPS 3 – 12 (THE TRANSITION METALS)

The elements from groups 3 to 12 are called the transition metals, and are all capable of conducting electricity (some better than others). They are called transition metals in part due to their capability to possess multiple oxidation states. Because of the presence of the D-shell of electrons in these metals, they may have anywhere from a +1 to a +6 oxidation state, resulting in the formation of many different compounds and bonds. Transition metals are moderately reactive, malleable, and can conduct electricity due to the capability of gaining and losing many electrons in their outer electron shell.

GROUPS 13 AND 14 (SEMI-METALLIC)

The elements in groups 13 and 14 are semi-metallic. They have moderate conductivity, and are very soft. Elements in group 13 have three valence electrons and elements in group 14 have four, allowing for five and four bonds respectively.

GROUP 15

This group is characterized by a shift from the top of this group (gases) to the bottom (semi-metallic). This group has five valence electrons and can form three bonds. The semi-metallic elements, such as arsenic and antimony, are relatively reactive.

GROUP 16

This group is also characterized by a shift from gases at the top of the group to semi-metallic at the bottom. This group has six valence electrons and is quite reactive. The need to obtain only two more electrons to fill the valence shell means that these elements are electronegative and typically form an anion with a charge of -2. As a result, these elements are reactive and tend to bond with the alkali or alkali earth metals.

GROUP 17 (HALOGENS)

The halogens are all gases and all contain seven electrons in their valence shell. They are extremely reactive, much like the alkali metals. Due to their reactivity and gaseous form at room temperature, they are often hazardous to humans. Inhaling chlorine or fluorine, for example, is usually deadly. The halogens will react in order to obtain a single additional electron to fill their valence shell and typically have a charge of -1.

GROUP 18 (THE NOBLE GASES)

The noble gases already contain a full valence shell. Because their electron orbitals are already full, the noble gases are largely unreactive, except for a few rare exceptions. The heavier noble gases (xenon and radon) can sometimes react with other species under high temperature and pressure conditions. The noble gases have no net charge.

Examples

1. Which of the following is not true of the alkali metals?

   A) They are more likely to be oxidized than reduced.

   B) They typically form +1 monatomic cations.

   C) Large amounts of energy are required to remove their first electron.

   D) They are highly reactive.

2. Which of the following statements is not true regarding the halogens in the periodic table?

   A) All of the halogens are extremely reactive.

   B) The halogen elements require 1 more electron to fill their valence shell.

   C) Halogen elements usually form ionic bonds with other elements.

   D) All of the halogens are very electronegative, except for astatine and iodine.

3. Which of the following elements has the highest first ionization energy?

   A) sodium

   B) sulfur

   C) carbon

   D) argon

   Answers: 1. C) 2. D) 3. C)

CHEMICAL BONDING

Molecules and Compounds

Atoms can exist on their own or bound together. When two or more atoms are held together by chemical bonds, they form a MOLECULE. If the molecule contains more than one type of atom, it is a **COMPOUND**. Molecules and compounds form the smallest unit of a substance—for example, if water (H_2O) is broken down into hydrogen and oxygen atoms, it no longer has the unique properties of water. Molecules and compounds always have the same ratio of elements. Water, for example, always has two hydrogens for every one oxygen.

Intramolecular Forces

A chemical bond is a force that holds two atoms together. There are two primary types of bolds: ionic and covalent.

In an **IONIC BOND**, one atom has lost electrons to the other, which results in a positive charge on one atom and a negative charge on the other atom. The bond is then a result of the electrostatic interaction between these positive and negative charges. For example, in the compound sodium chloride, sodium has lost an electron to chlorine, resulting in a positive charge on sodium and a negative charge on chlorine.

In a **COVALENT BOND**, electrons are shared between two atoms; neither atom completely loses or gains an electron. This can be in the form of one pair of shared electrons (a single bond), two pairs (a double bond), or three pairs of electrons shared (triple bond). In diatomic oxygen gas, for example, the two oxygen molecules share two sets of electrons.

Covalent bonds are often depicted using Lewis diagrams, in which an electron is represented by a dot and a shared pair of electrons is represented by a line.

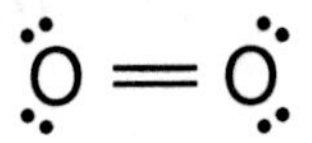

Figure 9.4. Lewis diagram of a covalent bond

Electrons within a covalent bond aren't always shared equally. More electronegative atoms, which exert a strong pull on the electrons, will hold onto the electrons longer than less electronegative atoms. For example, oxygen is more electronegative than hydrogen, so in H_2O (water) both oxygens have a slight negative charge, and the hydrogen has a slight positive charge. This imbalance is called **POLARITY**, and the small charge a **DIPOLE**.

Note that there is a commonality between the two types of bonding. In both ionic and covalent bonding types, the bond results in each atom having a full valence shell of electrons. When bonding, atoms seek to find the most stable electron configuration. In the majority of cases, this means filling the valence shell of the atom either through the addition or removal of electrons.

Intermolecular Forces

What causes water to stick together, forming a liquid at room temperature but a solid at lower temperatures? Why do we need more heat and energy to increase the temperature of water compared to other substances? The answer is **INTERMOLECULAR FORCES**: attractive or repulsive forces that occur between molecules. These are different from ionic and covalent bonds, which occur within a molecule.

There are two main types of intermolecular forces that you need to know for the test: Dipole-dipole interactions, and Van der Waals forces. In a **DIPOLE-DIPOLE INTERACTION**, the small charge on the atoms in a polar molecule interact with the charge on other polar molecules. When a hydrogen is bonded to a very electronegative atom, the resulting interaction is called **HYDROGEN BONDING**. This force can be seen between the oxygen and hydrogen atoms in water and is responsible for many of water's distinctive properties. Hydrogen bonds are the strongest of the intermolecular forces.

VAN DER WAALS FORCES are the sum of small force interactions between molecules that are a result of forces that **are not** covalent, ionic, or hydrogen bonding in nature. There are several distinct Van der Waals forces, but the most important is the **LONDON DISPERSION FORCE**, which arises from temporary dipoles created by the normal movement of electrons.

Chemical and Physical Properties

Substances, whether they are composed of individual atoms or molecules, all have unique properties that are grouped into two categories: physical and chemical. A change in a **PHYSICAL PROPERTY** does not result in a change in the chemical composition of a reactant, but only the physical structure. For example, a change of state is a physical reaction. A change in a **CHEMICAL PROPERTY** is one in which the molecular structure or composition of the compound has been changed. Physical and chemical properties are often influenced by intra- and intermolecular forces. For example, substances with strong hydrogen bonds will have higher boiling points.

Examples

1. Which of these statements is not true of covalent bonds?

    A) They include two overlapping atomic orbitals.

    B) The net formal charge on the resulting compound must be zero.

    C) They allow bonded atoms to achieve electron configurations comparable to those of noble gases.

    D) They may include more than one pair of shared electrons.

2. Which of the following molecules does not have an ionic bond?

A) $FeCl_2$

B) H_3PO_4

C) KOH

D) C_2H_6

3. In organic biomolecules such as proteins and DNA, interactions between the constituent pieces of the chain contribute substantially to the molecule's secondary structure. While these bonds are fairly strong, they frequently break to permit the molecule to bend and flex. The described interactions are most likely caused by:

A) hydrogen bonding

B) ionic bonding

C) covalent bonding

D) van der Waals forces

Answers: 1. C) 2. D) 3. C)

NAMING MOLECULES

A **CHEMICAL FORMULA** (sometimes called a molecular formula) describes the chemical composition of a compound or molecule using elemental symbols and integers to represent the number of each atom. There are two methods for writing a chemical formula. The first is the simplest, and just states the ratio of elements in a compound. For example, the compound acetic acid has the formula $C_2H_4O_2$, which means that a single molecule of acetic acid has 2 carbons, 4 hydrogens, and 2 oxygen atoms.

However, this chemical formula does not describe the structure of the compound. For this, it's necessary to use **FUNCTIONAL GROUP NOTATION**. When writing a chemical formula using functional group notation, the letters are moved around in the formula to reflect the correct order of the elements in the compound. In functional group notation, acetic acid is written as CH_3COOH. From this formula, it's clear that the first carbon in the molecule is attached to three hydrogen, and then to the next carbon, which is attached to the O-O-H chain.

Molecules can also be described using their **EMPIRICAL FORMULA**, which is just the molecule's chemical formula reduced to its simplest ratio. The empirical formula for acetic acid is CH_2O.

Chemical Names: Ionic Compounds

Ionic compounds are formed from one or more **CATIONS** (with a positive charge) and one or more **ANIONS** (with a negative charge). The naming rules for ionic compounds are as follows:

1. The cation is written first, followed by the anion. The cation has no suffix added. The anion has a suffix of –ide in the majority of cases (such as sodium chloride).

2. The stoichiometry of the molecule, as indicated by the subscripts, must produce a molecule that has no net charge. For example, $NaCl_2^-$, sodium dichloride, is not a valid compound.

3. The compound should be an empirical formula, meaning it should have the lowest subscripts possible. For example Na_2Cl_2 is not correct.

4. A polyatomic anion such as SO_4^{2-} does not have parentheses unless there are multiples of the anion. For example, $Na_2(SO_4)$ is not correct. However, $Al_2(SO_4)_3$ is correct because there are three sulfate anions.

Chemical Names: Covalent Compounds

The naming of covalent compounds is similar to ionic naming. In the naming of covalent compounds, the following rules apply:

1. The first element is named, along with a prefix indicating the number of atoms of that element in the molecular formula.

2. The second element is named, along with an appropriate suffix.

3. The first element, if having a value of 1, does not use the prefix mono-.

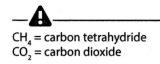

CH_4 = carbon tetrahydride
CO_2 = carbon dioxide

Table 9.1. Naming prefixes

NUMBER	PREFIX
1	mono
2	di
3	tri
4	tetra
5	penta
6	hexa
7	hepta
8	octa
9	nona

Examples

1. Which of these is not a properly named chemical by ionic nomenclature?

    A) potassium acetate

    B) lithium hydroxide

    C) lead nitrate

    D) calcium sulfite

2. Which of the following is the correct formula for chromium (III) oxide?

A) Cr_3O

B) CrO_3

C) Cr_3O_2

D) Cr_2O_3

3. What is the correct name for Na_2SO_4?

A) disodium sulfite

B) disodium sulfur oxide

C) sodium sulfate

D) sodium (II) sulfate

Answers: 1. C) 2. D) 3. C)

STATES OF MATTER

A STATE is a description of the physical characteristics of a material. There are four states: solid, liquid, gas, and plasma.

- A SOLID is a dense phase characterized by close bonds between all molecules in the solid; they have a definite shape and volume.

- A LIQUID is a fluid phase characterized by loose bonds between molecules in the liquid; they have an indefinite shape but a definite volume.

- A GAS is a very disperse phase characterized by the lack of, or very weak bonds, between molecules; gases have both an indefinite shape and volume.

- The PLASMA phase occurs when a substance has been heated and pressurized past its critical point, resulting in a new phase that has liquid and gas properties.

A substance will change phase depending on the temperature and pressure. As temperature increases, the phase will progress from solid to liquid to gas. As pressure increases, the opposite is true, and the phase will progress from gas to liquid to solid.

These phase changes have specific names, as shown below. Note that reciprocal changes will involve the same amount of energy, but moving from a less to a more energetic state uses energy while moving from a more to less energetic state will release energy.

- evaporation: liquid to gas (uses energy); occurs at boiling point

- condensation: gas to liquid (releases energy); occurs at boiling point

- melting: solid to liquid (uses energy); occurs at freezing point

- freezing: liquid to solid (releases energy); occurs at freezing point
- sublimation: solid to gas (uses energy)
- deposition: gas to solid (releases energy)

PHASE DIAGRAMS are used to show the relationships between phases, temperature, and pressure for a particular substance. In the phase diagram there are two points that are interesting to note. At the TRIPLE POINT, all three phases exist together, and at the CRITICAL POINT, the substance enters the plasma phase.

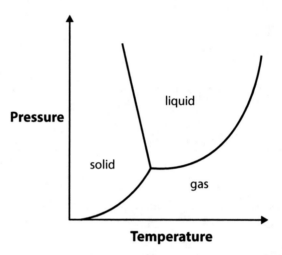

Figure 9.5. Phase diagram

Boiling Point and Freezing Point

The boiling point and freezing point of a molecule are related to its structure. There are three important factors that contribute to boiling and freezing points:

1. Strength of intermolecular forces: the greater the intermolecular force, the greater the boiling point of the substance will be.
2. Molecule size: as the molecule becomes larger, the boiling point of the molecule typically increases.
3. Molecule branching: as more branch points are present in the molecule, the molecule's boiling point will increase.

Let's look at an example. Methane has a molecular weight of 16 grams per mole, and water has a molecular weight of 18 grams per mole. Neither molecule is branched. As a result, factors 2 and 3 (as listed above), are not relevant. However, water has a boiling point of 100°C while methane has a boiling point of –164°C.

This large difference is a result of intermolecular forces. Water is a highly polar molecule that has strong intermolecular forces. On the other hand, methane is an uncharged, non-polar molecule with next to no intermolecular forces. Thus, the energy required to break the bonds between water molecules, and cause the phase change from liquid to vapor, is much greater than that for the methane molecule.

The Gas Laws

The interactions between each atom and molecule in a gas are extremely weak, and for this reason, gases have a low density compared to liquids and solids. However, due to their increased activity, the internal energy of a molecule in the gaseous phase is higher than that of a molecule in the liquid or solid phase.

When discussing gases, it's important to differentiate between real gases and ideal gases. **REAL GASES** are what we experience in the real world. These gases are compressible, have intermolecular interactions, and may react. An **IDEAL GAS** is an idealized version of a gas that simplifies calculations in chemistry. An ideal gas is assumed to follow these rules:

- Each gas molecule occupies a very small volume (close to zero) compared to the overall volume of the container.
- All collisions between gas molecules are perfectly elastic.
- There are no attractive or repulsive forces acting on the gas molecules.
- The gas molecules are in constant motion and move completely randomly.

A gas under these conditions will follow a number of laws that describe the relationship between pressure (P), volume (V), temperature (T), moles (n), and a value called the ideal gas constant (R). The value of the ideal gas constant will change depending on the units used for the other variables.

- Ideal gas law: $PV = nRT$
- Charles' Law: $\dfrac{V_1}{T_1} = \dfrac{V_2}{T_2}$

- Boyle's law: $P_1 V_1 = P_2 V_2$
- Avogadro's Law: $\dfrac{V_1}{n_1} = \dfrac{V_2}{n_2}$

Table 9.2. The ideal gas constant

R VALUE	UNITS
8.314	J/(mol·K)
0.08205	(L·atm)/(mol·K)
1.987	cal/(mol·K)

Standard temperature and pressure (STP) is 0°C (298 K) and 1 atm (101.35 kPA).

→

CONTINUE

Examples

1. What is the correct term for the energy required for a solid to become a liquid?

    A) latent heat of vaporization

    B) latent heat of fusion

    C) latent heat of fission

    D) latent heat of condensation

2. Which of the following is not a state of matter?

    A) plasma

    B) liquid

    C) solid

    D) crystal

3. Which of the following is likely to have the highest number of molecules?

    A) 1 liter of water vapor

    B) 1 liter of water

    C) 0.5 liter of ice

    D) 0.5 liter of an ice-water mixture

4. Which of the following is not true of a liquid?

    A) A liquid fills the volume of the container holding it.

    B) A liquid is fluid and can change shape.

    C) A liquid is always warmer than a solid.

    D) Molecules in a liquid can have attractive interactions.

5. The freezing point of a compound is the same as the:

    A) boiling point of the compound

    B) melting point of the compound

    C) triple point of the compound

    D) critical point of the compound

6. When the pressure is increased on a sample of gas with a constant temperature, its volume:

    A) stays the same

    B) increases

    C) decreases

    D) oscillates

7. A scientist has 1 mole of a sample of gas at 274°C and 1 atm of pressure. How much volume will it occupy?
($R = 0.0821$ L·atm/K·mol)

A) 18.5 liters

B) 19.9 liters

C) 22.4 liters

D) 25.2 liters

Answers: 1. B) 2. D) 3. B) 4. A) 5. B) 6. C) 7. C)

ACIDS AND BASES

In general, an ACID can be defined as a substance that produces hydrogen ions (H^+) in solution, while a BASE produces hydroxide ions (OH^-). Acidic solutions, which include common liquids like orange juice and vinegar, share a set of distinct characteristics: they have a sour taste and react strongly with metals. Bases, such as bleach and detergents, will taste bitter and have a slippery texture.

There are a number of different technical definitions for acids and bases, including the Arrhenius, Bronsted-Lowry, and Lewis acid definitions.

- The ARRHENIUS definition: An acid is a substance that produces H+ hydrogen ions in aqueous solution. A base is a substance that produces hydroxide ions OH– in aqueous solution.

- The BRONSTED-LOWRY definition: An acid is anything that donates a proton H+, and a base is anything that accepts a proton H+.

- The LEWIS definition: An acid is anything able to accept a pair of electrons, and a base is anything that can donate a pair of electrons.

Measuring the Strength of Acids and Bases

The PH of a solution is a measure of the acidity or basicity of the solution. It's found by taking the negative log of the concentration of hydrogen ions, making pH an exponential scale. The pH scale runs from 0 to 14 with a low pH being more acidic and a high pH more basic. A pH of 7 is that of water with no dissolved ions, and is considered neutral.

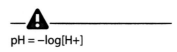

$$pH = -\log[H+]$$

CONTINUE

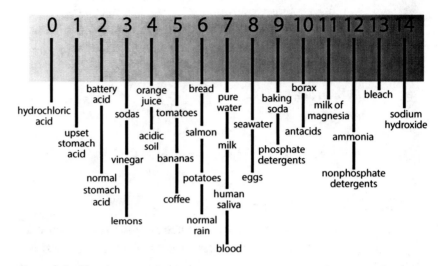

Figure 9.6. pH scale

Strong acids and bases will dissolve completely in solution, while weak acids and bases will only partially dissolve. Thus, strong acids and bases will have high or low pH values, respectively, and weak acids and bases will have pH values closer to 7.

Table 9.3. Strong and weak acids

STRONG ACIDS	WEAK ACIDS
Hydrobromic acid (HBr)	Acetic acid ($C_2H_4O_2$)
Hydrochloric acid (HCl)	Formic acid (HCOOH)
Sulfuric acid (H_2SO_4)	Butryic acid ($C_4H_8O_2$)

Acid Base Reactions

Acids and bases react with each other in solution to produce a salt and water, a process called NEUTRALIZATION. As a result of this reaction, if an equal amount of strong acid is mixed with an equal amount of strong base, the pH will remain at 7. For example, mixing hydrochloric acid and sodium hydroxide yields sodium chloride (a salt) and water, as shown below:

$$HCl(aq) + Na(OH)(aq) \rightarrow H_2O + NaCl(aq)$$

Examples

1. One of the characteristic properties of an acid is that it increases the concentration of:

   A) hydrogen ions

   B) hydroxyl ions

   C) hydroxide ions

   D) oxide ions

2. A solution with a pH of 12 is:

A) very acidic

B) neutral

C) very basic

D) slightly acidic

3. Proper blood pH level for humans is:

A) 7.0

B) 7.2

C) 7.6

D) 7.4

Answers: 1. A) 2. C) 3. D)

SOLUTIONS

In chemistry, the term MIXTURE describes a set of two or more substances that have been mixed together but are not chemically joined together. In a HOMOGENOUS mixture, the substances are evenly distributed; in a HETEROGENEOUS mixture, the substances are not evenly distributed.

A SOLUTION is a specific type of homogenous mixture in which all substances share the same basic properties and generally act as a single substance. In a solution, a SOLUTE is dissolved in a SOLVENT. For example, in salt water, salt is the solute and water is the solvent. The opposite process, in which a compound comes out of the solution, is called PRECIPITATION.

The CONCENTRATION of a solution—the amount of solute versus the amount of solvent—can be measured in a number of ways. Usually it's given as a ratio of solute to solvent in the relevant units. Some of these include:

- weight per volume (e.g., grams per liter)
- volume per volume (e.g., milliliter per liter)
- weight per weight (e.g., milligrams per gram)
- moles per volume (e.g., moles per liter)—also called MOLARITY
- moles per weight (e.g., moles per kilogram)—also called MOLALITY

Are the following mixtures homogenous or heterogeneous?
- lemonade
- concrete
- air
- trail mix
- salt water

Solubility

Solubility is a measure of how much solute will dissolve into a solvent. When a solution contains the maximum amount of solute possible, it is called a SATURATED SOLUTION. A solution with less solute is UNSATURATED, and a solution with more solute than can normally be dissolved in that solvent is SUPERSATURATED.

There are many factors that can affect the solubility of a compound, including temperature and pressure. Another factor affecting solubility is the COMMON ION EFFECT, which occurs in solutions with two compounds that share a common ion. When the two compounds are mixed into a solvent, the presence of the common ion reduces the solubility of each compound. For example, NaCl and $MgCl_2$ share the common ion of chlorine. When they are mixed in a solution, the maximum saturation of the chlorine ion in water will be reached before the saturation of either sodium or magnesium is reached. This causes a reduction in the overall solubility.

Examples

1. In a carbonated soda, carbon dioxide is dissolved in water. In this solution, water is the

   A) common ion

   B) solvent

   C) solute

   D) precipitant

2. How much ethanol should be added to 2.5 L of water to produce a solution with a molarity of 5 M?

   A) 2 mol

   B) 2.5 mol

   C) 7.5 mol

   D) 12.5 mol

   Answers: 1. B) 2. D)

REACTIONS

In a CHEMICAL REACTION, one set of chemical substances, called the REACTANTS, are transformed into another set of chemical substances called the PRODUCTS. This transformation is described in a chemical equation with the reactants on the left and products on the right. In the equation below, methane (CH_4) reacts with oxygen (O_2) to produce carbon dioxide (CO_2) and water (H_2O).

$$CH_4 + 2O_2 \rightarrow CO_2 + 2H_2O$$

When a reaction runs to COMPLETION, all the reactants have been used up in the reaction. If one reactant limits the use of the other reactants (i.e., if one reactant is used up before the others), it's called the LIMITING REACTANT. The YIELD is the amount of product produced by the reaction.

Balancing Equations

The integer values placed before the chemical symbols are the COEFFICIENTS that describe how many molecules of that substance are involved in the reaction. These values are important because in a chemical reaction, there is a conservation of mass. The inputs, or reactant mass, must equal the outputs, or products. For example, the reaction shown on the previous page includes one carbon, four hydrogen, and four oxygen on either side of the arrow.

In order to **BALANCE AN EQUATION**, you'll need to add the coefficients necessary to match the atoms of each element on both sides. In the reaction below, the numbers of bromine (Br) and nitrate ions (NO_3^-) do not match up:

$$CaBr_2 + NaNO_3 \rightarrow Ca(NO_3)_2 + NaBr$$

To balance the equation, start by adding a coefficient of 2 to the products to balance the bromine:

$$CaBr_2 + NaNO_3 \rightarrow Ca(NO_3)_2 + 2NaBr$$

There are now 2 sodium ions on the right, so another 2 need to be added on the left to balance it:

$$CaBr_2 + 2NaNO_3 \rightarrow Ca(NO_3)_2 + 2NaBr$$

Notice that adding this 2 also balances the nitrate ions, so the equation is now complete.

Types of Reactions

There are five main types of chemical reactions.

- In a **SYNTHESIS** reaction, two or more reactants will form a single product. $A + B \rightarrow C$

- In a **DECOMPOSITION** reaction, a single reactant will decompose into two products. Decomposition reactions typically require an input of energy. $A \rightarrow B + C$

- In a **SINGLE DISPLACEMENT** reaction, one reactant will dissociate, and its complement ion will react with another species in solution. $AB + C \rightarrow A + BC$

- In a **DOUBLE DISPLACEMENT** reaction, two reactants will dissociate and exchange complement ions. $AB + CD \rightarrow AC + BD$

- In a **COMBUSTION** reaction, a fuel (alkane or carbohydrate are typical) will react with oxygen to form carbon dioxide and water. $C_xH_yO_z + O_2 \rightarrow CO_2 + H_2O$

Oxidation and Reduction

An oxidation and reduction reaction (often called a redox reaction) is one in which there is an exchange of electrons. The species that loses electrons is **OXIDIZED**, and the species that gains electrons is **REDUCED**. The species that loses electrons is also called the **REDUCING AGENT**, and the species that gains electrons the **OXIDIZING AGENT**.

The movement of electrons in a redox reaction is analyzed by assigning each atom in the reaction an **OXIDATION NUMBER** (or state) that corresponds roughly to that atom's charge. (The actual meaning

OIL RIG
Oxidation
Involves
Loss
Reduction
Involves
Gain

of the oxidation number is much more complicated.) Once all the atoms in a reaction have been assigned an oxidation number, it's possible to see which elements have gained electrons and which elements have lost electrons. The basic rules for assigning oxidation numbers are given in the table below.

Table 9.4. Assigning oxidation numbers

SPECIES	EXAMPLE	OXIDATION NUMBER
Elements in their free state and naturally occurring diatomic elements	$Zn(s)$, O_2	0
Monoatomic ions	Cl^-	−1
Oxygen in compounds	H_2O	−2
Hydrogen in compounds	HCl	+1
Alkali metals in a compound	Na	+1
Alkaline earth metals in a compound	Mg	+2

RULES

The oxidation numbers on the atoms in a neutral compound sum to zero.	NaOH	Na: +1; O: −2; H: +1 $1 + -2 + 1 = 0$
The oxidation numbers of the atoms in an ion sum to the charge on that ion.	SO_3^{-2}	S: +4; O: −2 $4 + (-2)(3) = -2$

Reaction Stoichiometry

STOICHIOMETRY is the use of the relative amounts of reagents and products in a reaction to find quantities of those reagents and products. Stoichiometry can be used to find a number of variables, including the quantities of products and reagents involved in a reaction, and to identity the limiting reagent (the reagent that gets used up first).

An important unit to know when doing stoichiometry is the MOLE, which is defined the amount of a substance that contains 6.02×10^{23} particles (either individual atoms or molecules). On the periodic table, the atomic mass of an element is also the number of grams per mole of that element; these values can be used in stoichiometry to convert between moles and grams.

For example, in the single displacement reaction shown below, 1 mole of magnesium chloride is needed for every 2 moles of sodium to complete the reaction. This reaction creates 1 mole of magnesium and 2 moles of sodium chloride.

$$MgCl_2 + 2Na \rightarrow Mg + 2NaCl$$

So, if 50 grams of sodium are used up the reaction, stoichiometry can be used to find the number of grams of magnesium that are produced:

$$\frac{50 \text{ g Na}}{1} \times \frac{1 \text{ mol Na}}{23 \text{ g Na}} \times \frac{1 \text{ mol Mg}}{2 \text{ mol Na}} \times \frac{24.3 \text{ g Mg}}{1 \text{ mol Mg}} = 26.4 \text{ g Mg}$$

Examples

1. In a furnace, natural gas (methane) is burned to produce heat to keep a house warm. What sort of reaction is this?

   A) acid base reaction

   B) combustion reaction

   C) single displacement reaction

   D) synthesis reaction

2. If 4 moles of methane are used in the reaction below, how many moles of water will be produced?

   $CH_4 + 2O_2 \rightarrow CO_2 + 2H_2O$

   A) 2

   B) 8

   C) 12

   D) 16

3. Which of the following is a substance or compound that is entering into a reaction?

   A) mole

   B) reactant

   C) product

   D) yield

4. Sulfur trioxide (SO_3) is produced when sulfur is burned. Which of the following is the correct general reaction for this process?

   A) sulfur + nitrogen → sulfur trioxide

   B) sulfur + oxygen → sulfur dioxide

   C) sulfur dioxide + oxygen → sulfur trioxide

   D) sulfur + oxygen → sulfur trioxide

5. In a balanced equation,

   A) the mass of the reactants equals the mass of the products.

   B) the number of moles of reactants equals the number of moles of the products.

   C) the size of each molecule in the reaction remains the same.

   D) the number of moles of each element in the reaction remains the same.

6. Balance the following equation:

A) $2KClO_3 \rightarrow KCl + 3O_2$

B) $KClO_3 \rightarrow KCl + 3O_2$

C) $2KClO_3 \rightarrow 2KCl + 3O_2$

D) $6KClO_3 \rightarrow 6KCl + 3O_2$

Answers: 1. B) 2. B) 3. B) 4. D) 5. D) 6. C)

CHEMICAL EQUILIBRIUM

CHEMICAL EQUILIBRIUM is a state reached in reversible reactions in which the rate of forward reaction equals the rate of reverse reaction. Once equilibrium has been reached, it will appear as though the reaction has stopped because there is no noticeable change in the creation of products. However, this isn't true: at chemical equilibrium, reactions are still occurring, just at an equal rate.

Le Chatelier's Principle

LE CHATELIER'S PRINCIPLE states that a chemical reaction at equilibrium will respond to changes in concentration, pressure, volume, or temperature by shifting to reestablish equilibrium. This new equilibrium will favor either the reactants or the products relative to the original equilibrium.

An increase in the concentration of a reactant or product will shift the equilibrium to the other side (e.g., adding a reactant will result in the production of more products to offset the addition). Decreasing the concentration of a reactant or product will shift the reaction toward that side of the reaction (e.g., removing reactant will result in the production of more reactants and a corresponding decrease in the concentration of the products).

In a reaction involving gases, changes in pressure and volume can shift the equilibrium; the direction of the shift will depend on the number of moles of reactants and products. Decreasing the pressure (or increasing the volume) will result in a shift toward the side of the equation with more moles. Increasing the pressure (or decreasing the volume) will result in a shift toward the side of the equation with fewer moles.

Shifts in chemical equilibriums due to changes in temperature are determined by whether the equation is endothermic (uses energy) or exothermic (gives off energy). Increasing the temperature will favor the products in endothermic reactions and the reactants in exothermic reactions. The opposite is true when decreasing the temperature of a system.

Examples

1. According to Le Chatelier's principle, if hydrochloric acid (HCl) is removed from the reaction below, what will happen?

   $BaCl_2$ (aq) + H_2SO_4 (aq) → $BaSO_4$ (s) + 2HCl (aq)

   A) The reaction will shift to the left, and more reactants will be formed.

   B) The reaction will shift to the right, and more products will be formed.

   C) The reaction will not be able to reestablish equilibrium.

   D) The reaction will stop.

2. Which of the following statements about chemical equilibrium is true?

   A) Chemical equilibrium cannot be reestablished if the concentration of reactants is changed.

   B) In chemical equilibrium, all the reactants have been turned into products.

   C) Chemical equilibriums cannot be reached by reversible reactions.

   D) In chemical equilibrium, forward and reverse reactions are occurring at the same rate.

   Answers: 1. B) 2. D)

CHEMICAL KINETICS

Collision Theory

COLLISION THEORY refers to the idea that a chemical reaction cannot occur until two molecules which may react collide with one another. In a solid, although molecules are all touching one another, there is not much movement. As a result, chemical reactions in solid phase have a low reaction rate, or none at all. A solid usually only reacts when its surface comes into contact with a liquid or gas.

In liquids or gases, molecules are able to move freely, which allows greater interaction and an increased chance that two capable molecules will react. For this reason, the majority of chemical reactions occur in the liquid phase or the gas phase. However, even if two molecules collide that could react, most of the time they do not. In order for a reaction to take place, the reaction must have a minimum amount of energy, a quantity known as the reaction's ACTIVATION ENERGY.

Reaction Rates

Different reactions will occur at different rates. This REACTION RATE is determined by a number of factors, including the concentration of reactants, particle surface area, and temperature. Generally, increasing any of these variables will increase the reaction rate by providing more opportunities for particles to collide.

- Increasing the concentration of reactants introduces more particles to the system, meaning they are more likely to collide.
- Increasing particle surface area makes it more likely particles will come in contact with each other.
- Increasing the temperature increases the velocity of the particles, making them more likely to collide.

Catalysts

There are some substances, called CATALYSTS, that are able to reduce the activation energy of a reaction, which subsequently will increase the reaction rate. A chemical catalyst is commonly a metal or other elemental compound with many electrons in their valence shell; they assist in the stabilization of reaction intermediates. Common chemical catalysts include platinum, palladium, nickel, or cobalt.

A biological catalyst is known as an ENZYME. Common enzymes include cellulase, amylase, or DNA polymerase. Biological catalysts typically function by bringing two reactants close together. Many enzymes also have active sites in their protein chains that function similarly to a chemical catalyst, and assist in stabilizing reaction intermediates.

There are two types of catalysts subdivided by their phase: homogenous and heterogeneous. A HOMOGENOUS CATALYST is in the same phase as the reactants. Most enzymes are homogenous, and are soluble in the same phase as the reactants.

A HETEROGENEOUS CATALYST is not in the same phase as the reactants. An example of a heterogeneous catalyst is the platinum found in the catalytic converter in the exhaust stream of cars. The catalyst is in the solid phase, and the reactants are in the gas phase.

Examples

1. A reaction with a high activation energy will:
   A) require energy to begin
   B) require a catalyst to begin
   C) produce energy
   D) produce enzymes

2. A company is trying to make ammonia from the reaction of nitrogen (N_2) and hydrogen (H_2), but the reaction is progressing very slowly. Which of the following would be effective in increasing the reaction rate?

A) increasing the temperature

B) increasing the pressure

C) adding a catalyst

D) all of the above

Answers: 1. A) 2. D)

LAWS OF THERMODYNAMICS

THERMODYNAMICS is the study of energy in a system and its relationship to chemical reactions. The use of thermodynamics can help explain the rate at which a reaction will occur and whether a reaction will occur at all. There are three basic laws of thermodynamics:

The FIRST LAW OF THERMODYNAMICS states that the internal energy of a system (U) is equal to the heat in the system (Q) minus the work performed by the system (W): $U = Q - W$. This law also confirms the conservation of energy (that energy can neither be created nor destroyed).

This law is probably the most important for chemistry; it helps explain energy shifts in a reaction. For example, if the internal energy of reactants is greater than the internal energy of the products, energy must be released during the course of the reaction, either in the form of heat or work.

The SECOND LAW OF THERMODYNAMICS states that the entropy of a system increases with time and with action. In layman's terms, this law states that any action results in an increase of entropy, a property that describes disorder. The THIRD LAW OF THERMODYNAMICS states that the entropy of a substance approaches zero as the temperature approaches absolute zero (0 Kelvin).

Endothermic and Exothermic Reactions

There are three types of reactions: endothermic, exothermic, and isothermic reactions. An ENDOTHERMIC reaction requires heat in order to proceed while an EXOTHERMIC reaction releases heat during the course of the reaction. An ISOTHERMIC reaction has no net input or output of energy.

CONTINUE

1. In chemistry class, a student mixes two unknown chemicals in a beaker. He notices that the beaker becomes hot to the touch. What type of reaction must be taking place in the beaker?

   A) exothermic

   B) endothermic

   C) combustion

   D) single replacement

2. Which of these processes is exothermic?

   A) freezing water

   B) baking a cake

   C) melting iron

   D) breaking up a gaseous diatom

Answers: 1. A) 2. A)

NUCLEAR CHEMISTRY AND RADIOACTIVITY

The nuclei of some elements are unstable and will emit radioactive particles or energy in order to stabilize; together these emissions of particles and energy are called RADIOACTIVE DECAY or RADIATION. The three types of radiation that will be covered on the test include alpha, beta, and gamma radiation.

ALPHA PARTICLES consist of two protons and two neutrons (i.e., a helium nucleus). They are written as $_0^2He$. In beta decay, high energy electrons or positrons are emitted from the nucleus. BETA PARTICLES are written as $_{-1}^0\beta$ (for electrons) and $_{+1}^0\beta$ (for positrons). Lastly, GAMMA RADIATION is a high frequency (and thus high energy) electromagnetic radiation written as $_0^0\gamma$. All three types of radiation can cause serious health issues ranging from nausea to cancer; both alpha and beta particles are relatively large and thus can be stopped by simple protective barriers. Gamma radiation, however, can travel through most substances, including concrete; lead is usually needed to provide protection from gamma rays.

Half-Life

The time it takes for half a sample of a radioactive substance to decay is called the substance's HALF-LIFE ($t_{\frac{1}{2}}$). A sample of lead-210 has a half-life of 22.2 years, meaning a 100 gram sample of lead-210 would be reduced to 50 grams after 22.2 years; 25 grams after 44.4 years; 12.5 grams after 66.6 years; and so on.

Examples

1. Uranium 233 has a half-life of about 70 years. If an area is contaminated with this compound, how long will it take to reach less than 5% of its original concentration? Round to the nearest number.

   A) 3 half lives

   B) 4 half lives

   C) 5 half lives

   D) 6 half lives

2. In the nuclear reaction shown below, what is the missing product?

   $^{11}_{5}B \rightarrow$ product $+ ^{4}_{2}He$

   A) $^{9}_{5}B$

   B) $^{7}_{5}Li$

   C) $^{7}_{3}Li$

   D) $^{9}_{3}B$

   Answers: 1. C) 2. C)

10

PHYSICS

P hysics is the science of matter and energy and the interaction between the two. Physics is grouped into fields such as acoustics (the study of sound), optics (the study of light), mechanics (the study of motion), and electromagnetism (the study of electric and magnetic fields).

MECHANICS

Motion

$$d = \tfrac{1}{2}at^2 + v_i t \ (d = vt \text{ when } a = 0)$$

$$v_f = v_i + at$$

$$v_f^2 = v_i^2 + 2ad$$

---

m = mass
d = displacement
v = velocity
a = acceleration
t = time

Newtonian mechanics is the study of masses in motion using five main variables. **MASS** (m), as discussed above, is the amount of matter in an object; it is measured in kilograms (kg). **DISPLACEMENT** (d) is a measure of how far an object has moved from its starting point, usually given in meters (m). **VELOCITY** is the distance covered by an object over a given period of **TIME**, usually given in meters per second (m/s). Finally, the change in velocity over time is called **ACCELERATION** (a) and is measured in meters per second squared (m/s²).

Velocity and displacement are both **VECTORS,** meaning they have a magnitude (e.g., 4 m/s) and a direction (e.g., 45°). **SCALARS,** on the other hand, have only a magnitude. **DISTANCE** is a scalar: it describes how far something has traveled. So, if you run 1000 meters around a track and end up back where you started, your displacement is 0 meters, but the distance you covered was 1000 meters. **SPEED** is also a scalar; it is the distance traveled over the time the trip took.

The motion of objects with uniform acceleration is described by a set of equations that define the relationships between distance, velocity, time, distance, and acceleration. These equations can be used to solve for any of these five variables. When the object is moving in a single dimension, problems can be solved using the following steps:

1. Identify the variables given in the problem and the variable to be solved for.
2. Choose the equation that includes the variables from Step 1.
3. Plug the values from the problem into the equation and solve.

When the object is moving in two dimensions, it's necessary to separate the variables into their horizontal and vertical components because only variables in a single dimension can be used within the same equation. Often, it's necessary to solve for a variable in one dimension and use that value to solve for a variable in the second dimension.

Examples

1. How far will a car moving with a constant velocity of 40 mi/hr travel in 15 minutes?

   A) 2.7 miles

   B) 10 miles

   C) 40 miles

   D) 600 miles

2. A ball is dropped from a building with a height of 20 m. If there is no air resistance, how long will it take the ball to reach the ground ($g = 9.8$ m/s^2)?

   A) 2 s

   B) 4 s

   C) 5 s

   D) 10 s

   Answers: 1. B) 2. A)

Momentum

$$p = mv$$

$$J = \Delta P$$

p = momentum
J = impulse

$$m_1 v_{1_i} + m_2 v_{2_i} = m_1 v_{1_f} + m_2 v_{2_f} \text{ (elastic collision)}$$

$$m_1 v_{1_i} + m_2 v_{2_i} = (m_1 + m_2) v_f \text{ (inelastic collision)}$$

Multiplying an object's mass by its velocity gives a quantity called MOMENTUM (p), which is measured in kilogram meters per second ((kg·m)/s). Momentum is always conserved, meaning when objects collide, the sum of their momentums before the collision will be the same as the sum after (although their kinetic energy may not remain the same). Because momentum is derived from velocity, it is a vector. The change in momentum is called IMPULSE (J); it's measured in Newton seconds (N·s).

Examples

1. What is the momentum of an object of 1.5 kg mass moving with a velocity of magnitude 10 m/s?

    A) 1.5 (kg·m)/s

    B) 15 (kg·m)/s

    C) 150 (kg·m)/s

    D) 1500 (kg·m)/s

2. Two objects are traveling in the same direction at different speeds. Object 1 moves at 5 m/s and has a mass of 1 kg. Object 2 moves at a 2 m/s and has a mass of 0.5 kg. If object 1 collides with object 2 and they stick together, what will be the final velocity of the two objects?

    A) 2.5 m/s

    B) 3 m/s

    C) 4 m/s

    D) 7 m/s

    Answers: 1. B) 2. C)

FORCES

$$G = 6.67408 \times 10^{-11} \ \mathrm{m^3 \ kg^{-1} \ s^{-2}}$$

$$g = 9.8 \ \mathrm{m/s^2}$$

$$F_g = mg \ \text{(for falling objects)}$$

$$F_g = \frac{Gm_1 m_2}{r_2} \ \text{(for the gravitational force between two masses)}$$

$$F = ma$$

$$F_f = \mu_k F_N$$

Obviously, objects need a reason to get moving: they don't just start accelerating on their own. The "push" that starts or stops an object's motion is called a FORCE (F) and is measured in Newtons (N). Examples of forces include GRAVITY (created by mass of objects), FRICTION (created by the movement of two surfaces in contact with each other), TENSION (created by hanging a mass from a string or chain), and ELECTRICAL FORCE (created by charged particles). A force that creates circular motion is called a CENTRIPETAL FORCE.

Gravitational force is proportional to the masses of two objects and the distance between the center of mass of the two objects, not the distance between the surfaces.

Note that all of these forces are vectors with a magnitude and direction. Gravity, for example, always points down toward the earth, and friction always points in the opposite direction of the object's motion. On a FREE BODY DIAGRAM, forces are drawn as vectors, and vectors in the horizontal and vertical directions can be added to find the total force.

Newton's three laws of motion describe how these forces work to create motion:

LAW #1: An object at rest will remain at rest, and an object in motion will continue with the same speed and direction unless acted on by a force. This law is often called "the law of inertia."

LAW #2: Acceleration is produced when a force acts on a mass. The greater the mass of the object being accelerated, the greater the amount of force needed to accelerate the object.

LAW #3: Every action requires an equal and opposite reaction. This means that for every force, there is a reacting force both equal in size and opposite in direction. In other words, whenever an object pushes another object, it gets pushed back in the opposite direction with equal force.

Examples

1. An object is being acted on by only 2 forces as shown below. If the magnitudes of F1 and F2 are equal, which of the following statements must be true?

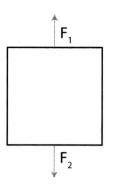

A) The velocity of the object must be zero.

B) The velocity of the object must be constant.

C) The velocity of the object must be increasing.

D) The velocity of the object must be decreasing.

2. An object is pulled across a rough surface with a force of 20 N. If the object moves with a constant velocity and the surface has a coefficient of kinetic friction equal to 0.2, what is the magnitude of the normal force acting on the object?

A) 4 N

B) 10 N

C) 20 N

D) 100 N

Answers: 1. B) 2. D)

CIRCULAR AND ROTATIONAL MOTION

Rotational Motion

$$\theta = \frac{1}{2}\alpha t^2 + \omega_i t$$

$$\omega_f = \omega_i + \alpha t$$

$$\omega_f^2 = \omega_i^2 + 2\alpha\theta$$

θ = angular displacement
ω = angular speed
a = angular acceleration

In addition to moving in a straight line, objects can also rotate. This ROTATIONAL MOTION is described using a similar set of variables and equations to those used for linear motion. However, the variables have been converted to represent rotational motion, as shown in the table below.

Table 10.1. Rotational motion

LINEAR VARIABLE	ROTATIONAL VARIABLE
displacement (d)	angular displacement (θ)
velocity (v)	angular speed (ω)
acceleration (a)	angular acceleration (a)

Example

The motor of an engine is rotating about its axis with an angular velocity of 100 rev/minute. After being switched off, it comes to rest in 15s. If the angular deceleration is constant, how many revolutions does the engine make before it comes to rest?

A) 10.5 rev

B) 11.5 rev

C) 12.5 rev

D) 13.5 rev

Answer: C)

CONTINUE

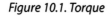

τ = torque

Torque

$$\tau = rF\sin(\theta)$$

TORQUE is a form of work that is applied in a circular motion; it is measured in newton meters (N·m). A wrench, for example, employs torque to apply force to turning a bolt. The specific definition of torque is a force that is applied over a distance and an angle to generate circular motion (as seen below). The amount of torque depends on the radius of the arm (r), the force applied (F), and the angle of the force (θ).

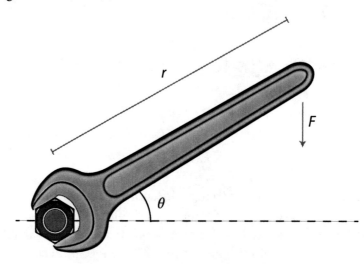

Figure 10.1. Torque

Example

A force of magnitude 10 N is applied at point A to cause a bar to rotate around point B, as shown below. What is the torque produced by the force?

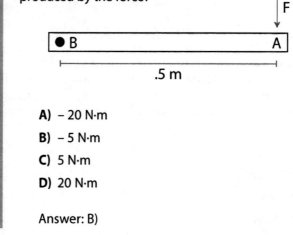

A) – 20 N·m

B) – 5 N·m

C) 5 N·m

D) 20 N·m

Answer: B)

Circular Motion

$$a = \frac{v^2}{r}$$

$$F = ma_c = m \times \frac{v^2}{r}$$

CIRCULAR MOTION is the movement of an object around central point. CENTRIPETAL ACCELERATION, which points toward the center of the circle, changes the direction of the object's velocity and keeps the object on a circular path. The force that creates centripetal acceleration can be tension (e.g., swing a weight on a string), friction(e.g., car tires on a turn), or other forces.

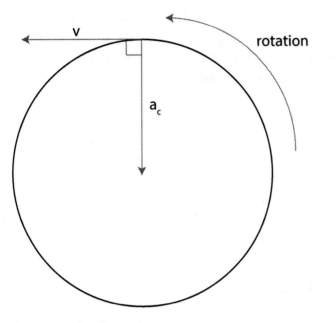

Figure 10.2. Circular motion

Example

An object of mass *m* undergoes uniform circular motion with a speed *v* at a distance *r* from the center of the circle. Which of the following will result in an increase in the centripetal force?

A) A decrease in *r* while maintaining the same speed.

B) An increase in *r* while maintaining the same speed.

C) A decrease in the speed of the mass by a factor of 4 and a decrease in *r* by a factor of 2.

D) An increase in the speed of the mass by a factor of 2 and an increase in *r* by a factor of 4.

Answer: A)

CONTINUE

ENERGY, WORK, AND POWER

Energy

$$KE = \frac{1}{2}mv^2$$

$$PE_g = mgh$$

In simple terms, energy is the capacity to do work; in other words, it's a measurement of how much force a system could apply. Energy is measured in Joules (J), which are $J = kg \cdot m^2/s^2$. There are two main categories of energy. The energy stored within an object due to its relative position is its POTENTIAL ENERGY: that object has the potential to do work. Potential energy can be created in a number of ways, including raising an object off the ground or compressing a spring. KINETIC ENERGY is present when an object is in motion. The sum of an object's kinetic and potential energies is called its MECHANICAL ENERGY.

Energy can be neither created nor destroyed; it can only be converted from one form to another. For example, when a rock is lifted some distance from the ground it has GRAVITATIONAL POTENTIAL ENERGY; when it's released, it begins to move toward the earth and that potential energy becomes kinetic energy. A pendulum is another example: at the height of its swing, the pendulum will have potential energy but no kinetic energy; at the bottom of its swing, it has kinetic energy but no more potential energy.

Generally, kinetic energy is the energy of an object in motion, and potential energy is the energy of an object at rest.

Examples

1. The mass of a rider and his cycle combined is 90 kg. What is the increase in kinetic energy if a 90 kg bike increases its speed from 6 km/h to 12 km/h?

   A) 300 J

   B) 350 J

   C) 375 J

   D) 400 J

2. A skier starts from rest at the top of a hill. If the height of the hill is 20 m, what is the speed of the skier at the bottom of the hill? (Assume no air resistance or friction.)

   A) 4 m/s

   B) 20 m/s

   C) 200 m/s

   D) 400 m/s

   Answers: 1. C) 2. B)

Work

$$W = Fd$$

$$P = \frac{W}{t}$$

WORK is defined in physics as a force exerted over a distance; work is also measured in Joules (J). Work has to take place over a distance: if an object is acted upon by a force, but does not move, then no work has been performed. For example, if someone pushes against a wall with 50 N of force, she has not performed any work. However, if she lifted a baseball off of the ground, then she performed work.

Work is a scalar quantity, and cannot be expressed in terms of a vector. However, the force applied to do work is a vector quantity, and thus the net force used to perform work can change depending on the angle at which it is applied.

POWER is force applied over time; it is measured in Watts.

Examples

1. A child pushes a truck across the floor at a velocity of 1 m/s for 5 m using 1 N of force. How much work did the child do?

   A) 0.25 J

   B) 5 J

   C) 2.5 J

   D) 25 J

2. In the same scenario described above, the child pushes the truck for 5 s. How much power did the child deliver to the truck?

   A) 0.05 W

   B) 0.25 W

   C) 0.5 W

   D) 1 W

   Answers: 1. B) 2. D)

THERMODYNAMICS

TEMPERATURE is a measure of the average kinetic energy of the atoms or molecules of a substance. Substances with a higher temperature have more kinetic energy, meaning their molecules are moving at a higher velocity. Lowering the temperature of the substance will slow the speed of the molecules. The SI unit for temperature is Celsius, but it also measured in Fahrenheit and Kelvin.

HEAT is the transfer of energy between substances; it is measured in Joules. When the air warms a block of ice, or a soda gets cold in the fridge, that transfer of energy is heat. Heat always moves from warmer substances to colder ones. Heat can be transferred

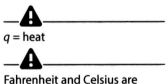

q = heat

Fahrenheit and Celsius are reference scales, while Kelvin is an absolute scale.

in several different ways. One is CONDUCTION, which occurs when heat is transferred between neighboring molecules; conduction is what makes a person's hand cold when she holds ice. During CONVECTION, heat is transferred away from an object by the movement of gases or fluids, for example when warm air rises from a radiator.

Heat is not an intrinsic property. It would not be correct to say that an object contains 100 Joules of heat. It would be correct to say that an object has transmitted 100 Joules of heat.

Heat Capacity

$$q = mc\Delta T$$

The HEAT CAPACITY of an object is best defined as its resistance to temperature change. A material with a higher heat capacity will have a lower change in temperature when exposed to a greater amount of heat. For example, water has one of the highest heat capacities of 4.18 J/(g·K), meaning 4.18 Joules are needed to increase the temperature of one gram of water by one degree Kelvin. On the other hand, most metals have low heat capacities. Copper has a heat capacity of just 0.39 J/(g·K). This means that if copper and water are exposed to the same amount of heat, copper will heat up more than 10 times faster than water will.

> ### Example
> If 27.53 J of heat are needed to increase the temperature of a 15 g mass by 7.3 K, what is the mass's heat capacity?
>
> **A)** 0.251 J/(g·K)
>
> **B)** 1.835 J/(g·K)
>
> **C)** 3.977 J/(g·K)
>
> **D)** 13.398 J/(g·K)
>
> Answer: A)

FLUID MECHANICS

Pressure

$$P = \rho g h$$

P = pressure
ρ = density

PRESSURE is the force applied over a specific area; it is measured in Pascal's, atmospheres, or bars. When an object is submersed in a fluid, the weight of the fluid will exert pressure on that object. The magnitude of the pressure depends on the acceleration due to gravity (g), the depth of the object (h), and the fluid's density.

Fluid pressure is affected by depth, not by shape.

The DENSITY (ρ) of a material is defined as its mass per unit volume. For example, water has a density of 1 gram per cubic centimeter, or 1 gram per milliliter. The SPECIFIC DENSITY or specific gravity of a material is defined as its density when compared to water. In this case, water has a set value of 1. Gold has a specific gravity of 19.3, which means that it is 19.3 times denser than water.

Example

Objects A, B, C, and D are submersed in water as shown below. Which of the following statements is true?

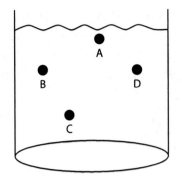

A) The pressure at B is less than the pressure at A.

B) The pressure at A is equal to the pressure at C.

C) The pressure at B and D are equal.

D) The pressure at points A, B, C, and D are equal.

Answer: C)

Buoyancy

BUOYANCY is the ability of an object to float in a fluid that has a greater density than the object. For example, wood might float in water, but a steel marble will not, due to the much higher density of the steel marble compared to the wood.

The buoyant force of an object is a principle first determined by Archimedes, who stated that, "The strength of the buoyant force is equal to the weight of the fluid displaced by the object." Thus, the magnitude of the upward buoyant force on a floating object can be found by calculating the volume of displaced fluid.

Example

When a block is completely submerged in a vessel filled to the top with liquid, the amount of liquid that overflows the vessel—

A) has equal weight to that of the block.

B) has equal volume to that of the block.

C) has the same relative density as that of the block.

D) has the same mass as that of the block.

Answer: B)

CONTINUE

Fluid Flow

$$A_1 v_1 = A_2 v_2$$

$$P_1 + \rho g h_1 + \frac{1}{2}\rho v_1^2 = P_2 + \rho g h_2 + \frac{1}{2}\rho v_2^2$$

When fluid is flowing through a pipe, the area of the pipe and the fluid's velocity have an inverse relationship. Thus, if a pipe gradually becomes thinner, then the water flowing through it will become faster. Based on this understanding, the **BERNOULLI EQUATION** establishes the flow rate of a fluid through a pipe depending on the energy of a fluid flowing through a pipe, the height of the pipe, and the corresponding pressure.

Example

A fluid whose density remains constant is flowing through a tube with radius r_1. It then moves into a section of the tube with a radius r_2. If $r_2 > r_1$, what effect will the increase in radius have?

A) Decrease the speed of the fluid.

B) Increase the speed of the fluid.

C) Increase the volume of fluid that flows past a given point.

D) Decrease the volume of fluid that flows past a given point.

Answer: A)

WAVES

Types of Waves

A **WAVE** is a periodic motion that carries energy through space or matter. There are two main types of waves: mechanical and electromagnetic. **MECHANICAL WAVES** travel through a physical medium; ripples in a pond and sound waves traveling through the air are both examples of mechanical waves. **ELECTROMAGNETIC WAVES** do not require a medium to travel because they consist of oscillating magnetic and electric fields. These waves are classified on the **ELECTROMAGNETIC SPECTRUM** and include visible light, x-rays, and radio waves.

Waves can also be classified by how the particles in the wave vibrate. **LONGITUDINAL WAVES** cause particles to vibrate parallel to the movement of the wave; **TRANSVERSE WAVES** cause particles to vibrate perpendicular to the movement of the wave.

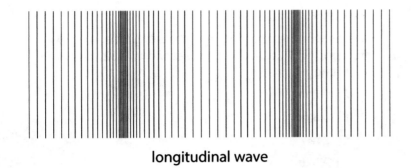

longitudinal wave

transverse wave

Figure 10.3. Types of waves

Example

Which of the following requires a medium to travel?

A) visible light

B) microwaves

C) radio waves

D) sound waves

Answer: D)

Characteristics of Waves

$$v = \lambda f = \frac{\lambda}{T}$$

$$T = \frac{1}{f}$$

The four major characteristics of waves are wavelength, amplitude, period, and frequency. The WAVELENGTH (λ) is the distance from the peak of one wave to the next (or from the trough of one wave to the next). The AMPLITUDE (A) of a wave is the distance from the top of the wave to the bottom. Both wavelength and amplitude are measured in meters (the SI unit for distance).

The PERIOD (T) of a wave is the time it takes the wave to complete one oscillation; it is usually measured in seconds. The FREQUENCY (f) of a wave is the number of oscillations that occur per second; it is measured in Hertz (Hz). The period and frequency of a wave are inverses of each other: the shorter the period of a wave, the higher its frequency.

Example

A wave with a speed of 10 m/s is traveling on a string at a frequency of 20 oscillations per second. What is the wave's wavelength?

A) 0.2 m

B) 0.5 m

C) 2 m

D) 200 m

Answer: B)

Properties of Waves

Waves of all kinds exhibit particular behaviors. Waves can interact either to create CONSTRUCTIVE INTERFERENCE, where the resulting wave is bigger than either original wave, or DESTRUCTIVE INTERFERENCE, which creates a wave that is smaller than either original wave. Waves will also bend when passing through a slit, a process called DIFFRACTION. Waves will also REFRACT, or bend, when they pass from one medium into another.

Example

What is the maximum possible amplitude of the wave created by the interference of a wave with an amplitude of 0.5 m and a wave with an amplitude of 2 m?

A) 0 m

B) 0.5 m

C) 2.5 m

D) 5 m

Answer: C)

Sound

I = intensity

$I_0 = 1 \times 10^{-12}$ W/m² (smallest intensity that can be heard by the human ear)

$$DB = 10\log\left(\frac{I}{I_0}\right)$$

SOUND is comprised of waves that are usually produced by the vibration of an object, such as the strings of an instrument or the human vocal cords. The vibrations cause the air to vibrate as well, which creates a pressure variation in the air, creating a longitudinal wave. When humans hear a sound, it is the detection of the pressure variation by our ear drums. The speed of a sound wave depends on the medium that it is moving through. In air, sound has a speed of about 340 meters per second or 761 miles per hour.

Humans can typically detect sound waves between 20 Hz to 20,000 Hz. Sound waves with a lower frequency have a "lower"

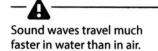

Sound waves travel much faster in water than in air.

pitch to human ears and sound waves with a high frequency have a "high" pitch to human ears.

Sound INTENSITY (I) is the sound power over a specific area; it's measured in W/m² or decibels (DB). Intensity represents the amount of energy carried by the sound wave; the louder the sound (and larger the amplitude), the greater the intensity. However, sound wave energy is inversely proportional to the distance from which it is heard. Thus, as you move away from a sound source, the intensity of the sound decreases exponentially.

⚠ The decibel scale is a logarithmic scale: it is not linear.

Example

Sound waves will move fastest through which medium?

A) water

B) air

C) a vacuum

D) wood

Answer: D)

PERIODIC MOTION

An oscillation is a PERIODIC MOTION that occurs at a specific frequency. Examples of objects that oscillate include pendulum clocks, springs, and the strings in musical instruments.

Springs

$$F = -kx$$

A SPRING is a coil of metal or other ductile material that, when compressed or stretched, will return to its original shape if not held by a force. The force required to stretch or compress a spring is related to the distance the spring will be displaced and its spring constant (k). The greater the spring constant, the stiffer the spring. The springs which make up the suspension of a car, for example, have very high spring constants, in the range of 3000 – 5000 Newtons per meter, whereas the spring that is used in a ballpoint pen might have a spring constant value of 2 – 3 Newtons per meter.

⚠ x = displacement
k = spring constant

Example

What is the magnitude of the force required to compress a spring 35 cm if the spring has a spring constant of 55 Newtons per meter?

A) 6.74 N

B) 19.25 N

C) 674 N

D) 1925 N

Answer: B)

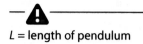

Pendulums

$$f = \frac{1}{2\pi}\left(\frac{\sqrt{g}}{L}\right)$$

A **PENDULUM** is a mass hanging on a string that is swinging back and forth. In a pendulum, as the mass reaches its lowest point, the velocity is the greatest. As it reaches its height on either side, the stored potential energy is the highest, but at its peak the velocity is exactly equal to zero. The frequency of a pendulum is dependent on two things: the gravitational force and the length of the rope.

Examples

Which of the following would increase the frequency of a pendulum?

A) moving the pendulum to a planet with a higher acceleration due to gravity

B) making the length of the pendulum longer

C) adding more mass to the end of the pendulum

D) increasing the angle of the initial release point

Answer: A)

LIGHT

LIGHT is a form of electromagnetic radiation that makes up a small spectrum of all the electromagnetic waves. Visible light is the wavelength range of 400 to 800 nanometers, and is one of the few types of radiation that is able to penetrate the Earth's atmosphere.

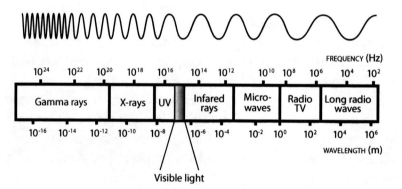

Figure 10.4. Electromagnetic spectrum

Properties of Light

$$n_1\sin\theta_1 = n_2\sin\theta_2$$

$$n = \frac{c}{v_s}$$

Light, which is an electromagnetic wave, has a number of special properties because it acts as both a particle and a wave—a phenomenon called the **WAVE-PARTICLE DUALITY OF LIGHT**. Light will reflect off some materials: the **INCIDENT RAY** will bounce off a surface, and the incident angle will be equal to the angle of reflection. Light will also bend when it passes from one media to another in a process called **REFRACTION**. The angle of refraction can be found using Snell's law and the material's index of refraction (*n*).

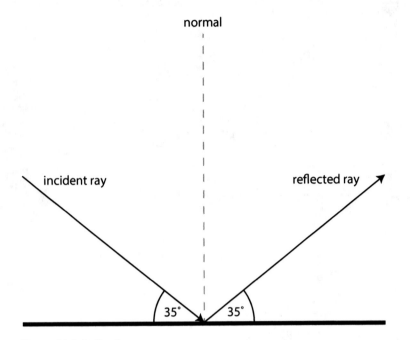

Figure 10.5. Reflection

Light waves can experience both interference and diffraction like any other wave. Because light is made up of discrete packets of energy (called quanta), light also sometimes acts as a particle. For example, when light strikes a metal surface, the packets of energy can eject electrons from atoms in a process called the **PHOTOELECTRIC EFFECT**.

CONTINUE

Example

A ray of light is directed at a reflective surface as shown below.

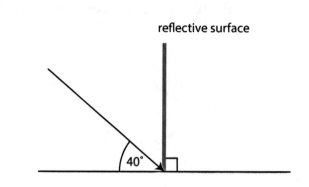

What angle does the reflected ray make with respect to the normal?

A) 0°

B) 40°

C) 50°

D) 90°

Answer: B)

ELECTRICITY

Electric Charge

q = charge

$$k = 9 \times 10^9 \text{ N} \times \text{m}_2/\text{C}_2$$

$$F = k\frac{q_1 q_2}{r^2}$$

An electric charge is generated due to the difference in CHARGE (q) potential between protons, which have a +1 charge, and electrons, which have a –1 charge. The charges on a proton or electron are elementary, meaning that they cannot be further subdivided into smaller units. The charge is measured in coulombs (C). A single electron has a charge of –1.6 × 10⁻¹⁹ C. One proton has the exact same amount of charge, but of the opposite sign. Electricity is generated by the flow of electrons through a conducting coil, such as copper or steel.

Charged particles are naturally attracted to or repulsed from each other based on their charge. An electron will repel another electron, and a proton will repel another proton. An electron and proton will be attracted to one another. COULOMB'S LAW is used to predict the strength of the attractive or repulsive force between two particles. A positive value of force indicates that the particles are being repelled from one another.

Example

Two particles are separated by a distance of 0.5 m. If one particle has a charge of 1 μC and the other particle has a charge of −2 μC, what is the magnitude of the force between the particles ($k = 9 \times 10^9$ Nm²/C²)?

A) 9×10^{-3} N

B) 7.2×10^{-2} N

C) 7.2×10^{10} N

D) 9×10^9 N

Answer: B)

Electric Fields

$$\Delta V = Ed$$

Charged particles create an **ELECTRIC FIELD** (E) in which they will exert an electric force on other charged particles. The strength of an electric field is measured in newtons per coulomb and is proportional to the charge of the particle experiencing the force (i.e., a particle with a higher charge will experience a larger force, and vice versa).

Moving a particle through an electric field will change the potential electrical energy of that particle in an amount proportional to the displacement and force of the electric field. The difference in potential electrical energy between two points is known as **VOLTAGE** (V), which is measured in volts.

$$E = \frac{F}{q}$$

Example

A particle is placed in a uniform electric field of magnitude 1×10^4 N/C. If the particle experiences a force of 0.1 N, what is the magnitude of the charge on the particle?

A) 0.1 μC

B) 1 μC

C) 10 μC

D) 100 μC

Answer: C)

Circuits

$$V = IR$$

$$P = IV = \frac{V^2}{R}$$

In an electric **CIRCUIT**, a closed loop is formed that is connected to the positive and negative ends of a voltage source. The voltage source provides the charge potential that drives electrons through the circuit to create electricity. The movement of electrons is called **CURRENT**, which is measured in Amps (A).

I = current
R = resistance
P = power

Current in a circuit can be thought of as analogous to water in a pipe.

A **RESISTOR** is an electrical component that provides resistance to the flow of current through an electric circuit. A resistor is usually composed of a series of materials that are not conducive to electron flow. The units of resistance are Ω. According to Ohm's law, current and resistance are inversely related, and both are proportional to voltage.

⚠ Resistors in series are additive. Resistors in parallel have a lower total resistance than any individual resistor.

Resistors in a circuit can be wired in series or in parallel. In a **SERIES** circuit, the current can only follow one path, while in a **PARALLEL** circuit the current can follow multiple pathways.

Table 10.2. Series and parallel circuits

	SERIES	PARALLEL
Current	$I_1 = I_2 = I_3 = \ldots = I_n$	$I_t = I_1 + I_2 + \ldots + I_n$
Voltage	$V_t = V_1 + V_2 + \ldots + V_n$	$V_1 = V_2 = V_3 = \ldots = V_n$
Resistance	$R_t = R_1 + R_2 + \ldots + R_n$	$\frac{1}{R_t} = \frac{1}{R_1} + \frac{1}{R_2} + \ldots + \frac{1}{R_n}$

Examples

1. What is the current running through a 2 Ω resister in a circuit with a 10 V battery?

   A) 2 A

   B) 5 A

   C) 20 A

   D) 50 A

2. If a circuit wired in series includes five 10 Ω resisters, what is the total resistance of the circuit?

   A) 2 Ω

   B) 10 Ω

   C) 50 Ω

   D) 500 Ω

   Answers: 1. B) 2. C)

MAGNETISM

MAGNETIC FIELDS can be produced by moving electric charges or can be the result of the alignment of subatomic particles in a substance. The SI unit for magnetism is the Tesla, named after the Russian inventor Nikola Tesla. Electricity and magnetism are closely related: moving particles (like electricity) will create magnetic fields. Similarly, magnetic fields will exert a force on moving charged particles, and a moving magnetic field will create an electric current.

All magnets have a north and a south pole. As with charges, like poles repel each other and opposite poles attract each other; the magnitude of this force is directly proportional to the strength of the magnets and inversely proportional to their distance. Magnetic field lines always flow from north to south.

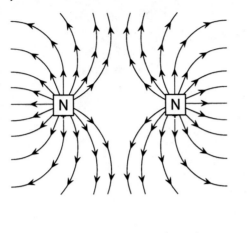

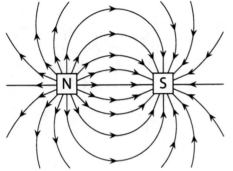

Figure 10.6. Magnetic field lines

Example

The north poles of two magnets are held near each other. At which distance will the magnets experience the most force?

A) 0.1 m

B) 1 m

C) 10 m

D) 100 m

Answer: A)

11

EARTH AND SPACE SCIENCES

ASTRONOMY

Astronomy is the study of celestial objects and everything that occurs outside of the Earth's atmosphere. This includes everything from planets and stars to, at times, the nature of the universe itself.

The TEAS will not heavily test astronomical concepts, but it will be helpful to know basic terminology:

- A **PLANET** is an astronomical object which is large enough to have its own gravity but not large enough to undergo thermonuclear fusion. It is also large enough to have cleared the local area of other celestial objects smaller than it.

- A **STAR** is a luminous plasma ball which is being held together by nothing but its own gravity. The Sun is a star, as are the vast majority of lights seen in the night sky.

- A **SOLAR SYSTEM** is a star and all of the objects which are orbiting that star. The objects do not necessarily have to be planets.

- A **GALAXY** is a system of stars, interstellar gas, dust, dark matter, and stellar remnants which are bound together by an immense gravity field.

- The **SUN** is the star found at the center of our solar system. It is also the primary source of energy for the planets which orbit it (including the Earth).

- **HELIOCENTRIC** is a term that describes a system which has a sun as its center (such as our solar system).

- A **ROTATION** is the circular movement of a given object around a single point (usually the center of the object).

- **REVOLUTION** might be considered another term for

orbit, astronomically speaking. This term is used when one object moves around another one.

- An ELLIPTICAL PATH (or elliptical orbit) is a type of orbit around an object which is roughly egg-shaped, rather than being perfectly spherical.

The Planets

Our solar system includes eight planets which follow elliptical orbits around the sun. The immense graviational field of the sun holds the plants in orbit, and the output of electromagnetic radiation from the sun is what provides the energy from which life on Earth is derived.

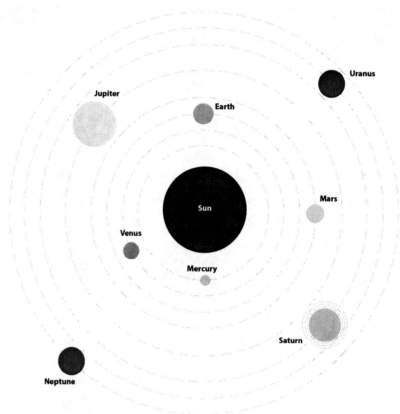

Figure 11.1. Solar system

MERCURY is the planet closest to the sun; it is not much larger than the Earth's moon. On the day side, the temperatures reach around 840°F while on the night side temperatures can drop to very far below freezing. There is nearly no atmosphere on Mercury and thus nothing to protect it from impacts of meteors.

VENUS is the second planet from the sun. It is even hotter than Mercury, and the atmosphere is toxic due to a greenhouse effect (which also traps heat). The pressure on the surface of the planet is immense. Venus has a very slow rotation around its axis and spins in the opposite direction from most of the planets of the solar system. Venus is one of the brightest objects in the sky (other than the moon and the sun).

EARTH is the third planet from the sun. This is a water dominant planet, with around two-thirds of the surface covered by water, and is the only known planet which has life on it. The atmosphere consists primarily of nitrogen and oxygen. The movement of the Earth is responsible for many familiar characteristcs:

- The Earth rotates along its axis while at the same time, moving counterclockwise around the sun.
- A day is the time it takes the Earth to make one rotation around its axis, which tilts at an angle of 23.5 degrees.
- A year is the time it takes the Earth to make one revolution around the sun.
- The cycle of night and day is created by the Earth's rotation on its axis.
- The seasons are created by the movement of the Earth around the sun combined with the tilt of the Earth's axis, which determines the amount of sunlight that reaches the Earth's surface.

MARS is the fourth planet from the sun and is a cold and dry planet. The dust which makes up the surface of the planet is a form of iron oxide, which is also what gives the planet its red color. The topography of Mars is very similar to that of Earth, and ice has been found in some locations on Mars. Additionally, though the atmosphere is currently too thin for water to exist on the surface in liquid form, it is theorized that water was abundant on the planet in the past.

JUPITER is the largest planet in the solar system and the fifth planet from the sun. The planet itself is primarily gaseous, being composed of hydrogen and helium (along with other gases in smaller amounts). The Great Red Spot is an enormous storm which has been ongoing on the planet for hundreds of years. The planet has dozens of moons and a very strong magnetic field.

The sixth planet from the sun, **SATURN**, is known for the rings which orbit it. The planet is primarily gaseous, being comprised of helium and hydrogen. The planet has multiple moons.

URANUS is the seventh planet from the sun. The equator of Uranus is at a right angle to the orbit of the planet, so it appears to be on its side. This planet is about the same size as Neptune. Uranus has faint rings, multiple moons, methane, and a blueish-green tint.

The eighth planet from the sun, **NEPTUNE**, is characterized by its cold temperature and its very strong winds. Neptune is about seventeen times the size of Earth. The planet was originally discovered when scientists theorized that the irregular orbit of

Uranus was the result of a gravitational pull from an undiscovered planet.

In recent years, PLUTO, formerly the ninth planet from the sun, has been reclassified from a true planet to a dwarf planet. Pluto is smaller than the Earth's moon, and it has an orbit near the outer edge of the local solar system. Its orbit around the sun takes around 248 Earth years. The planet itself is rocky and very, very cold. Its atmosphere is extremely thin.

The Sun

Made of hot plasma, our sun, like other stars, is essentially a gigantic reactor where nuclear reactions occur naturally. Around one million Earths could fit into the sun, which accounts for 99.8 percent of the mass in the entire solar system. Astronomers consider our sun to be a type G, main sequence star, which means that it's a fairly typical star. While it is no giant star, it's actually estimated to be brighter than about 85 percent of the stars in our galaxy, since most of the stars in existence are red dwarfs.

Located in the "suburbs" of the MILKY WAY GALAXY, about two-thirds of the way out from the center, the sun came into being 4.6 billion years ago. Most scientists think that our sun, as well as the rest of our solar system, formed from a large cloud of rotating dust and gas. Due to gravity, this cloud collapsed into a rotating disk and most of the material was drawn into the center. This material grew increasingly hot and dense until nuclear fusion was initiated and our sun was officially born.

Our sun is considered a Population I star, which means that it's relatively young and rich in elements that are heavier than helium. Elements heavier than helium (He) all the way up the Periodic Table to iron (Fe) are produced through the process of nuclear fusion, which happens inside stars. Elements heavier than iron are produced during supernova explosions, which occur when very massive stars die. It is thought that the birth of our solar system was triggered by shock waves from one or more such supernovae, due to the presence of elements like gold and uranium, which are higher on the Periodic Table than iron.

Though the sun often appears from afar as a uniform object, it is not. First, temperatures across the sun are not consistent. The sun's exterior burns at about 10,000° Fahrenheit, but its core—where nuclear reactions take place—can climb up to 27 million degrees Fahrenheit. Second, the sun's "body" doesn't rotate uniformly, either. Due to convective motion and the CORIOLIS EFFECT, the star rotates faster at its equator than its poles. Finally, though it is an almost perfect sphere, the sun actually doesn't have a definite boundary—though for practical purposes, the edge of the photosphere (the sun's apparent visible surface) is considered its boundary.

Although it is largely comprised of hydrogen (74.9 percent in its **PHOTOSPHERE**—the outer shell of the sun which radiates light) and helium (23.8 percent), heavier elements like oxygen, carbon, iron, and neon make up less than 1 percent each of the photosphere. The composition of the inner sun is more variable, as it has changed from possessing more hydrogen to possessing more helium, via the process of nuclear fusion which converts hydrogen into helium.

The sun has multiple regions: its **CORE**, where the thermal energy which heats the sun (and then escapes out into space in the form of sunlight or kinetic energy) is produced; the **RADIATIVE ZONE**, which extends from the core to 70 percent of the sun's surface and scatters light coming from the sun's core; the **TACHOLINE**, which separates the radiative and convective zones and may cause the sun's magnetic field; and the **CONVECTIVE ZONE**, which features convection cells of gas to carry the sun's heat outward to the photosphere, where it escapes into space.

However, as is evident during total solar eclipses, the sun actually has one more layer—an atmosphere. Counterintuitively, the sun's atmosphere is actually hotter than the photosphere. The atmosphere has several parts: the **CHROMOSPHERE**, where temperature increases with altitude; a thin transition region, the **CORONA**, where solar winds are produced; and the **HELIOSPHERE**, which is a magnetic bubble extending beyond the orbit of Pluto to the edge of our solar system.

The sun has a magnetic field which can vary greatly and be very strong in some spots, though on average it is about twice as strong as Earth's. The sun's non-uniform magnetic field is largely a byproduct of its non-uniform rotation, and these distortions are the main causes behind some of the most interesting phenomena associated with the sun: **SUNSPOTS** (temporary areas of reduced surface temperature), **SOLAR FLARES** (the most violent eruptions), and **CORONAL MASS EJECTIONS** (where billion of tons of matter spew out into space).

EARTH SCIENCES

The earth sciences include all the sciences that study the Earth. These disciplines look at topics as varied as the structure of the Earth's crust, the movement of Earth's oceans, and the causes of Earth's weather.

Geology
Geology is the study of the solid components of the Earth. The Earth is not a uniform mass: it has many different layers and a disparate topography. Among the layers of the Earth are the crust, the asthenosphere, the mantle, and the core. The thinnest of those layers is the **CRUST**, which is also the outermost layer (and the layer

that humanity calls home). The crust is not uniform and, in fact, has a unique topology. Valleys, mountains, plains, and basins are all variations in the height and thickness of the crust. Together with the topmost layer of the mantle (the most solid part of the mantle), the core forms the LITHOSPHERE.

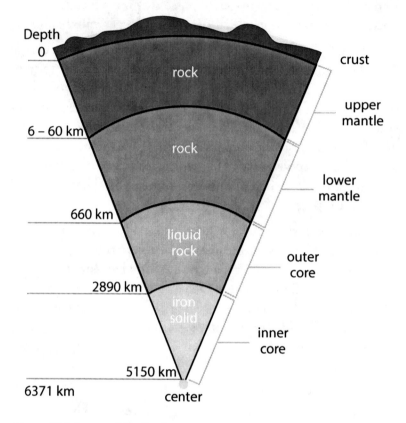

Figure 11.2. Layers of the Earth

The crust is composed of TECTONIC PLATES which move over the asthenosphere. This movement is what explains many natural phenomena, including volcanoes, the creation and destruction of mountains, changes in the sea floor, and earthquakes. The crust is usually only stable for a small time frame, geologically speaking, as these events are constanly occurring across the Earth's surface.

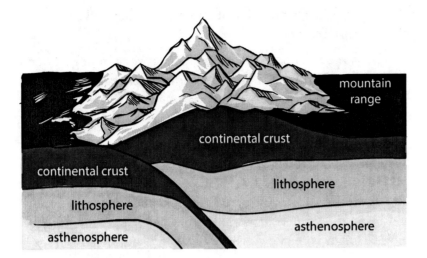

Figure 11.3. The Earth's crust

Rocks on the Earth are also changing. Generally, rocks are made up of a combination of different inorganic crystalline substances known as **MINERALS**. Each type of mineral will have a specific chemical makeup and will have properties that are unique to them. Here are some of the most common minerals:

- Bauxite is a type of rock composed primarily of aluminum oxides which have been hydrated.
- Quartz is the most abundant mineral in the crust of the Earth. This is the most common and simplest form of all silicates. It is an oxide of silicon.
- Talc is a common and soft mineral which can be scratched with a fingernail.
- Pyrite is a mineral comprised of iron and sulfur. Pyrite is commonly known as "fool's gold" because of its resemblance to its actual gold.
- Graphite is a form of carbon. You may recognize this as being used in pencils and some other commercial applications.

Also included in this list would be all the types of precious stones: emerald, ruby, opal, diamond, sapphire, etc.

There are three main types of rocks: igneous, sedimentary, and metamorphic. **IGNEOUS ROCKS** have been formed through the melting and cooling of minerals within the mantle beneath the surface of the Earth. These can surface, initially, as lava. Some common examples of igneous rocks are granite, basalt, and solid volcanic lava.

SEDIMENTARY ROCKS are formed from the accumulation of sediment, often at the bottom of bodies of water, which is then compressed to form rocks. This sediment can derive from biological detritus, weathering of rocks, or the chemical breakdown of minerals.

METAMORPHIC ROCKS are rocks that have gone through a transformation. When rock is put under immense heat and pressure, both physical and chemical changes can occur within it. Some of the examples of this type of rock include slate, gneiss, and marble.

Rocks are subject to several destructive forces. WEATHERING is the process of rocks and soil breaking down through contact with the atmosphere and waters of the Earth. This occurs without movement. EROSION is the process of rocks and soil breaking down and being moved and deposited somewhere else through nature processes such as the flowing of water, wind, and storms.

DEPOSITION is a process through which soil and rocks are added to a mass through transport as a result of erosion and a loss of kinetic energy. Deposition would be rocks breaking off of a mountain because of a hard storm and then "depositing" them down at the bottom of the mountain when they no longer have enough kinetic energy to move.

Oceanography

The HYDROSPHERE is the term which is used for the collective water of the Earth. This includes everything from oceans to lakes, ponds, and rivers. On the Earth, the hydrosphere is about 70 percent of the surface. This water contains minerals and salts which have been dissolved, and the vast majority of the water is held in four ocean basins. Seas, porous rocks, ice caps, lakes, and rivers contain the rest of the water on Earth. From smallest to largest, the oceans are the Arctic Ocean, the Indian Ocean, the Atlantic Ocean, and the Pacific Ocean.

The OCEANS play a large role in maintaining the environment of the Earth. Oceans are able to absorb and release heat and, thus, they help to regulate both the climate and the weather. Because of the tilt and rotation of the Earth, sunlight strikes the Earth's surface unevenly. Oceans trap this heat and distribute it around the planet. This uneven heating also helps create ocean currents.

Oceanography itself is a pretty broad topic and is a term used to describe the study of the ocean as well as oceanic ecosystems, currents, fluid dynamics, plate tectonics, and marine organisms. One of the current major areas of study in oceanography is the ACIDIFICATION of the ocean, which is a term used to describe the decreasing pH of the ocean due to carbon dioxide emissions.

Meteorology

The ATMOSPHERE is a term for the layer of gases which surround planets (or any large body with a significant amount of mass) and which are being held in place by the gravity of those planets. The atmosphere of the Earth has multiple layers which reflect, refract, and absorb the light energy being emitted from the sun. These processes cause the movement of energy that creates the weather and climate of the Earth. The study of the atmosphere, weather, and climate is called METEOROLOGY.

The atmosphere of the Earth consists of many elements, but it is primarily composed of nitrogen (78 percent) and oxygen (21 percent). About 1 percent of the atmosphere is made up of other gases, such as carbon dioxide, ozone, and argon.

There are multiple layers of the atmosphere, all of which are separated from each other by pauses (which have the largest variation in characteristics): exosphere, thermosphere, mesosphere, stratosphere, and troposphere.

The EXOSPHERE is the most distant part of the atmosphere. This is where satellites are orbiting the planet and where molecules have the potential to escape into space itself. The very bottom of the exosphere is known as the thermopause. The thermopause is about 375 miles above the surface of the Earth. The outermost boundary of the exosphere is about 6200 miles above the surface of the Earth.

The THERMOSPHERE is the next layer when coming toward Earth from space. This layer is between 53 and 375 miles above the surface of the Earth and is known colloquially as the upper atmosphere. The gases in this layer are very thin, but they become denser the closer you get to the Earth. That energy is what leads to high temperatures: the top of this layer is around −184° Fahrenheit while the bottom is around 3600° Fahrenheit.

Between thirty-one and fifty-three miles above the surface of the Earth lies a denser layer of atmosphere and gases called the MESO-SPHERE. The temperatures in this layer are around 5° Fahrenheit. Gases here are usually thick enough to stop most small meteors that enter the atmosphere of the Earth, causing them to burn up. This layer, along with the stratosphere, are collectively known as the middle atmosphere. The boundary between the two layers is called the stratopause.

The STRATOSPHERE is from thirty-one miles to eight miles above the surface of the Earth. About 19 percent of the gases in the atmosphere are contained in the stratosphere, which has a very low water content. The temperature of this layer increases with the height; the heat is a byproduct of the creation of ozone in this layer. This is the layer which absorbs much of the energy coming in from the sun (particularly ultraviolet radiation and x-ray radiation). The barrier between this layer and the troposphere is the tropopause.

The TROPOSPHERE is the lowest layer. This is where weather takes place. It goes from the surface of the Earth to between four and twelve miles above the surface. (The exact height of this layer varies.)

The density of gas in the troposphere decreases with the height, and the air becomes thinner (which is why mountaintops have thin air).

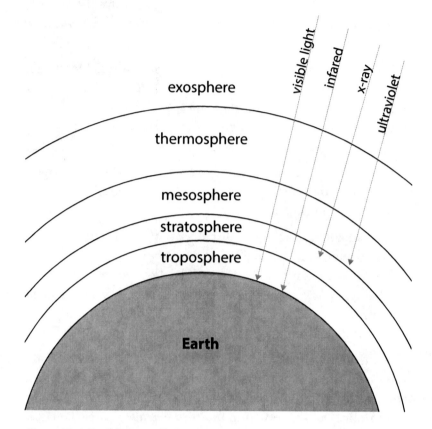

Figure 11.4. Earth's atmosphere

The layer which humans live in is known as the troposphere, which is also the layer in which weather takes place. **WEATHER** is a temporary (e.g., day to day) atmospheric condition such as rain, snow, or heat waves. Note that this is different from **CLIMATE**, which is the condition in a particular area over a long period of time. (Think about how the northwestern United States is generally cold and rainy, or how the southwest is hot and dry.)

Some of the variables which are governed by weather conditions include the weight of the air (barometric pressure), air temperature, humidity, air velocity, clouds, and the levels of precipitation. Instruments are commonly used to help determine the relative levels of all of these variables. Below are some common weather measurement instruments:

- A **THERMOMETER** is a tool which is used to measure the temperature of the air, usually using either mercury or alcohol.
- A **BAROMETER** is used to measure the pressure of the air. If the pressure is going up, calm weather is coming. If the pressure if going down, expect rain.
- A **PSYCHROMETERS** is a device used to measure relative humidity through the use of evaporation.

- An **ANEMOMETER** is an instrument which measures wind speed using a series of cups which catch the wind and then turn a dial.

- A **RAIN GAUGE** is used to determine how much rain has fallen in a given period of time.

- **WIND VANES** are used to help determine the direction of the wind.

- A **HYGROMETER** is an instrument which is used to help measure the humidity of the air.

- **WEATHER MAPS** show the atmospheric conditions over geographical areas.

- A **COMPASS** is an instrument which is used primarily for navigation and can be used to determine directions.

- **WEATHER BALLOONS** are commonly used to help measure the conditions of weather in the upper atmosphere.

Most meteorologists will utilize readings from a weather map and a number of these tools in order to determine what air masses are moving around in the troposphere. Air masses are defined as sections of air that have a uniform content of moisture and temperature. The way that these air masses move and interact with each other determine the weather and, thus, are what most meteorologists use when determining changes in the weather.

Examples

1. Fill in the blanks: Nuclear fusion is the _____ of atomic nuclei and it happens in _____ while nuclear fission is the _____ of atomic nuclei and it happens in _____.

   A) splitting, stars, combining, nuclear power plants

   B) combining, stars, splitting, nuclear power plants

   C) splitting, nuclear power plants, combining, stars

   D) combining, nuclear power plants, splitting, stars

2. Which of the following statements is true?

   A) The sun's rate of rotation is consistent throughout its surface, but its temperature is not.

   B) The sun's temperature is consistent throughout its surface, but its rate of rotation is not.

   C) Both the sun's temperature and rate of rotation are consistent throughout its surface.

   D) Neither the sun's temperature nor rate of rotation are consistent throughout its surface.

CONTINUE

3. The Earth's crust and upper mantle form the
   A) outer core
   B) inner core
   C) lithosphere
   D) asthenosphere

4. The layer of the atmosphere which absorbs most of the sun's ultraviolet radiation is the
   A) exosphere
   B) thermosphere
   C) stratosphere
   D) troposphere

   Answers: 1. B) 2. D) 3. C) 4. C)

PART IV: ENGLISH AND LANGUAGE USAGE

34 questions | 34 minutes

The English and Language Usage section will test your understanding of the basic rules of grammar. The first step in getting ready for this section of the test is to review parts of speech and the rules that accompany them. The good news is that you have been using these rules since you first began to speak; even if you don't know a lot of the technical terms, many of these rules may be familiar to you. Some of the topics you might see include:

- matching pronouns with their antecedents
- matching verbs with their subjects
- ensuring that verbs are in the correct tense
- spelling irregular, hyphenated, and commonly misspelled words
- using correct capitalization
- distinguishing between types of sentences
- correcting sentence structure
- changing passive to active voice

12

PARTS OF SPEECH

NOUNS AND PRONOUNS

NOUNS are people, places, or things. They are typically the subject of a sentence. For example, in the sentence *The hospital was very clean*, the noun is *hospital*; it is a place. PRONOUNS replace nouns and make sentences sound less repetitive. Take the sentence *Sam stayed home from school because Sam was not feeling well*. The word *Sam* appears twice in the same sentence. Instead, you can use a pronoun and say *Sam stayed at home because he did not feel well*. Sounds much better, right?

Because pronouns take the place of nouns, they need to agree both in number and gender with the noun they replace. So, a plural noun needs a plural pronoun, and a feminine noun needs a feminine pronoun. In the previous sentence, for example, the plural pronoun *they* replaced the plural noun *pronouns*. There will usually be several questions on the English and Language Usage section that cover pronoun agreement, so it's good to get comfortable spotting pronouns.

Examples

Wrong: If a student forgets their homework, it is considered incomplete.

Correct: If a student forgets his or her homework, it is considered incomplete.

Student is a singular noun, but *their* is a plural pronoun. So, this first sentence is grammatically incorrect. To correct it, replace *their* with the singular pronoun *his* or *her*.

Wrong: Everybody will receive their paychecks promptly.

Correct: Everybody will receive his or her paycheck promptly.

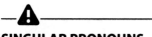

SINGULAR PRONOUNS
- I, me, mine, my
- you, your, yours
- he, him, his
- she, her, hers
- it, its

PLURAL PRONOUNS
- we, us, our, ours
- they, them, their, theirs

Everybody is a singular noun, but *their* is a plural pronoun. So, this sentence is grammatically incorrect. To correct it, replace *their* with the singular pronoun *his* or *her*.

Wrong: When a nurse begins work at a hospital, you should wash your hands.

Correct: When a nurse begins work at a hospital, he or she should wash his or her hands.

This sentence begins in third-person perspective and finishes in second-person perspective. So, this sentence is grammatically incorrect. To correct it, ensure the sentence finishes in third-person perspective.

Wrong: After the teacher spoke to the student, she realized her mistake.

Correct: After Mr. White spoke to his student, she realized her mistake (*she* and *her* referring to student).

Correct: After speaking to the student, the teacher realized her own mistake (*her* referring to teacher).

This sentence refers to a teacher and a student. But whom does *she* refer to, the teacher or the student? To improve clarity, use specific names or state more specifically who spotted the mistake.

VERBS

Remember the old commercial, *Verb: It's what you do*? That sums up verbs in a nutshell. A *verb* is the action of a sentence; verbs *do* things. Verbs must be conjugated to match the context of the sentence; this can sometimes be tricky because English has many irregular verbs. For example, *runs* is an action verb in the present tense that becomes *ran* in the past tense; the linking verb *is* (which describes a state of being) becomes *was* in the past tense.

Table 12.1. Conjugations of the verb *to be*

	PAST	PRESENT	FUTURE
SINGULAR	was	is	will be
PLURAL	were	are	will be

As mentioned, verbs must use the correct tense, and that tense must make sense in the context of the sentence. For example, the sentence *I was baking cookies and eat some dough* sounds strange, right? That's because the two verbs *was baking* and *eat* are in different tenses. *Was baking* occurred in the past; *eat*, on the other hand, occurs in the present. Instead, it should be *ate some dough*.

Like pronouns, verbs must agree in number with the noun they refer back to. In the example above, the verb *was* refers back to the singular *I*. If the subject of the sentence was plural, it would need to be modified to read *They were baking cookies and ate some dough*.

Note that the verb *ate* does not change form; this is common for verbs in the past tense.

Examples

Wrong: The cat chase the ball while the dogs runs in the yard.

Correct: The cat chases the ball while the dogs run in the yard.

Cat is singular, so it takes a singular verb (which confusingly ends with an s); dogs is plural, so it needs a plural verb.

Wrong: The cars that had been recalled by the manufacturer was returned within a few months.

Correct: The cars that had been recalled by the manufacturer were returned within a few months.

Sometimes, the subject and verb are separated by clauses or phrases. Here, the subject cars is separated from the verb phrase were returned, making it more difficult to conjugate the verb.

Correct: The deer hid in the trees.

Correct: The deer are not all the same size.

The subject of these sentences is a collective noun, which describes a group of people or items. This noun can be singular if it's referring to the group as a whole, or plural if it refers to each item in the group as a separate entity.

Correct: The doctor and nurse work in the hospital.

Correct: Neither the nurse nor her boss was scheduled to take a vacation.

Correct: Either the patient or her parents need to sign the release forms.

When the subject contains two or more nouns connected by and, that subject is plural and requires a plural verb. Singular subjects joined by or, either/or, neither/nor, or not only/ but also remain singular; when these words join plural and singular subjects, the verb should match the closest subject.

Wrong: Because it will rain during the party last night, we had to move the tables inside.

Correct: Because it rained during the party last night, we had to move the tables inside.

All the verb tenses in a sentence need to agree both with each other and with the other information in the sentence. In the first sentence above, the tense doesn't match the other information in the sentence: last night indicates the past (rained) not the future (will rain).

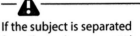

Think of the subject and the verb as sharing a single *s*. If the noun ends with an *s*, the verb shouldn't, and vice versa.

If the subject is separated from the verb, cross out the phrases between them to make conjugation easier.

ADJECTIVES AND ADVERBS

ADJECTIVES are words that describe a noun. Take the sentence *The boy hit the ball*. If you want to know more about the noun *boy*, then you could use an adjective to describe him: *The little boy hit the ball*. An adjective simply provides more information about a noun or subject in a sentence.

For some reason, many people have a difficult time with adverbs, but don't worry! They are really quite simple. ADVERBS and adjectives are similar because they provide more information about a part of a sentence; however, adverbs do not describe nouns—that's an adjective's job. Instead, adverbs describe verbs, adjectives, and even other adverbs. For example, in the sentence *The doctor had recently hired a new employee*, the adverb *recently* tells us more about how the action *hired* took place.

Adjectives, adverbs, and MODIFYING PHRASES (groups of words that together modify another word) should always be placed as close as possible to the word they modify. Separating words from their modifiers can create incorrect or confusing sentences.

Examples

Wrong: Running through the hall, the bell rang and the student knew she was late.

Correct: Running through the hall, the student heard the bell ring and knew she was late.

The phrase *running through the hall* should be placed next to *student*, the noun it modifies.

Wrong: Of my two friends, Clara is the most smartest.

Correct: Of my two friends, Clara is more smart.

The first sentence above has two mistakes. First, the word *most* should only be used when comparing three or more things. Second, the adjective should only be modified with *more/most* or the suffix *-er/-est*, not both.

OTHER PARTS OF SPEECH

PREPOSITIONS express the location of a noun or pronoun in relation to other words and phrases in a sentence. For example, in the sentence *The nurse parked her car in a parking garage*, the preposition *in* describes the position of the car in relation to the garage. Together, the preposition and the noun that follow it are called a PREPOSITIONAL PHRASE. In the example above, the prepositional phrase is *in a parking garage*.

CONJUNCTIONS connect words, phrases, and clauses. The conjunctions summarized in the acronym FANBOYS—For, And, Nor, But, Or, Yet, So—are called COORDINATING CONJUNCTIONS and are used to join INDEPENDENT CLAUSES (clauses that can stand alone as a complete sentence). For example, in the sentence *The nurse prepared the patient for surgery, and the doctor performed the surgery*, the conjunction *and* joins together the two independent clauses. Other conjunctions, like *although, because,* and *if,* join together an independent and DEPENDENT CLAUSE (which cannot stand on its own). In the sentence *She had to ride the subway because her car was broken*, the conjunction *because* joins together the two clauses.

INTERJECTIONS, like *wow* and *hey*, express emotion and are most commonly used in conversation and casual writing.

> ⚠ An independent (or main) clause can stand alone as its own sentence. A dependent (or subordinate) clause must be attached to an independent clause to make a complete sentence.

Examples

Choose the word that best completes the sentence.

1. Her love _____ blueberry muffins kept her coming back to the bakery every week.

   A) to

   B) with

   C) of

   D) about

   The correct preposition is *of* (choice C).

2. Christine left her house early on Monday morning, _____ she was still late for work.

   A) but

   B) and

   C) for

   D) or

   In this sentence, the conjunction is joining together two contrasting ideas, so the correct answer is *but* (choice A).

13

SENTENCE STRUCTURE

PUNCTUATION

The basic rules for using the major punctuation marks are given in the table below.

Table 13.1. How to use punctuation

PUNCTUATION	USED FOR ...	EXAMPLE
period	ending sentences	Periods go at the end of complete sentences.
question mark	ending questions	What's the best way to end a sentence?
exclamation point	ending sentences that show extreme emotion	I'll never understand how to use commas!
comma	joining two independent clauses (always with a coordinating conjunction)	Commas can be used to join clauses, but they must always be followed by a coordinating conjunction.
	setting apart introductory and nonessential words and phrases	Commas, when used properly, set apart extra information in a sentence.
	separating items in a list	My favorite punctuation marks include the colon, semicolon, and period.
semicolon	joining together two independent clauses (never with a conjunction)	I love exclamation points; they make sentences seem so exciting!
colon	introducing a list, explanation, or definition	When I see a colon I know what to expect: more information.

apostrophe	form contractions	It's amazing how many people can't use apostrophes correctly.
	show possession	Parentheses are my sister's favorite punctuation; she finds commas' rules confusing.
quotation marks	indicate a direct quote	I said to her, "Tell me more about parentheses."

CAPITALIZATION

- The first word of a sentence is always capitalized.
- The first letter of a proper noun is always capitalized. (We're going to Chicago on Wednesday.)
- Titles are capitalized if they precede the name they modify. (President Obama met with Joe Biden, his vice president.)
- Months are capitalized, but not the names of the seasons. (Snow fell in March even though winter was over.)

SENTENCE CLASSIFICATION

Types of Clauses

A sentence can be classified as simple, compound, complex, or compound-complex based on the type and number of clauses it has.

Table 13.2. Types of clauses

SENTENCE TYPE	NUMBER OF INDEPENDENT CLAUSES	NUMBER OF SUBORDINATE CLAUSES
simple	1	0
compound	2+	0
complex	1	1+
compound-complex	2+	1+

A **SIMPLE SENTENCE** consists of only one independent clause. Because there are no dependent clauses in a simple sentence, it can simply be a two-word sentence, with one word being the subject and the other word being the verb (e.g., *I ran.*). However, a simple sentence can also contain prepositions, adjectives, and adverbs. Even though these additions can extend the length of a simple sentence, it is still considered a simple sentence as long as it doesn't contain any dependent clauses.

COMPOUND SENTENCES have two or more independent clauses and no dependent clauses. Usually a comma and a coordinating conjunction (*and, or, but, nor, for, so,* and *yet*) join the independent clauses, though semicolons can be used as well. For example, the sentence *My computer broke, so I took it to be repaired* is compound.

COMPLEX SENTENCES have one independent clause and at least one dependent clause. In the complex sentence *If you lie down with dogs, you'll wake up with fleas*, the first clause is dependent (because of the subordinating conjunction *if*), and the second is independent.

COMPOUND-COMPLEX SENTENCES have two or more independent clauses and at least one subordinate clause. For example, the sentence *Even though David was a vegetarian, he went with his friends to steakhouses, but he focused on the conversation instead of the food*, is compound-complex.

🔒

On the test you'll have to both identify and construct different kinds of sentences.

⚠️

Can you write a simple, compound, complex, and compound-complex sentence using the same independent clause?

Examples

Classify: San Francisco in the springtime is one of my favorite places to visit.

Although the sentence is lengthy, it is simple because it contains only one subject and verb (*San Francisco... is*) modified by additional phrases.

Classify: I love listening to the radio in the car because I can sing along as loud as I want.

The sentence has one independent clause (*I love... car*) and one dependent (*because I . . . want*), so it's complex.

Classify: I wanted to get a dog, but I have a fish because my roommate is allergic to pet dander.

This sentence has three clauses: two independent (*I wanted... dog* and *I have a fish*) and one dependent (*because my... dander*), so it's compound-complex.

Classify: The game was canceled, but we will still practice on Saturday.

This sentence is made up of two independent clauses joined by a conjunction (*but*), so it's compound.

Clause Placement

In addition to these classifications, sentences can also be defined by the location of the main clause. In a PERIODIC SENTENCE, the main idea of the sentence is held until the end. In a CUMULATIVE SENTENCE, the independent clause comes first, and any modifying words or clauses follow it. Note that this type of classification—periodic or cumulative—is not used in place of the simple, compound, complex, or compound-complex classifications. A sentence can be both cumulative and complex, for example.

Examples

Classify: To believe your own thought, to believe that what is true for you in your private heart is true for all men, that is genius.

In this sentence the main independent clause—*that is genius*—is held until the very end, so it's periodic. It's also simple because it has one independent clause.

Classify: We need the tonic of wildness—to wade sometimes in marshes where the bittern and meadow-hen lurk, and hear the booming of the snipe; to smell the whispering sedge where only some wilder and more solitary fowl builds her nest, and the mink crawls with its belly close to the ground.

Here, the main clause—*we need the tonic of wildness*—is at the beginning, so the sentence is cumulative. It's also simple because it has one main clause.

ACTIVE AND PASSIVE VOICE

Sentences can be written in active voice or passive voice. ACTIVE VOICE means that the subjects of the sentences are performing the action of the sentence. In a sentence in PASSIVE VOICE, the subjects are being acted on. So, the sentence *Justin wrecked my car* is in the active voice because the subject (*Justin*) is doing the action (*wrecked*). The sentence can be rewritten in passive voice by using a *to be* verb: *My car was wrecked by Justin*. Now the subject of the sentence (*car*) is being acted on. Notice that it's possible to write the sentence so that the person performing the action is not identified: *My car was wrecked*.

Generally, good writing will make more use of the active than passive voice. However, passive voice can sometimes be the better choice. For example, if it's not known who or what performed the action of the sentence, it's necessary to use passive voice.

Examples

1. Rewrite the following sentence in active voice: *I was hit with a stick by my brother.*

    To rewrite a sentence in active voice, first take the person or object performing the action (usually given in a prepositional phrase) and make it the subject. Then, the subject of the original sentence becomes the object and the *to be* verb disappears: *My brother hit me with a stick.*

2. Rewrite the following sentence in passive voice: *My roommate made coffee this morning.*

    To rewrite a sentence in passive voice, the object (*coffee*) becomes the subject, and the subject gets moved to a prepositional phrase at the end of the sentence. Lastly, the *to be* verb is added: *The coffee was made this morning by my roommate.*

POINT OF VIEW

A sentence's **POINT OF VIEW** is the perspective from which it is written. Point of view is described as either first, second, or third person.

Table 13.3. Point of view

PERSON	PRONOUNS USED	WHO'S ACTING?	EXAMPLE
first	I, we	the writer	I take my time when shopping for shoes.
second	you	the reader	You prefer to shop online.
third	he, she, it, they	the subject	She buys shoes from her cousin's store.

Using first person is best for writing in which the writer's personal experiences, feelings, and opinions are an important element. Second person is best for writing in which the author directly addresses the reader. Third person is most common in formal and academic writing; it creates distance between the writer and the reader. A sentence's point of view has to remain consistent throughout the sentence.

Look for pronouns to help you identify which point of view a sentence is using.

Example

Wrong: If someone wants to be a professional athlete, you have to practice often.

Correct: If you want to be a professional athlete, you have to practice often.

Correct: If someone wants to be a professional athlete, he or she has to practice often.

In the first sentence, the person shifts from third (*someone*) to second (*you*). It needs to be rewritten to be consistent.

HOMOPHONES AND SPELLING

The TEAS will include questions that ask you to identify the correct **HOMOPHONE**, which is a set of words that are pronounced similarly but have different meanings. Bawl and ball, for example, are homophones. You will also be tested on spelling, so it's good to familiarize yourself with commonly misspelled words.

CONTINUE

COMMON HOMOPHONES

- Bare/bear
- Brake/break
- Die/dye
- Effect/affect
- Flour/flower
- Heal/heel
- Insure/ensure
- Morning/mourning
- Peace/piece
- Poor/pour
- Principal/principle
- Sole/soul
- Stair/stare
- Suite/sweet
- Their/there/they're
- Wear/where

Examples

Choose the sentence that contains the correct spelling of the underlined word.

1. Her excellent <u>manors</u> and friendly personality <u>made</u> it easy for her to win new clients.

2. Her excellent <u>manners</u> and friendly personality <u>made</u> it easy for her to win new clients.

3. Her excellent <u>manors</u> and friendly personality <u>maid</u> it easy for her to win new clients.

4. Her excellent <u>manners</u> and friendly personality <u>maid</u> it easy for her to win new clients.

People's behavior towards others are *manners*, while a *manor* is a country house. A *maid* is a person who cleans and *made* is the past tense of make. **So, the correct answer is 2.**

1. The nurse has three <u>patents</u> to see before lunch.

2. The nurse has three <u>patience</u> to see before lunch.

3. The nurse has three <u>patients</u> to see before lunch.

4. The nurse has three <u>pateince</u> to see before lunch.

The correct spelling of *patients* is found in answer choice 3.

PART V: TEST YOUR KNOWLEDGE

14

PRACTICE TEST ONE

Reading

The next five questions are based on the following passage.

In recent decades, jazz has been associated with New Orleans and festivals like Mardi Gras, but in the 1920s jazz was a booming trend whose influence reached into many aspects of American culture. In fact, the years between World War I and the Great Depression were known as the Jazz Age, a term coined by F. Scott Fitzgerald in his famous novel *The Great Gatsby*. Sometimes also called the Roaring Twenties, this time period saw major urban centers experience new economic, cultural, and artistic vitality. In the United States, musicians flocked to cities like New York and Chicago, which would become famous hubs for jazz musicians. Ella Fitzgerald, for example, moved from Virginia to New York City to begin her much-lauded singing career, and jazz pioneer Louis Armstrong got his big break in Chicago.

Jazz music was played by and for a more expressive and free populace than the United States had previously seen. Women gained the right to vote and were openly seen drinking and wearing revealing clothing. This period marked the emergence of the flapper, a woman determined to make a statement about her new role in society. Jazz music also provided the soundtrack for the explosion of African American art and culture now known as the Harlem Renaissance. In addition to Fitzgerald and Armstrong, numerous musicians, including Duke Ellington, Fats Waller, and Bessie Smith, promoted their distinctive and complex music as an integral part of the emerging African American culture.

1. Which of the following is the author's main purpose for writing this passage?

   A) to explain the role jazz musicians played in the Harlem Renaissance

   B) to inform the reader about the many important musicians playing jazz in the 1920s

   C) to discuss how jazz influenced important cultural movements in the 1920s

   D) to provide a history of jazz music in the 20th century

2. *Jazz music also provided the soundtrack for the explosion of African American art and culture now known as the Harlem Renaissance.*

   The sentence above appears in the second paragraph of the passage. This sentence is best described as which of the following?

   A) theme

   B) topic

   C) main idea

   D) supporting idea

3. The passage is reflective of which of the following types of writing?

    A) technical

    B) expository

    C) persuasive

    D) narrative

4. Which of the following conclusions may be drawn directly from the second paragraph of the passage?

    A) Jazz music was important to minority groups struggling for social equality in the 1920s.

    B) Duke Ellington, Fats Waller, and Bessie Smith were the most important jazz musicians of the Harlem Renaissance.

    C) Women were able to gain the right to vote with the help of jazz musicians.

    D) Duke Ellington, Fats Waller, and Bessie Smith all supported women's right to vote.

5. Which of the following is the topic sentence for the whole passage?

    A) In recent decades, jazz has been associated with New Orleans and festivals like Mardi Gras, but in the 1920s jazz was a booming trend whose influence was reaching into many aspects of American culture.

    B) Sometimes also called the Roaring Twenties, this time period saw major urban centers experiencing new economic, cultural, and artistic vitality.

    C) The Jazz Age brought along with it a more expressive and free populace.

    D) Jazz music also provided the soundtrack for the explosion of African American art and culture now known as the Harlem Renaissance.

The next six questions are based on the passage below.

Popcorn is often associated with fun and festivities, both in and out of the home. It's eaten in theaters, usually after being salted and smothered in butter, and in homes, fresh from the microwave. But popcorn isn't just for fun—it's also a multi-million dollar industry with a long and fascinating history.

While popcorn might seem like a modern invention, its history actually dates back thousands of years, making it one of the oldest snack foods enjoyed around the world. Popping is believed by food historians to be one of the earliest uses of cultivated corn. In 1948, Herbert Dick and Earle Smith discovered old popcorn dating back 4,000 years in the New Mexico Bat Cave. For the Aztec Indians that called the caves home, popcorn (or *momochitl*) played an important role in society, both as a food staple and in ceremonies. The Aztecs cooked popcorn by heating sand in a fire; when it was heated, kernels were added and would pop when exposed to the heat of the sand.

The American love affair with popcorn began in 1912, when popcorn was first sold in theaters. The popcorn industry flourished during the Great Depression by advertising popcorn as a wholesome and economical food. Selling for 5 to 10 cents a bag, it was a luxury that the downtrodden could afford. With the introduction of mobile popcorn machines at the World's Columbian Exposition in the late 1800s, popcorn moved from the theater into fairs and parks. Popcorn continued to rule the snack food kingdom until the rise in popularity of home televisions during the 1950s.

The popcorn industry reacted to their decline in sales quickly by introducing pre-popped and un-popped popcorn for home consumption. However, it wasn't until microwave popcorn became commercially available in 1981 that at-home popcorn consumption began to grow exponentially. With the wide availability of microwaves in the United States, popcorn also began popping up in offices and hotel rooms. The home still remains the most popular popcorn eating spot, though: today, 70 percent of the 16 billion quarts of popcorn consumed annually in the United States is eaten at home.

6. The author's description of the growth of the popcorn industry is reflective of which of the following types of text structure?

   A) cause-effect

   B) comparison-contrast

   C) sequence

   D) problem-solution

7. *Popcorn is often associated with fun and festivities, both in and out of the home.*

   The sentence above appears as the first sentence of the passage. This sentence is best described as which of the following?

   A) theme

   B) topic

   C) main idea

   D) supporting idea

8. Which of the following conclusions may be drawn directly from the third paragraph of the passage?

   A) People ate less popcorn in the 1950s than in previous decades because they went to the movies less.

   B) Without mobile popcorn machines, people would not have been able to eat popcorn during the Great Depression.

   C) People enjoyed popcorn during the Great Depression because it was a luxury food.

   D) During the 1800s, people began abandoning theaters to go to fairs and festivals.

9. The author intends to do which of the following by using the words *The American love affair with popcorn began in 1912*?

   A) entertain

   B) express feelings

   C) persuade

   D) inform

10. Which of the following is the author's main purpose for writing this passage?

    A) to explain how microwaves affected the popcorn industry

    B) to show that popcorn is older than many people realize

    C) to illustrate the history of popcorn from ancient cultures to modern times

    D) to demonstrate the importance of popcorn in various cultures

11. Based on the passage, which of the following is the most likely inference?

    A) Popcorn tastes better when it is cooked on heated sand.

    B) The popcorn industry will continue to thrive in the United States.

    C) If movie theaters go out of business, the popcorn industry will also fail.

    D) Archaeologists would likely find other examples of ancient cultures eating popcorn if they looked hard enough.

The next three questions are based on the passage below.

Mason was one of those guys who just always seemed at home. Stick him on a bus, and he'd make three new friends; when he joined a team, it was only a matter of time before he was elected captain. This particular skill rested almost entirely in his eyes. These brown orbs seemed lit from within, and when Mason focused that fire, it was impossible not to feel its warmth. People sought out Mason for the feeling of comfort he so easily created, and anyone with a good joke would want to tell it to Mason. His laughter started with a spark in his eyes that traveled down to create his wide, open smile.

CONTINUE

12. Based on a prior knowledge of literature, the reader can infer that this passage was taken from which of the following?

   A) a short story collection

   B) a science magazine

   C) an academic journal

   D) a history textbook

13. Which of the following is the author's intent in the passage?

   A) entertain

   B) express feelings

   C) persuade

   D) inform

14. Which of the following is a logical conclusion that can be drawn from this description?

   A) Mason wishes people would tell him more jokes.

   B) Mason is very good at sports.

   C) Mason does not like when strangers approach him.

   D) Mason has many friends.

The next two questions are based on the following memo.

The following memo was sent by the Human Resources Department to each department leader within the company.

MEMO

From: Human Resource Department

To: Department Leaders

Date: December 6, 2013

Subject: Personal Use of Computers

   Management has been conducting standard monitoring of computer usage, and we are dismayed at the amount of personal use occurring during business hours. Employee computers are available for the sole purpose of completing company business and for nothing else. These rules must be respected. If employees are found to be using computers for personal use during work hours, disciplinary action will be taken. Personal use should occur in emergency situations only, and in these cases use should be limited to 30 minutes. Please communicate these requirements to all personnel in your department.

15. Which of the following is the main purpose of this email?

   A) to notify employees that their computer use is being monitored

   B) to inform a group of employees about disciplinary action that has been taken

   C) to provide information about the computer usage policy to department leaders

   D) to explain in which emergency situations it is appropriate for employees to use computers

16. Which of the following inferences may be logically drawn from the memo?

   A) Department leaders will be punished if employees are found to be using computers inappropriately.

   B) Employees will likely leave the company rather than stop using their computers for personal business.

   C) Management will allow some flexibility about the rules for computer use for department leaders.

   D) Management will not hesitate to initiate disciplinary action against employees who use computers inappropriately.

The next four questions are based on the following passage.

It could be said that the great battle between the north and south we call the Civil War was a battle for individual identity. The states of the South had their own culture, one based on farming, independence, and the rights of both man and state to determine their own paths. Similarly, the North had forged its own identity as a center of centralized commerce and manufacturing. This clash of lifestyles was bound to create tension, and this tension was bound to lead to war. But people who try to sell you this narrative are wrong. The Civil War was not a battle of cultural identities—it was a battle about slavery. All other explanations for the war are either a direct consequence of the South's desire for wealth at the expense of her fellow man or a fanciful invention to cover up this sad portion of our nation's history. And it cannot be denied that this time in our past was very sad indeed.

17. Which of the following describes this type of writing?

    A) technical

    B) expository

    C) persuasive

    D) narrative

18. Which of the following excerpts from the passage contains an opinion?

    A) It could be said that the great battle between the North and South we call the Civil War was a battle for individual identity.

    B) The states of the South had their own culture, one based on farming, independence, and the rights of both man and state to determine their own paths.

    C) The Civil War was not a battle of cultural identities—it was a battle about slavery.

    D) And it cannot be denied that this time in our past was very sad indeed.

19. Which of the following is a likely motive for the author?

    A) to convince readers that slavery was the main cause of the Civil War

    B) to illustrate the cultural differences between the North and the South before the Civil War

    C) to persuade readers that the North deserved to win the Civil War

    D) to demonstrate that the history of the Civil War is too complicated to be understood clearly

20. Which of the following indicates how the author would likely state his position on the Civil War?

    A) The Civil War was the result of cultural differences between the north and south.

    B) The Civil War was caused by the south's reliance on slave labor.

    C) The North's use of commerce and manufacturing allowed it to win the war.

    D) The South's belief in the rights of man and state cost them the war.

→

CONTINUE

21. According to the index below, where might the reader find information about truthfulness?

Ethics, 225 – 275
     self-determination, 227 – 231
     veracity, 232 – 235
     justice, 236 – 241
     beneficence, 242 – 249

A) 227 – 231

B) 232 – 235

C) 236 – 241

D) 242 – 249

The next two questions are based on the figure below.

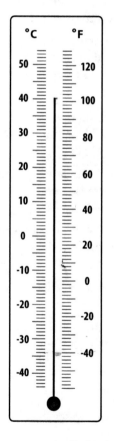

22. If the thermometer indicated a temperature of −40°F, what would the temperature be in degrees Celsius?

A) −6°C

B) −4°C

C) −20°C

D) 85°C

23. If the reading in the thermometer shown dropped 10°C, what would the temperature be in degrees Fahrenheit?

A) 82°F

B) 85°F

C) 92°F

D) 100°F

The next three questions are based on the figure showing the inventory at Gigi's Diner below.

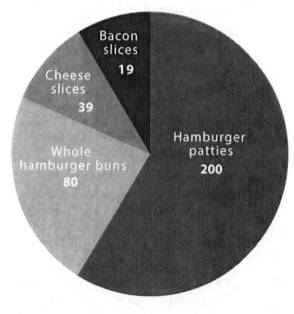

24. Which food does Gigi's have the least of?

A) bacon slices

B) cheese slices

C) hamburger buns

D) hamburger patties

25. According to the graph above, how many more hamburger buns does Gigi's need in order to make 200 hamburgers?

A) 120

B) 161

C) 181

D) 200

26. Which of the following is the number of hamburgers Gigi's could make if each burger includes 1 bacon slice and 2 cheese slices?

A) 18

B) 19

C) 39

D) 80

27. The president's speech was eloquent and touched many voters with its wit and flair.

Which of the following is the definition of the word *eloquent*?

A) persuasive

B) humorous

C) loud

D) well-spoken

The next three questions are based on the figure below.

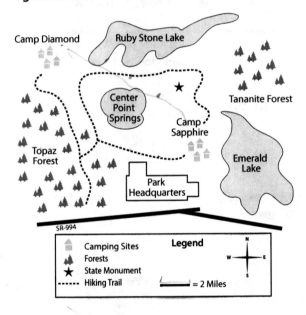

28. Which direction is Topaz Forest in relation to Emerald Lake?

A) north

B) south

C) east

D) west

29. Approximately how many miles is Camp Diamond from Camp Sapphire (by path)?

A) 0.16 miles

B) 1.6 miles

C) 16 miles

D) 160 miles

30. Which location is directly south of Tannanite Forest?

A) Ruby Stone Lake

B) Camp Sapphire

C) Emerald Lake

D) Camp Diamond

The next two questions are based on the table below.

Table 14.1. Shoe store prices

RETAILER	BASE PRICE	SHIPPING & HANDLING	TAXES	
Wholesale Footwear	$59.99	$10.95	$7.68	78 60
Bargain Sales	$65.99	$5.95	$5.38	71
Famous Shoes	$79.99	0.00	$4.89	
Fancy Shoes	$89.99	$2.95	$8.99	

31. Dennis wants to buy shoes and has $80 to spend. Which retailer(s) can he afford to buy from?

A) Wholesale Footwear

B) Wholesale Footwear and Bargain Sales

C) Wholesale Footwear, Bargain Sales, and Famous Shoes ✗

D) Fancy Shoes ✗

32. If Dennis bought his shoes online and didn't have to pay any taxes, shoes from which retailer would cost the least?

A) Wholesale Footwear 69

B) Bargain Sales 76

C) Famous Shoes 79.99

D) Fancy Shoes 91

33. A student needs to find the definition of a word in her history textbook. Which of the following will be the most helpful?

A) preface

B) glossary

C) appendix

D) index

34. A student wants to look online to find unbiased information about organic foods. Analyze the following websites and their taglines to determine which site he should use.

A) www.dangerinthegrocerystore.com; "The truth about the toxic chemicals in your produce."

B) www.growbetter.com; "Your one-stop shop for agricultural pesticides and fertilizers."

C) www.betterfood.org; "A non-profit that provides nutritional support to needy families."

D) www.foodandnutrition.gov; "An official site of the United States Surgeon General."

35. According to the table of contents below, which of the following lists includes only subheadings?

Chapter 2: Early American History

1. Early Settlement

   A. Plymouth

   B. Jamestown

2. The American Revolution

   A. American Victories

   B. British Victories

3. A New Century

   A. The Constitutional Convention

   B. The Ratification Years

A) Plymouth, Jamestown, British Victories, and A New Century

B) American Victories, British Victories, A New Century, and The Ratification Years

C) American Victories, British Victories, The Constitutional Convention, and The Ratification Years

D) Early Settlement, The American Revolution, A New Century, and The Ratification Years

36. Read and follow the directions below.

---

1. You start with $20 in your wallet.

2. You spend $5 on lunch.

3. You receive $20 for mowing your neighbor's yard.

4. You spend $10 on a new shirt.

5. You receive $10 for driving a friend to work.

6. You spend $30 on fuel for your vehicle.

How much money do you have left?

A) $0

B) $5

C) $10

D) $20

The next two questions are based on the table below.

Table 14.2. Tee shirt prices

COMPANY	PRICES
Maximum Tees	$15.99 for the first 100 shirts; $12.99 for each additional shirt
Wholesale Tees	$16.50 per shirt
Total Tees	$19.99 for the first 50 shirts; $14.99 for each additional shirt
Classic Tees	$16.50 for the first 50 shirts; $11.50 for each additional shirt

37. An ecological protection group wants to buy 50 shirts. Which company will provide the least expensive order?

A) Maximum Tees

B) Wholesale Tees

C) Total Tees

D) Classic Tees

38. A sports team wants to place an order for 100 shirts. Ordering from which company will cost them the least amount of money?

A) Maximum Tees

B) Wholesale Tees

C) Total Tees

D) Classic Tees

39. After following the directions below, how much water is left?

1. You have 3 gallons of water.
2. You use 0.5 gallons to water your plant.
3. You use 1 gallon to refill your dog's water bowl.
4. You put 0.5 gallons in an ice tray to make ice cubes.

A) 0 gallons

B) 0.5 gallons

C) 1 gallon

D) 1.5 gallons

40. When connecting line A to port B, make sure that port C is **completely** closed. If port C is left open, fluid will leak as soon as line A is connected. Once line A and port B are **fully** connected, port C can be opened as needed.

The bold text in the directions above indicate which of the following?

A) brand names

B) emphasis

C) commands

D) proper nouns

41. Elaine was feeling <u>lethargic</u> after a poor night's sleep, but she still managed to get to work on time.

Which of the following is the definition of the underlined word in the sentence above?

A) tired

B) confused

C) angry

D) rushed

42. Analyze the headings below. Which of the following headings is out of place?

Chapter 6: Art of the Middle Ages

I. The Stories Behind Famous Paintings

II. Notable Sculpting Techniques

III. Recipes for Common Dishes

IV. Textiles and Tapestries

A) The Stories Behind Famous Paintings

B) Notable Sculpting Techniques

C) Recipes for Common Dishes

D) Textiles and Tapestries

43. Miguel was concerned that his <u>laceration</u> would need stitches.

Which of the following is the definition of the underlined word in the sentence above?

A) deep cut

B) minor wound

C) broken bone

D) swollen joint

CONTINUE →

44. Read and follow the directions below.

> 1. Start at the center of town.
>
> 2. Drive north 10 miles.
>
> 3. Turn left and drive west 5 miles.
>
> 4. Turn left and drive south 2 miles.
>
> 5. Turn right and drive west 1 mile.

Which of the following is now your distance from the center of town?

A) 12 miles north, 6 miles west

B) 8 miles north, 6 miles west

C) 12 miles north, 4 miles west

D) 8 miles north, 4 miles west

45. Examine the headings below. Based on the pattern, which of the following is a reasonable heading to insert in the blank spot?

> **Chapter 3: Planning Your Vacation**
>
> 1.   Getting There
>
>   A. Air Travel
>
>   B. Traveling by Train
>
>   C. _____
>
>   D. Taking the Bus
>
> 2.   Accommodations
>
> 3.   Dining

A) Choosing a Destination

B) Navigating the Airport

C) Finding a Hotel

D) Road Trips

46. The couple's "plan" was little more than just a desire to travel. They showed up at the airport with no tickets, no itinerary, and no destination in mind.

The use of quotes in the text above signifies which of the following?

A) foreign phrases

B) emphasized words

C) dialogue

D) words used ironically

47. The guide words at the top of a dictionary page are *lexicon* and *lipid*. Which of the following words is an entry on this page?

A) luminous

B) leper

C) license

D) livid

48. Read and follow the directions below.

> 1.   You start with one red marble and two green marbles in a pouch.
>
> 2.   Remove one red marble.
>
> 3.   Add one green marble.
>
> 4.   Add one red marble.
>
> 5.   Add one green marble.
>
> 6.   Remove one red marble.
>
> 7.   Remove one green marble.
>
> 8.   Add three red marbles.
>
> 9.   Add two green marbles.

Which of the following is the number of marbles now in the pouch?

A) five red, three green

B) three red, five green

C) four red, four green

D) six red, two green

Mathematics

1. $43 + 2 - 1 =$

   A) 46

   B) 44

   C) 45

   D) 42

2. $72 - 23 - 6 =$

   A) 54

   B) 48

   C) 43

   D) 37

3. A sporting goods store is offering an additional 30% off all clearance items. Angie purchases a pair of running shoes on clearance for $65.00. If the shoes originally cost $85.00, what was her total discount?

   A) 53.5%

   B) 46.5%

   C) 22.9%

   D) 39.2%

4. Which of the following is not a rational number?

   A) -4

   B) $\frac{1}{5}$

   C) $0.8\overline{33}$

   D) $\sqrt{2}$

5. What is 1230.932567 rounded to the nearest hundredths place?

   A) 1200

   B) 1230.9326

   C) 1230.93

   D) 1230

6. What is the absolute value of -9?

   A) -9

   B) 9

   C) 0

   D) -1

7. Add $0.98 + 45.102 + 32.3333 + 31 + 0.00009$.

   A) 368.573

   B) 210.536299

   C) 109.41539

   D) 99.9975

8. $(9 \div 3) \times (8 \div 4) =$

   A) 1

   B) 6

   C) 72

   D) 576

9. $7.95 \div 1.5 =$

   A) 2.4

   B) 5.3

   C) 6.2

   D) 7.3

10. Melissa is ordering fencing to enclose a square area of 5625 square feet. How many feet of fencing does she need?

    A) 75

    B) 150

    C) 300

    D) 5,625

11. If a discount of 25% off the retail price of a desk saves Mark $45, what was the desk's original price?

    A) $135

    B) $160

    C) $180

    D) $210

12. What number is 5% of 2000?

    A) 50

    B) 100

    C) 150

    D) 200

13. Adam owns 4 times as many shirts as he has pairs of pants, and he has 5 pairs of pants for every 2 pairs of shoes. What is the ratio of Adam's shirts to Adam's shoes?

A) 25 shirts: 1 pair shoes

B) 10 shirts : 1 pair shoes

C) 20 shirts : 1 pair shoes

D) 15 shirts : 2 pairs shoes

14. Solve for x and y: $15x + 2y = 3$ and $12x + y = -3$.

A) $(x, y) = (-1, 9)$

B) $(x, y) = (1, -15)$

C) $(x, y) = (1, -6)$

D) $(x, y) = (-\frac{1}{6}, -1)$

15. Jane earns $15 per hour babysitting. If she starts out with $275 in her bank account, which of the following equations represents how many hours she will have to babysit for her account to reach $400?

A) $-400 = 15h - 275$

B) $400 = \frac{15}{h} + 275$

C) $400 = 15h$

D) $400 = 15h + 275$

16. Patrick is coming home from vacation in Costa Rica and wants to fill one of his suitcases with bags of Costa Rican coffee. The weight limit for his suitcase is 22 kilograms, and the suitcase itself weighs 3.2 kilograms. If each bag of coffee weighs 800 grams, how many bags can he bring in his suitcase without going over the limit?

A) 2

B) 4

C) 23

D) 27

17. A bag contains twice as many red marbles as blue marbles, and the number of blue marbles is 88% of the number of green marbles. If g represents the number of green marbles, which of the following expressions represents the total number of marbles in the bag?

A) $3.88g$

B) $3.64g$

C) $2.64g$

D) $2.32g$

18. If $|3x+2| = 5$, which of the following options are the correct values of x?

A) $\left(1, \frac{-7}{3}\right)$

B) $\left(-1, \frac{7}{3}\right)$

C) $(3, 7)$

D) $\left(\frac{7}{3}, \frac{3}{7}\right)$

19. If $\frac{|2k + 4|}{8} = 2$, which of the following values of k satisfies this equation?

A) $(12, 2)$

B) $(4, 5)$

C) $(3, 6)$

D) $(-10, 6)$

20. Which inequality is equivalent to $\frac{2x + 7}{9} < 2$?

A) $3x < \frac{21}{3}$

B) $x > -3$

C) $x < \frac{11}{2}$

D) $2x > 1$

21. $\frac{4}{5} \times \frac{14}{25} \times \frac{125}{7} \times \frac{4}{2} =$

A) 16

B) $\frac{24}{25}$

C) 32

D) 18

22. $\frac{2}{9} \times \frac{3}{25} \times \frac{125}{6} \times \frac{3}{10} =$

A) $\frac{6}{30}$

B) $\frac{1}{6}$

C) 6

D) $\frac{11}{30}$

23. $\frac{1}{5} + \frac{4}{25} =$

A) $\frac{8}{25}$

B) $\frac{5}{29}$

C) $\frac{9}{25}$

D) $\frac{5}{20}$

24. Alan bought a pizza which had 8 slices. He ate 3 slices of pizza for lunch, and left the remaining pizza for Jenny. What fraction of pizza did Alan leave for Jenny?

A) $\frac{3}{8}$

B) $\frac{1}{2}$

C) $\frac{4}{5}$

D) $\frac{5}{8}$

25. $\left(\frac{3}{4} + \frac{1}{5}\right) - \left(\frac{2}{3} + \frac{3}{2}\right) =$

A) $\frac{7}{8}$

B) $\frac{-73}{60}$

C) $\frac{73}{60}$

D) $\frac{-26}{30}$

26. Which inequality is equivalent to $3x + 2 > 5$?

A) $x < 1$

B) $x > -1$

C) $x > 1$

D) $x > 3$

27. $\frac{2}{9} + \left(\frac{5}{6} - \frac{1}{2}\right) =$

A) $\frac{5}{12}$

B) $\frac{7}{9}$

C) $\frac{5}{9}$

D) $\frac{8}{45}$

28. Which of the following does the roman numeral CLVII equal?

A) 202

B) 157

C) 752

D) 257

29. Simplify the following expression: $5\frac{1}{3} - 2\frac{1}{3}$

A) $5\frac{1}{3}$

B) $5\frac{2}{3}$

C) 5

D) 3

30. Convert the following into a fraction:

$5.25 + 1.5 =$

A) $5\frac{3}{4}$

B) $7\frac{3}{4}$

C) $6\frac{3}{4}$

D) $7\frac{1}{4}$

31. Convert 0.28 into a fraction.

A) $\frac{9}{25}$

B) $\frac{7}{45}$

C) $\frac{7}{25}$

D) $\frac{8}{15}$

32. Convert $\frac{5}{20}$ into decimal form.

   A) 0.55

   B) 0.35

   C) 0.15

   D) 0.25

Use the chart below to answer questions 33 and 34.

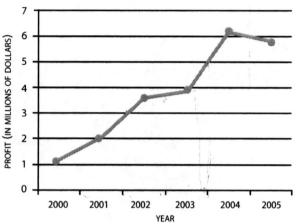

33. Referencing the line graph, approximately how much did profit increase from 2003 to 2004 in dollars?

   A) 2.3 million

   B) 6.2 million

   C) 3.9 million

   D) 3.2 million

34. Approximately how much more profit was earned in 2001 than in 2000?

   A) 2.2 million

   B) 1.0 million

   C) 3.5 million

   D) 6.1 million

Science

1. Blood is prevented from changing direction in the veins by—

   A) pressure generated from the heart

   B) valves

   C) vacuum generated from the heart

   D) squeezing at the vein by nearby skeletal muscle

2. The liquid part of the blood is called—

   A) plasma

   B) blood fluid

   C) serous fluid

   D) serum

3. Which of the following is true regarding the periodic table?

   A) Groups have the same number of valence electrons and similar chemical properties.

   B) Periods are vertical columns.

   C) Atomic radius increases as you go from left to right.

   D) Alkali metals are frequently found by themselves in nature.

4. Blood cells that are responsible for transportation of oxygen are called—

   A) leukocytes

   B) thrombocytes

   C) erythrocytes

   D) plasma cells

5. What is another name for the Adam's apple?

   A) vocal box

   B) thyroid cartilage

   C) cricoid cartilage

   D) hyoid bone

6. When exhaling, the diaphragm—

   A) relaxes

   B) contracts

   C) moves down and in

   D) stays in the same position

7. A double bond between two atoms, for example the double bond between oxygen in O_2, has how many electrons?

   A) 2

   B) 4

   C) 6

   D) 8

8. What is the anterior bone of the lower leg?

   A) ulna

   B) fibula

   C) tibia

   D) radius

9. Assuming every variable unmentioned in the Ideal Gas Law remains constant, which is true?

   A) as the temperature increases, the pressure of a gas must decrease

   B) as the number of molecules in a gas increases, the temperature must increase

   C) as volume increases, the number of molecules must increase

   D) as pressure increases, volume must increase

10. The humerus and ulna form the—

    A) shoulder joint

    B) elbow joint

    C) wrist joint

    D) knee joint

11. The patella is also called the—

    A) breastbone

    B) kneecap

    C) finger bone

    D) funny bone

12. The bone that is stationary during movement is called the—

    A) insertion

    B) agonist

    C) origin

    D) antagonist

13. Which of the following is the process that produces a liquid from a gas?

    A) vaporization

    B) condensation

    C) sublimation

    D) denitrification

14. What is the primary function of the quadriceps muscle?

    A) extend the knee joint

    B) flex the knee joint

    C) extend the hip joint

    D) flex the hip joint

15. Which part of the brain is responsible for higher brain functions?

    A) the pons

    B) the cerebral cortex

    C) the cerebellar cortex

    D) medulla

16. How many thoracic spinal nerves are there in the human body?

    A) eight

    B) nine

    C) twelve

    D) fourteen

17. Which of the following is not a specialized sense?

    A) touch

    B) balance

    C) sight

    D) hearing

18. In which region of the small intestine are most of the nutrients absorbed?

    A) the jejunum

    B) the ileum

    C) the duodenum

    D) the colon

19. Which type of nutrient is broken down by trypsin?

    A) protein

    B) fat

    C) sugar

    D) carbohydrates

20. Chemical bonding—

    A) uses electrons that are closest to the nucleus of the atoms bonding

    B) always uses electrons from only one of the atoms involved

    C) uses all the electrons in all atoms involved

    D) uses the valence electrons of all the atoms involved

21. Which of the following would have the most dramatic effect in changing the reaction rate?

    A) decreasing the temperature by two-fold

    B) increasing the pressure by two-fold

    C) decreasing the activation energy by three-fold

    D) decreasing the concentration of reactants by two-fold

22. Group one in the periodic table has
_____ valence electrons and are
_____ reactive than Group two.

   A) zero; more

   B) zero; less

   C) one; less

   D) one; more

23. Enzymes are created from amino acid
chains. As such, what might prevent the
action of an enzyme?

   A) a pH close to 7

   B) a high temperature

   C) the lack of hydrogen ions in solution

   D) a lack of ATP in the cell

24. If a scientist wants to determine the rate at
which an enzyme works, what could he or
she measure?

   A) the rate at which the enzyme is
   degraded

   B) the rate at which the product
   disappears

   C) the rate at which the reactants
   disappear

   D) the rate at which the products appear

25. According to the graph below, which is the
most effective enzyme?

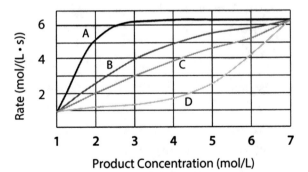
Product Concentration (mol/L)

   A) A

   B) B

   C) C

   D) D

26. What is true of elements found in the same
group (column) in the Periodic Table?

   A) They have the same atomic mass.

   B) They have the same level of reactivity.

   C) They have the same number of protons.

   D) The have the same number of valence
   electrons.

27. Compounds that are acidic will be able to
lower the pH of a solution by doing which
of the following?

   A) accepting H+ ions

   B) releasing H+ ions

   C) binding with acidic species in solution

   D) reducing oxidative species in solution

28. Which of the following elements is the
most electronegative?

   A) chlorine

   B) iron

   C) magnesium

   D) silicon

29. According to Newton's first law, how fast
will a 10 kilogram object accelerate when
pushed with 50 newtons of force?

   A) 2.5 m/s^2

   B) 5.0 m/s^2

   C) 8.0 m/s^2

   D) 15.0 m/s^2

30. Upon touching a chair cushion and then
a metal plate, John notices that the metal
plate feels much colder than the cushion,
although the surrounding air temperature
is the same. What is an explanation for this?

   A) The chair cushion has a higher heat
   capacity than the metal plate.

   B) The metal plate has a higher heat
   transfer rate than the chair cushion.

   C) The metal plate is able to absorb more
   heat from the air than the cushion.

   D) The chair cushion produces some
   internal heat.

31. If a pitcher throws a baseball into the air, and notices that it takes 5 seconds to reach its peak, how long will the baseball need to fall back to the ground? Neglect air resistance.

   A) 2.5 seconds

   B) 9.8 seconds

   C) 5.0 seconds

   D) 10.0 seconds

32. Which of the following is true regarding DNA in the human body?

   A) DNA is used as an energy source.

   B) DNA is used as a template for creation of proteins.

   C) Each sperm has forty-six chromosomes.

   D) DNA is made of amino acids.

33. How many kingdoms of life are there?

   A) three

   B) six

   C) seven

   D) nine

34. Alleles for brown eyes (B) are dominant over alleles for blue eyes (b). Assume both parents have brown eyes, but have one allele each of both B and b. What is the percent chance that their offspring have brown eyes?

   A) 100

   B) 75

   C) 66

   D) 50

35. Plants absorb carbon dioxide (CO_2) to create sugar for energy. What is the primary byproduct of this process?

   A) oxygen

   B) nitrogen

   C) carbon monoxide

   D) carbon

36. What prevents ultraviolet radiation produced by the sun from damaging life on earth?

   A) the ozone layer

   B) greenhouse gases

   C) the vacuum between earth and the sun

   D) the water layer

37. Which of the following is not present in an animal cell?

   A) nucleus

   B) mitochondria

   C) cytoplasm

   D) cell wall

38. Mitosis is the process of cell division to create new cells. What is the process of cell division required to create new sex cells, or gametes?

   A) telosis

   B) meiosis

   C) kinesis

   D) phoresis

39. What are the two main parts of the human body's central nervous system?

   A) the heart and the spinal cord

   B) the brain and the spinal cord

   C) the peripheral nerves and the brain

   D) the spinal cord and the peripheral nerves

40. Which of the following is not an organ system in humans?

   A) the endocrine system

   B) the respiratory system

   C) the vascular system

   D) the muscular system

41. Humans can turn glucose into ATP, the basic energy molecule in the body. What is a byproduct of this process?

    A) carbon dioxide

    B) oxygen

    C) nitrogen

    D) phosphorus

42. Which of the following does NOT correctly match the part of the cell and its primary function?

    A) mitochondria: production of ATP through oxidative phosphorylation

    B) nucleus: DNA replication and transcription

    C) smooth endoplasmic reticulum: translation of mRNA into proteins

    D) Golgi apparatus: Packaging and transportation of proteins within and in/out of cells

43. What is the primary difference between a cell membrane and a cell wall?

    A) A cell membrane is flexible and a cell wall is rigid.

    B) A cell membrane is not found in plants, whereas a cell wall is.

    C) A cell membrane is not found in animals, whereas a cell wall is.

    D) A cell membrane is composed of protein, whereas a cell wall is composed of sugar.

44. What skill is a scientist using when he or she observes the ways in which different mammals climb trees?

    A) drawing conclusions

    B) interpreting data

    C) making observations

    D) making a hypothesis

45. When conducting an experiment, the factor that is being measured is called what?

    A) independent variable

    B) dependent variable

    C) conclusion

    D) controlled variable

46. Which of the following questions is the best high-level scientific question?

    A) Who is credited with inventing the electromagnet?

    B) How many penguins live in Antarctica?

    C) Is the boiling or freezing point of water affected by how much salt is in it?

    D) When did dinosaurs become extinct?

47. What is the correct order of the steps in the scientific method?

    A) ask a question, analyze results, make a hypothesis, test the hypothesis, draw conclusions, communicate results

    B) make a hypothesis, test the hypothesis, analyze the results, ask a question, draw conclusions, communicate results

    C) ask questions, make a hypothesis, test the hypothesis, analyze results, draw conclusions, communicate results

    D) ask a question, make a hypothesis, test hypothesis, draw conclusions, analyze results, communicate results

48. When determining the mass of an ant, you should use—

    A) meters

    B) grams

    C) liters

    D) kilograms

CONTINUE

1. She told them to _____ their room before they left for the party.

   Which of the following correctly completes the sentence?

   A) cleaned

   B) tidy

   C) clears

   D) neat

2. They left for the party, but Rebecca had to return home because _____ forgot her purse.

   Which of the following is the correct pronoun for the sentence above?

   A) he

   B) they

   C) we

   D) she

3. Which of the following is punctuated incorrectly?

   A) The dentist told her patient he needed to return later in the week because he had more cavities.

   B) The dentist told her patient he needed to return later in the week, because he had more cavities.

   C) The dentist told her patient he needed to return later in the week; because he had more cavities.

   D) The dentist told her patient he needed to return later in the week—because he had more cavities.

4. Which of the following sentences does not contain an error in?

   A) To the laundromat, take the laundry please.

   B) Please take the laundry to the laundromat.

   C) Take the laundry please to the laundromat.

   D) The laundry please take to the laundromat.

5. Which of the following provides an example of correct subject-verb agreement?

   A) The head zookeeper, who has been with the zoo for over twenty years, have agreed to set up a new enclosure for the elephants.

   B) Of all the elephants owned by the zoo, only some has been approved to move to the new enclosure.

   C) The rest of the elephants has been given to a well-respected rescue organization.

   D) The rescue organization, which takes in animals from zoos across the country, has agreed not to sell the elephants to another zoo.

6. Which of the following is a simple sentence?

   A) He threw the ball across the field to his friend.

   B) He threw the ball to the dog, and the dog ran after it.

   C) He threw the ball across the field because he wanted to see if he could.

   D) He threw the ball across the field; it landed in a ditch.

7. Which underlined word is spelled correctly?

   A) The threat from the storm was immenent, and an evacuation order was issued.

   B) The hurricane made landfall early in the morning, but damage was minimal.

   C) The storm shelter was constructd of heavy concrete for safety.

   D) The tornado sirens were desined to be heard for miles.

8. The teacher was irate and told the students they'd be punished if no one confessed.

Which of the following is the meaning of *irate* in the sentence above?

A) sad

B) happy

C) angry

D) frightened

9. I had worked a very long shift, _____ I still had to run errands after work.

Which conjunction best completes the sentence?

A) nor

B) or

C) but

D) so

10. He ran quickly while training hard for the race that weekend.

The word *quickly* serves as which of the following parts of speech in the sentence above?

A) verb

B) adjective

C) noun

D) adverb

11. Which of the following sentences is an example of correct subject-verb agreement?

A) The dogs ran from one end of the fence to the other, barking loudly.

B) The dogs was running from one end of the fence to the other, barking loudly.

C) The dogs barks loudly, runs from one end of the fence to the other.

D) The dog runs from one end of the fence to the other and bark loudly.

12. Which of the following sentences follows the rules of capitalization?

A) We went to Paris, Rome, and London on our vacation in june.

B) We went to paris, rome and London on our vacation in June.

C) We went to Paris, Rome and London on our Vacation in June.

D) We went to Paris, Rome and London on our vacation in June.

13. The conscientious driver always checked her mirrors before she switched lanes.

Which of the following is the meaning of *conscientious* as it is used in the sentence above?

A) thoughtful

B) considerate

C) careful

D) cruel

14. Which of the following is an example of a complex sentence?

A) I forgot my homework because I was in such a hurry to get to the bus stop.

B) I forgot my homework, but my teacher said I can turn it in tomorrow.

C) I forgot my homework on the dining room table next to my backpack and my lunch.

D) I forgot my homework, yet I had put it next to my backpack the night before.

15. Which of the following sentences is an example of the third-person perspective?

A) You need to check on the patient in room 302.

B) Check on the patient in room 302.

C) He checked on the patient in room 302.

D) I will check on the patient in room 302.

CONTINUE

16. Which of the following sentences is punctuated correctly?

A) Which school will you be attending in the fall, Harvard or Yale?

B) Which school will you be attending in the fall, Harvard or Yale.

C) Which school will you be attending in the fall Harvard or Yale?

D) Which school will you be attending in the fall; Harvard or Yale?

17. Which of the following sentences is punctuated correctly?

A) You need to call the lab, check the test results, and contact the patient's doctors.

B) You need to call the lab check the test results, and contact the patients doctors.

C) You need to: call the lab, check the test results, and contact the patient's doctors.

D) You need to—call the lab, check the test results and contact the patients doctors.

18. The patient came to the office _____ of respiratory distress.

Which of the following is the correct completion of the sentence above?

A) complaning

B) complaining

C) compllaining

D) compllaning

19. The letters were quite _____ and contained intimate details.

Which of the following correctly completes the sentence above?

A) personal

B) personnal

C) personnel

D) personel

20. He waited _____

Which of the following allows the above sentence to be completed as a simple sentence?

A) for the bus.

B) for the bus, but it was running late.

C) for the bus, so he could get to work on time.

D) for the bus because he had an appointment.

21. Which of the following sentences contains the correct spelling of the underlined word?

A) The heart rate <u>veries</u> for a number of reasons.

B) The heart rate <u>varies</u> for a number of reasons.

C) The heart rate <u>varries</u> for a number of reasons.

D) The heart rate <u>varys</u> for a number of reasons.

22. Which of the following sentences follows the correct rules of capitalization?

A) Mr. Smith is a patient at the Penner Hospital.

B) Mr. Smith is a Patient at the Penner Hospital.

C) Mr. Smith is a patient at the penner Hospital.

D) Mr. smith is a patient in the Penner Hospital.

23. Which of the following sentences is punctuated correctly?

A) We went to the store; where we shopped for groceries.

B) We went to the store, where we shopped for groceries.

C) We went to the store, where we shopped for groceries?

D) We went to the store, where we shopped for groceries,

24. Which of the following phrases follows the rules of capitalization?

A) Mr. Jones, who is a Senator

B) the representative from maine

C) President Clinton

D) Vice-president Biden

25. Which of the following sentences is punctuated correctly?

A) He returned the books, to the library, using the drop slot by the front door.

B) He returned the books to the library; using the drop slot by the front door.

C) He returned the books to the library using the drop slot by the front door.

D) He returned the books to the library. Using the drop slot by the front door.

26. Which of the following sentences is the most clear and correct?

A) Because of her injury, Jessica had to wear a brace on her knee during practice.

B) Jessica had to wear a brace on her knee because of her injury during practice.

C) During practice, Jessica had to wear a brace because of her injury on her knee.

D) On her knee, Jessica had to wear a brace during practice because of her injury.

27. Which of the following is a simple sentence?

A) After they finished their homework, they left for the zoo.

B) They left for the zoo after finishing their homework.

C) They left for the zoo after they finished their homework.

D) They left for the zoo, but they had already finished their homework.

28. The dress was beautiful, but it was too expensive for her budget.

The word *expensive* serves as which of the following parts of speech in the sentence above?

A) adjective

B) preposition

C) conjunction

D) article

29. He went to the doctor on the other side of town on the first of june.

Which word in the sentence should be capitalized?

A) Doctor

B) Town

C) June

D) First

30. She hurried that morning, _____ she wouldn't be late for her first day at work.

Which word best completes the sentence?

A) because

B) for

C) but

D) so

31. She threw the ball to the dog.

The word *to* serves as which of the following parts of speech in the sentence above?

A) noun

B) conjunction

C) verb

D) preposition

32. Which of the following sentences is an example of the second-person point of view?

A) You need to take the patient his medication.

B) I took the patient his medication.

C) The patient needs his medication.

D) She already gave him his medication.

33. Which of the following sentences is punctuated correctly?

A) Today, we will learn proper hand-washing procedures for hospital employees.

B) Today we will learn proper hand-washing procedures, for hospital employees.

C) Today: we will learn proper hand-washing procedures for hospital employees.

D) Today, we will learn proper, hand-washing procedures for hospital employees.

34. Take the _____ blood pressure.

Which of the following is the correctly spelled word to complete the sentence?

A) patience

B) patients

C) patent's

D) patient's

35. Which of the following sentences contains a correct example of subject-verb agreement?

A) We have taken the patients to their rooms.

B) We takes the patients to their rooms.

C) He has took the patients to their rooms.

D) They has taken the patients to their rooms.

Answer Key – Reading

1. C)	13. A)	25. A)	37. A)
2. D)	14. D)	26. B)	38. D)
3. B)	15. C)	27. D)	39. C)
4. A)	16. D)	28. D)	40. B)
5. A)	17 C)	29. C)	41. A)
6. C)	18. C)	30. C)	42. C)
7. B)	19. A)	31. B)	43. A)
8. A)	20. B)	32. A)	44. B)
9. D)	21. B)	33. B)	45. D)
10. C)	22. B)	34. D)	46. D)
11. B)	23. A)	35. C)	47. C)
12. A)	24. A)	36. B)	48. B)

Answer Key – Mathematics

1. B)

We need to remember the order of operations (PEMDAS) to solve this question. First of all, we solve the problem inside the parentheses, and then the exponents. In this particular question, 43 + 2 comes first, which equals 45. Now, the expression becomes (45 − 1). Then, we subtract 1 from 45. As there is no exponent in this equation, this gives us 44.

2. C)

We need to remember the order of operations (PEMDAS) to solve this question. First of all, we solve the problem inside the parentheses, and then the exponents. In this particular question, 72 − 23 comes first, which equals 49. Now, the expression becomes (49 − 6). Then, we subtract 6 from 49. As there is no exponent in this equation, this gives us 43.

3. B)

First, take the additional 30% off the clearance price:

$$\$65.00 \times \frac{70}{100} = \$45.50$$

Next, find what percentage of $85.00 is $45.50:

$$\frac{\$45.50}{\$85.00} = \frac{x}{100}$$

$$(\$45.50)(100) = (\$85.00)(x)$$

$$x = \frac{(\$45.50)(100)}{\$85.00} = 53.5$$

Angie is paying 53.5% the original price, which means she received a 100% − 53.5% = 46.5% discount.

4. D)

A rational number is one which can be written in the form of a simple fraction. If we observe closely, only option D) gives us a number which cannot be written in the form of a fraction.

5. C)

We are asked to round off this given number to the nearest hundredths place. Considering the numbers on the right of the decimal, our answer comes out to be 1230.93.

6. B)

We know that the absolute value of any negative number gives the positive of that same number (i.e. absolute value of −9 is +9).

7. C)

There are two ways to solve this question. First, you can add all the given numbers and find the exact answer. This method is time-consuming and is less efficient.

The second method to solve this question is by adding only the numbers on the left of the decimal and then comparing your answer with the answer choices that you are given. We add 45, 32, and 31 to get 45 + 32 + 31 = 108. Now, we can easily interpret that our answer must be very close to 108 when we add the decimal points as well for each given number. In the answer choices, only option C) gives us the number closest to 108. (Note that this method of approximation saves time but it is not very accurate if all the answer choices are very close to each other.)

8.   B)

This is a very simple question. All you need to know is the PEMDAS rule. First of all, solve the problems inside the parentheses, and then we multiply the answers of each.

9 divided by 3 equals 3.

8 divided by 4 equals 2.

We multiply 3 and 2 to get our final answer: $3 \times 2 = 6$

9.   B)

This is a simple division question. When we divide 7.95 by 1.5, we get 5.3 as answer. In order to re-confirm your answer, you can cross-check by multiplying 5.3 by 1.5, and it would be 7.95.

10.   C)

Use the area to find the length of a side of the square:

$A = l \times w = l^2$

$5{,}625 \text{ ft}^2 = l^2$

$l = \sqrt{5{,}625 \text{ ft}^2} = 75 \text{ ft}$

Now multiply the side length by 4 to find the perimeter:

$P = 4l$

$P = 4(75 \text{ ft}) = 300 \text{ ft}$

11.   C)

From the given information in the question, we know that 25% of the actual price of a desk is $45. If we write this in the form of an equation, it becomes:

$\left(\frac{25}{100}\right) \times x = \$45$ (25% of x equals $45)

$x = \frac{45}{0.25} \rightarrow \$180$

Therefore, the actual price of the desk equals $180.

12.   B)

In order to find 5% of 2000, we need to multiply 2000 by $\frac{5}{100}$ i.e., $2000 \times 0.05 = 100$

13.   B)

Multiply the ratios so that pants cancel out in the numerator and denominator:

$$\frac{4 \text{ shirts}}{1 \text{ pants}} \times \frac{5 \text{ pants}}{2 \text{ pairs shoes}} = \frac{20 \text{ shirts}}{2 \text{ pairs shoes}}$$

Divide by the greatest common factor to reduce the ratio:

$$\frac{20 \text{ shirts}}{2 \text{ pairs shoes}} \div 2 = \frac{10 \text{ shirts}}{1 \text{ pair shoes}}$$

14.   A)

You can use elimination to solve this system of equations. First, multiply the second equation by 2:

$2(12x + y = -3)$

$24x + 2y = -6$

Now, subtract this equation from the first equation to eliminate y:

$$\begin{aligned} 15x + 2y &= 3 \\ - (24x + 2y &= -6) \\ \hline -9x &= 9 \end{aligned}$$

Next, divide by 9 to solve for x:

$\frac{5y}{5} = \frac{-30}{5}$ should be: $-9x/9 = 9/9$

$x = -1$

Then, plug this value for x into one of the equations to solve for y:

$15(-1) + 2(y) = 3$

$2y = 18$

$y = 9$

15.   D)

The money Jane earns is equal to $15 times the number of hours she babysits: $15h$

The total money in Jane's bank account is equal to the money she started with plus the money she earns: $275 + 15h$

Set this expression equal to $400:

$400 = 275 + 15h$

16.   C)

$22 \text{ kg} - 3.2 \text{ kg} = 18.8 \text{ kg}$ remaining for coffee

$18.8 \text{ kg} = 18{,}800 \text{ g}$

$18{,}800 \text{ g} \times \frac{1 \text{ bag of coffee}}{800 \text{ g}} = 23.5$ bags of coffee

Round down to 23 bags.

17. B)

There are twice as many red marbles as blue marbles, so (red) = 2(blue).

The number of blue marbles is 88% the number of green marbles, so (blue) = 0.88g.

Substitute this expression for blue marbles in the one above:

(red) = 2(0.88g)

(red) = 1.76g

The total number of marbles is equal to red plus blue plus green:

(red) + (blue) + g

1.76g + 0.88g + g

3.64g

18. A)

We re-write the given equation as:

$|3x + 2| = 5$

$+ (3x + 2) = 5$ or $-(3x + 2) = 5$

$3x = 5 - 2$ or $-3x - 2 = 5$

$x = 1$ or $x = -\frac{7}{3}$

Therefore, $(1, -\frac{7}{3})$.

19. D)

The given equation can be re-written as:

$\frac{|2k + 4|}{8} = 2 \rightarrow |2k + 4| = 16$

$+ (2k + 4) = 16 \rightarrow 2k = 12 \rightarrow k = 6$

$Or -(2k + 4) = 16 \rightarrow -2k - 4 = 16 \rightarrow$

$-2k = 20 \rightarrow k = -10$

Therefore, $k = -10, 6$

20. C)

Consider the given inequality:

$\frac{2x + 7}{9} < 2$

Multiplying by 9 on both sides, we get:

$2x + 7 < 18$

Subtracting 7 on both sides, we get:

$2x < 18 - 7$

$2x < 11$

Dividing by 2 on both sides, we get:

$x < \frac{11}{2}$

21. A)

This question looks like a lengthy multiplication question, but actually it's not. We know that $25 \times 5 = 125$. Similarly, $7 \times 2 = 14$. This means that the denominators of all the fractions are cancelled out by numerators of the second and third fractions, and we are left with only $4 \times 4 = 16$.

22. B)

A simple trick in solving these complex fraction-multiplication questions is to look for the numbers which can cancel each other. For example, in this given question, we see that $3 \times 3 = 9$ which cancels the 9 of the denominator. Similarly, $\frac{125}{25} = \frac{5}{1} = 5$.

The net result of this multiplication after cancellation of numerators and denominators becomes:

$\frac{2}{6} \times 5 \times \frac{1}{10} = \frac{1}{6}$

23. C)

Adding the given fractions, we get:

$\frac{1(5) + 4}{25} \rightarrow \frac{5 + 4}{25} \rightarrow \frac{9}{25}$

24. D)

As we know that there were a total of 8 slices of pizza, this means that each slice was $\frac{1}{8}$ of the total pizza. Alan ate 3 slices, i.e., $\frac{1}{8} + \frac{1}{8} + \frac{1}{8} = \frac{3}{8}$.

Remaining pizza $= 1 - \frac{3}{8} \rightarrow \frac{8 - 3}{8} \rightarrow \frac{5}{8}$

25. B)

Finding the sum of the expressions in parentheses first, we get:

$\left(\frac{3}{4} + \frac{1}{5}\right) \rightarrow \frac{15 + 4}{20} = \frac{19}{20}$

$\left(\frac{2}{3} + \frac{3}{2}\right) \rightarrow \frac{4 + 9}{6} \rightarrow \frac{13}{6}$

$\frac{19}{20} - \frac{13}{6} = \frac{19(6) - 13(20)}{120} \rightarrow \frac{-146}{120} \rightarrow -\frac{73}{60}$

26. C)

$3x > 5 - 2$

$3x > 3$

$x > 1$

27. C)

Finding the difference of the fractions given in the parentheses first, we get:

$\frac{5}{6} - \frac{1}{2} = \frac{5 - (3)}{6} = \frac{2}{6} = \frac{1}{3}$

$\frac{2}{9} + \frac{1}{3} \rightarrow \frac{2 + 3}{9} \rightarrow \frac{5}{9}$

28. B)

157 (correct: C = 100, L = 50, V = 5, I = 1)

29. D)

$5\frac{1}{3} - 2\frac{1}{3}$

$5.33 - 2.33 = 3$

30. C)

Answer is $6\frac{3}{4}$

$5\frac{1}{4} + 1\frac{1}{2} = 6 + \frac{1}{4} + \frac{2}{4} = 6\frac{3}{4}$

31. C)

$0.28 = \frac{28}{100}$

The lowest common denominator is 4.

$\frac{28}{4} = 7$

$\frac{100}{4} = 25$

$= \frac{7}{25}$

32. D)

5 divided by 20 equals .25.

33. A)

The question is straightforward, but the exact dollar amounts are a little more difficult to interpret. Since the question asks for *approximately* how much, we know we have a little wiggle room and the answer choices will not be very similar. So if we see one that is possibly right, we know we have our answer.

In 2003, the profit was just a little bit under $4 million, so we know it is about 3.8 or 3.9. In 2004, the profit jumps to just over $6 million, so we know it is probably about 6.1 or 6.2.

In either case, 6.1 − 3.8 = 2.3, as does 6.2 − 3.9 = 2.3, so we know answer choice A) is correct. Even if you arrived at an estimate of 6.2 − 3.8 = 2.4, that is certainly *approximate* for this exam.

34. B)

The question asks for the difference in profit between 2001 and 2000. In 2001, approximately $2.2 million was earned and in 2000, approximately $1.2 million was earned.

2.2 − 1.2 = 1 million

Answer Key – Science

1. B)	13. B)	25. A)	37. D)
2. A)	14. A)	26. D)	38. B)
3. A)	15. B)	27. B)	39. B)
4. C)	16. C)	28. A)	40. C)
5. B)	17. A)	29. B)	41. A)
6. A)	18. A)	30. B)	42. C)
7. B)	19. A)	31. C)	43. A)
8. C)	20. D)	32. B)	44. C)
9. C)	21. C)	33. B)	45. B)
10. B)	22. C)	34. B)	46. C)
11. B)	23. B)	35. A)	47. C)
12. C)	24. D)	36. A)	48. B)

Answer Key – English and Language Usage

1. B)	10. D)	19. A)	28. A)
2. D)	11. A)	20. A)	29. C)
3. A)	12. D)	21. B)	30. D)
4. B)	13. C)	22. A)	31. D)
5. D)	14. A)	23. B)	32. A)
6. A)	15. C)	24. C)	33. A)
7. B)	16. A)	25. C)	34. D)
8. C)	17. A)	26. A)	35. A)
9. C)	18. B)	27. B)	

15

PRACTICE TEST TWO

Reading

The next four questions are based on the passage below.

Skin colors and markings have an important role to play in the world of snakes. Those intricate diamonds, stripes, and swirls help animals hide from predators and advertise to mates. Perhaps most importantly (for us humans, anyway), the markings can also indicate whether the snake is venomous. While it might seem counterintuitive for a poisonous snake to stand out in bright red or blue, that fancy costume tells any approaching predator that eating him would be a bad idea.

If you see a flashy looking snake out in the woods, though, those markings don't necessarily mean it's poisonous: some snakes have found a way to ward off predators without the actual venom. The California kingsnake, for example, has very similar markings to the venomous coral snake with whom it frequently shares a habitat. However, the kingsnake is actually nonvenomous; it's merely pretending to be dangerous to eat. A predatory hawk or eagle, usually hunting from high in the sky, can't tell the difference between the two species, and so the kingsnake gets passed over and lives another day.

1. The passage is reflective of which of the following types of writing?

   A) technical

   B) expository

   C) persuasive

   D) narrative

2. *Skin colors and markings have an important role to play in the world of snakes.*

   The sentence above appears in the first paragraph of the passage. This sentence is best described as which of the following?

   A) theme

   B) topic

   C) main idea

   D) supporting idea

3. Which of the following conclusions may be drawn directly from the second paragraph of the passage?

   A) The kingsnake is dangerous to humans.

   B) The coral snake and the kingsnake are both hunted by the same predators.

   C) It's safe to handle snakes in the woods because you can easily tell whether they're poisonous.

   D) The kingsnake changes its marking when hawks or eagles are close by.

4. Which of the following is the author's main purpose in writing this passage?

A) to explain how the markings on a snake are related to whether it is venomous

B) to teach readers the difference between coral snakes and kingsnakes

C) to illustrate why snakes are dangerous

D) to demonstrate how animals survive in difficult environments

The next seven questions are based on the passage below.

Credit scores, which range from 300 to 850, are a single value that summarizes an individual's credit history. Pay your bills late? Your credit score will be lower than someone who gets that electric bill filed on the first of every month. Just paid off your massive student loans? You can expect your credit score to shoot up. The companies that compile credit scores actually keep track of all the loans, credit cards, and bill payments in your name. This massive amount of information is summed up in a credit report, which is then distilled to a single value: your credit score.

Credit scores are used by many institutions that need to evaluate the risk of providing loans, rentals, or services to individuals. Banks use credit scores when deciding when to hand out loans; they can also use them to determine the terms of the loan itself. Similarly, car dealers, landlords, and credit card companies will likely all access your credit report before agreeing to do business with you. Even your employer can access a modified version of your credit report (although it will not have your actual credit score on it).

When it comes to credit, everyone begins with a clean slate. The first time you access any credit—be it a credit card, student loan, or rental agreement—information begins to accumulate in your credit report. For this reason, having no credit score can often be just as bad as having a low one. Lenders want to know that you have a history of borrowing money and paying it back on time. After all, if you've never taken out a loan, how can a bank know that you'll pay back its money? So, having nothing on your credit report can result in low credit limits and high interest rates.

With time, though, credit scores can be raised. With every payment, your credit report improves and banks will be more likely to loan you money. These new loans will in turn raise your score even higher (as long as you keep making payments, of course).

In general, there are a number of basic steps you can take to raise your credit score. First, ensure that payments are made on time. When payments are past due, it not only has a negative impact on your score, but new creditors will be reluctant to lend while you are delinquent on other accounts.

Being smart about taking on debt is another key factor in keeping your credit score high. As someone who is just starting off in the financial world, there will be multiple offers to open accounts, say for an introductory credit card or short-term loan. You may also find that as your score increases, you receive offers for larger and larger loans. (Predatory lenders are a scourge on the young as well as the old.) But just because banks are offering you those loans doesn't make them a good idea. Instead, you should only take on debt you know you can pay back in a reasonable amount of time.

Lastly, keep an eye on unpaid student loans, medical bills, and parking tickets, all of which can take a negative toll on your credit score. In fact, your credit score will take a major hit from any bill that's sent to a collection agency, so it's in your best interest to avoid letting bills get to that point. Many organizations will agree to keep bills away from collection agencies if you set up a fee payment system.

5. Which of the following excerpts from the passage contains an opinion?

   A) Credit scores, which range from 300 to 850, are a single value that summarizes an individual's credit history.

   B) Many organizations will agree to keep bills away from collection agencies if you set up a fee payment system.

   C) After all, if you've never taken out a loan, how can a bank know that you'll pay back its money?

   D) Predatory lenders are a scourge on the young as well as the old.

6. Which of the following is a likely motive for the author?

   A) to help readers understand and improve their credit scores

   B) to warn banks about the dangers of lending to people with no credit score

   C) to persuade readers to take out large loans in order to improve their credit scores

   D) to explain to readers how the process of taking out a bank loan works

7. *With every payment, your credit report improves and banks will be more likely to loan you money.*

   The sentence above appears in the fourth paragraph of the passage. This sentence is best described as which of the following?

   A) theme

   B) topic

   C) main idea

   D) supporting idea

8. The author's description of how credit scores work in the first paragraph is reflective of which of the following types of text structure?

   A) cause-effect

   B) comparison-contrast

   C) sequence

   D) problem-solution

9. Which of the following conclusions may be drawn directly from the third paragraph of the passage?

   A) It is possible to wipe your credit report clean and start over with a blank slate.

   B) A person with a large amount of debt can likely get a loan with a low interest rate because they have demonstrated they are trustworthy.

   C) Someone who has borrowed and paid back large sums of money will get a loan with more favorable terms than someone who has never borrowed money before.

   D) A college student with no credit cards or debt likely has a high credit score.

10. The author intends to do which of the following by using the words *Even your employer can access a modified version of your credit report (although it will not have your actual credit score on it)*.

    A) entertain

    B) express feelings

    C) persuade

    D) inform

11. Which of the following is an example of a supporting detail in the passage?

    A) In general, there are a number of basic steps you can take to raise your credit score.

    B) When it comes to credit, everyone begins with a clean slate.

    C) Similarly, car dealers, landlords, and credit card companies will likely all access your credit report before agreeing to do business with you.

    D) Predatory lenders are a scourge on the young as well as the old.

CONTINUE

The next five questions are based on the following passage.

Notice to All Students

It has come to the attention of the administration that many of you are angered about recent changes to the dormitory curfew policy. As you should be aware, the administration has instituted a temporary curfew for those living in the Walcher Dormitory due to the recent spike in on-campus crime. While we understand the reasons for your concern, we will continue to enforce this curfew as it was described in earlier notices. The details are given again below for clarification:

- The curfew will be in effect from March 1 – March 31.
- Students who enter or leave the dormitory between 1:00 a.m. and 5:00 a.m. will be subject to disciplinary action.
- Students who need to be exempted from the curfew may apply with Dr. Fowler at fowler@university.edu. Exemptions will only be given for students with work responsibilities or health issues. Other than emergency situations, students **must** have an official curfew exemption form in order to claim an exemption.

The administration thanks you for your understanding and patience.

12. According to the notice above, which of the following students would be subject to disciplinary action?
    A) a student who enters the dormitory at 4:00 a.m. with an official curfew exemption form
    B) a student who leaves the dormitory at 6:00 a.m. to go running
    C) a student who enters the dormitory at 1:30 a.m. after staying late at a party
    D) a student who leaves the dormitory at 3:00 a.m. for a medical emergency

13. Which of the following is the administration's main purpose for writing this notice?
    A) to tell students that the curfew will be enforced despite their objections
    B) to introduce students to the rules for the curfew
    C) to outline how exemptions to the curfew will be handed out
    D) to explain to students what disciplinary action will be taken against students who violate the curfew

14. Which of the following inferences may be logically drawn from the notice?
    A) Students who violate curfew will be expelled from school.
    B) This type of curfew has been successfully implemented before.
    C) The administration is attempting to punish students using a curfew.
    D) Students have been protesting the new curfew.

15. Other than emergency situations, students _must_ have an official curfew form from Dr. Fowler in order to claim an exemption.

    The underlined text in the sentence above indicates which of the following?
    A) brand names
    B) emphasis
    C) definitions
    D) proper nouns

16. Which of the following is the administration's intent in the notice?
    A) entertain
    B) express feelings
    C) persuade
    D) inform

The next three questions are based on the passage below.

Whenever Vi entered that old house, it felt like she was coming home. Even though she hadn't lived there in almost twenty years, the memories of the years she had spent there felt as fresh as the newly fallen snow that blanketed the yard. When she walked through the living room she didn't see the rickety old chairs and peeling paint—she saw the many evenings she'd enjoyed there with her mom, dad, and kid sister. To her the old dining room didn't smell like dust and moldy table linens; it smelled like home-cooked meals.

Vi's sister, on the other hand, worried about the more practical matters. That dust and mold had been accumulating in the house ever since their mother moved out, and it didn't seem like their father planned to do anything about it. She hired cleaners, plumbers, and painters, but her father just sent them away.

17. Which of the following are likely motives for the author?

   A) She wants the reader to dislike Vi and her sister.

   B) She wants the reader to understand the differences between Vi and her sister.

   C) She wants the reader to sympathize with Vi's father.

   D) She wants the reader to believe Vi and her sister should do more to help their father.

18. Which of the following inferences may be logically drawn from the passage?

   A) Vi and her sister had an unhappy childhood.

   B) Vi and her sister are going to force their father to sell his house.

   C) Vi and her sister disagree about how to help their father.

   D) Vi and her sister don't ever talk to their mother.

19. Based on a prior knowledge of literature, the reader can infer that this passage was taken from which of the following?

   A) a novel

   B) a science magazine

   C) an academic journal

   D) a history textbook

The next three questions are based on the passage below.

There's no denying the cuteness of a puppy—those big eyes and boundless energy can bring joy to even the sourest of days. It's that sense of joy that brings so many future pet owners to pet stores and dog breeders to pick out their newest family members.

But puppies don't stay puppies forever. In just a few short years, that little bouncing bundle of fur will grow into a full-size dog, and unfortunately, many families just aren't ready to handle that responsibility. Every year, tens of thousands of dogs end up in shelters once they reach adulthood. Perhaps the dog grew larger than the owners expected, or the owners weren't able to provide the training that turns a puppy into a well-behaved adult. Whatever the reason, animal rescue shelters are overrun with adult dogs that need good homes.

CONTINUE

20. Which of the following is the most likely motive for the author?

   A) She wants readers to stop adopting dogs.

   B) She wants readers to adopt older dogs.

   C) She wants readers to adopt only from pet stores and dog breeders.

   D) She wants readers to do a better job of training their puppies.

21. Which of the following is the author's intent in the passage?

   A) entertain

   B) express feelings

   C) persuade

   D) inform

22. The reader can infer that this passage was taken from which of the following?

   A) an advertisement for a local pet store

   B) a commercial for a dog training school

   C) a local news story about stray dogs

   D) a brochure for an animal rescue shelter

Chapter 2: Do-It-Yourself Home Renovations
I. The Living Room
    A. Installing Wood Floors
    B. Installing Carpet
    C. Building Custom Bookshelves
II. The Bathroom
    A. Installing Tile
    B. _____
III. The Kitchen
    A. Choosing Countertops
    B. Building Custom Cabinets

---

23. Examine the headings above. Based on the pattern, which of the following is a reasonable heading to insert in the blank spot?

   A) Weatherproofing the Patio

   B) Adding Insulation in the Attic

   C) Choosing a New Dishwasher

   D) Updating Plumbing and Fixtures

24. An editor wants to make sure that a writer is using a particular word correctly. Which of the following resources would be the most appropriate for her to use?

   A) Wikipedia

   B) The American Guide to Grammar and Usage

   C) The Personal Website of Author Alex Fickles

   D) Ten Style Rules for Non-Fiction Writers

---

1. Starting from the hotel, drive 2 miles north to work.

2. From work, drive 3 miles east to the gym.

3. From the gym, drive 5 miles west to the theater

4. From the theater, drive 4 miles south to a restaurant.

---

25. Read the directions above. After following the directions, how far would you be from the hotel?

   A) 2 miles south, 8 miles west

   B) 6 miles south, 2 miles west

   C) 2 miles south, 2 miles west

   D) 6 miles north, 8 miles west

The next two questions refer to the table of contents below.

Advanced Mathematics
1. Pre-Calculus, p. 137 – 225
    A. Quadratic Equations, p. 137 – 178
    B. Trigonometry, p. 179 – 225
2. Calculus, p. 226 – 314
    A. Limits, p. 226 – 240
    B. Derivatives, p. 241 – 289
    C. Integrals, p. 290 – 314
2. Differential Equations, p. 315 – 452

26. Which of the following topics would be covered on page 237?

    A) limits

    B) integrals

    C) trigonometry

    D) differential equations

27. On which of the following pages would you find information on integrals?

    A) 145

    B) 215

    C) 302

    D) 412

The next three questions refer to the map below.

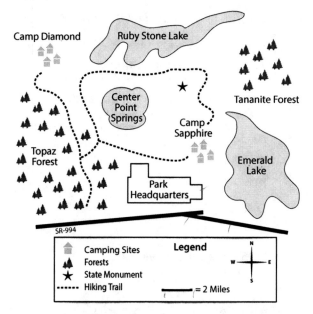

28. According to the map above, which direction is Ruby Stone Lake in relation to Camp Diamond?

    A) north

    B) south

    C) east

    D) west

29. According to the map, which geographical feature is due west of Camp Sapphire?

    A) Tananite Forest

    B) Topaz Forest

    C) Emerald Lake

    D) Ruby Stone Lake

30. According to the map, how many miles is it from Park Headquarters to the center of Emerald Lake?

    A) 0.6 miles

    B) 6 miles

    C) 60 miles

    D) 600 miles

31. My little sister has always been <u>impetuous</u> and will often cancel our plans at the last minute.

    Which of the following is the definition of the underlined word in the sentence above?

    A) forgetful

    B) impulsive

    C) imperious

    D) terrifying

32. I told Alan, "There's no way I can be there on time," but he insisted on meeting at 7:00 p.m.

    The use of quotes in the text above signifies which of the following?

    A) foreign phrases

    B) emphasized words

    C) dialogue

    D) words used ironically

CONTINUE

The next two questions are based on the pie chart below.

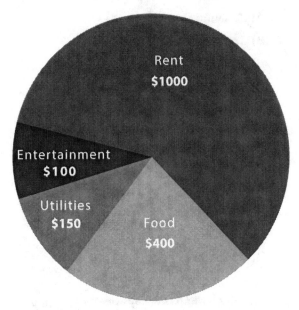

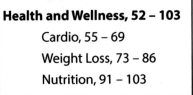

Health and Wellness, 52 – 103

Cardio, 55 – 69

Weight Loss, 73 – 86

Nutrition, 91 – 103

35. According to the index above, which of the following pages would include information on weight loss?

A) 62

B) 75

C) 87

D) 98

---

1. You start with 5 pennies in your pocket.

2. You find 1 penny on the ground.

3. You trade 5 pennies for 1 nickel.

4. You find 3 pennies under the bed.

36. After following the directions above, how many pennies do you have?

A) 3

B) 4

C) 5

D) 6

33. According to the chart above, how many dollars are spent on food and utilities each month?

A) $150

B) $400

C) $550

D) $1500

34. According to the previous graph, what accounts for the largest expense per month?

A) entertainment

B) utilities

C) food

D) rent

Table 15.1. Tee shirt prices

RETAILER	PRICE PER DOZEN	COLOR
Maximum Tees	$15.99	red
Wholesale Tees	$12.99	blue
Total Tees	$19.99	green

45. Tina needs to purchase a dozen red or blue shirts but has only $14. According to the previous table, which company can she order from?

A) Maximum Tees

B) Wholesale Tees

C) Total Tees

D) none of the companies

37. The teacher not only <u>condoned</u> the student's behavior but also actively encouraged it.

Which of the following is the definition of the underlined word in the sentence above?

A) allowed

B) punished

C) ignored

D) questioned

The next two questions are based on the nutrition label below.

Nutrition Facts

Serving Size 172 g

Amount Per Serving

Calories 200   Calories from Fat 8

	% Daily Value*
Total Fat 1g	1%
Saturated Fat 0g	1%
Trans Fat	
Cholesterol 0g	0%
Sodium 7mg	0%
Total Carbohydrate 36g	12%
Dietary Fiber 11g	45%
Sugars 6g	
Protein 13g	

Vitamin A	1%	•	Vitamin B	1%
Calcium	4%	•	Iron	24%

*Percent Daily Values are based on a 2,000 calorie diet. Your daily values may be higher or lower depending on your calorie needs.

NutritionData.com

38. Two servings of the food described in the nutrition label above would include how many grams of dietary fiber?

   A) 11 g

   B) 22 g

   C) 45 g

   D) 90 g

39. A single serving of the food described on the nutrition label above provides the highest percent daily value of which of the following?

   A) iron

   B) calcium

   C) total carbohydrates

   D) total fat

The next two questions are based on the table below.

Table. 15.2. Bookstore prices

RETAILER	PRICE PER BOOK	SHIPPING & HANDLING
Bargain Books	$14.99	$0.99 per book
Your Favorite Books	$16.50	$0.50 per book
Books on Sale	$13.99	$2.99 for first 50 books; no charge for any after that
Books by the Pound	$17.99	No shipping and handling

40. A teacher wants to order twenty-five books for her class. Which store should she order from to pay the lowest amount for the books and shipping?

   A) Bargain Books

   B) Your Favorite Books

   C) Books on Sale

   D) Books by the Pound

41. A principal wants to order 150 books for her school. Which store should she order from to pay the lowest amount for books and shipping?

   A) Bargain Books

   B) Your Favorite Books

   C) Books on Sale

   D) Books by the Pound

42. A customer wants to find unbiased reviews of Gino's Pizzeria, a local restaurant. Which of the following resources should the customer consult?

   A) a local paper's review of Gino's Pizzeria

   B) www.ginospizza.com; *The Official Site of Gino's Pizzeria*

   C) an advertisement from one of the Gino's Pizzeria's competitors

   D) a brochure from a local tourism board

→

CONTINUE

The next two questions are based on the thermometer below.

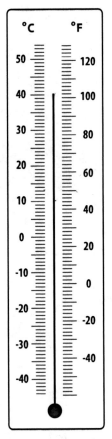

43. If the thermometer indicated a temperature of 50°F, which of the following would be the temperature in degrees Celsius?

A) 0°C

B) 3°C

C) 10°C

D) 13°C

44. If the thermometer shown above dropped 30°C, which of the following would be the temperature in degrees Fahrenheit?

A) 14°F

B) 24°F

C) 44°F

D) 54°F

The next two questions are based on the phone book excerpt below.

L 272 LAUNDRIES To Advertise Call 1-555-929-1255 - Area Code is 555 Unless Otherwise Specified

LAUNDRIES

A+ Laundry & Cleaners
1279 S Parkfield Dr................**121-7755**

Coin City Laundry
1662 Crown Pkwy................**999-3232**

Daily Spin Quality Cleaners
3773 Bell Springs Dr................**117-1958**

Magic Coin Laundry
9722 S Parkfield Dr................**151-0003**

Opal's Cleaners
4355 Central Park Dr................**121-7825**

Satin Touch Laundry Center
1116 Bathaven Ct................**533-1115**

LAUNDRIES-SELF SVCE.

Quik-E-Wash
7879 Springfield Dr................**111-1985**

Royal Cleaners
1492 Columbus Ct................**567-0010**

Spin Cycle Laundry
Self Service Coin Laundromat
Full Service Wash n' Fold
Advanced Washers and Dryers
3475 Baythorne Dr................**567-0010**

Super Spin Laundry
4789 Iron Clark Dr................**122-1811**

Total Clean Laundry Center
9134 Bay Breeze Cir................**145-8889**

Wash Center USA
415 Purple Park Dr................**555-1212**

LAWN & GARDEN EQUIP.

AAA Lawn Service and Sales
1212 Greenleaf Dr................**311-1218**

Bard's Stone & Feed
1117 Maple Crossing................**757-0110**

Calm Winds Nursery
47134 N Lakeville Dr................**729-1991**

Earth Friendly Gardeners
5234 Orchard Valley Dr................**445-3335**

Palm Planet
1410 Elm St................**131-1571**

Summer Stone Outdoors
525 Parkside Dr................**888-3995**

LAWN & GROUNDS MAINT.

ALL SEASON LAWN MAINTENANCE
Lawn & Grounds Maintenance
Tree Removal
Landscape Design
Stonework & Fencing
Call 555-123-7879

American Landscape
9822 Dreamy Lane................**121-7755**

Capitol Lawn and Design
1237 Georgia Crest Dr................**912-3200**

Edward's Irrigation Repair
2010 Blue Jay Ln................**151-0003**

GARDENSCAPE
Mowing, Maintenance & Landscaping
Residential and Commercial
1105 Spring Creek Dr................**615-1001**

Green Giant Lawncare
0427 Phoenix St................**227-1368**

Happy Plant Lawnworks
8081 Red Bird Ct................**151-0003**

JTW Landscape Service
39009 Williamsburg Dr................**227-1368**

Perfecto Lawncare & Maintenance
0320 Kendrix Ct................**431-2906**

Stonewall Complete Landscapes
0525 E Penny Lane................**391-5580**

46. Where is Spin Cycle Laundry located?

A) 4789 Iron Clark Dr.

B) 9134 Bay Breeze Cir.

C) 1116 Bathaven Ct.

D) 3475 Baythorne Dr.

47. At which number can a customer reach Bard's Stone and Feed?

A) 757-0110

B) 311-1218

C) 123-7879

D) 151-0003

48. The output from the cup factory was so <u>prodigious</u> it was able to provide cups for the whole state.

Which of the following is the definition of the underlined word in the sentence above?

A) fleeting

B) fortunate

C) massive

D) timely

Mathematics

1. $3 \times (2 \times 4^3) \div 4 =$
   A) 81
   B) 64
   C) 127
   D) 96

2. $(5 \times 3) \times 1 + 5 =$
   A) 20
   B) 21
   C) 90
   D) 13

3. $(5^3 + 7) \times 2 =$
   A) 1264
   B) 264
   C) 139
   D) 164

4. Evaluate the expression $\frac{4x}{x-1}$ when $x = 5$.
   A) 3
   B) 4
   C) 5
   D) 6

5. Round 707.456 to the nearest tenths place.
   A) 708.0
   B) 710
   C) 707.5
   D) 700

6. Subtract the following numbers and round to the nearest tenths place:

   134.679
   − 45.548
   − 67.8807

   A) 21.3
   B) 21.25
   C) −58.97
   D) −59.0

7. What is the median of the following list of numbers: 4, 5, 7, 9, 10, and 12?
   A) 6
   B) 7.5
   C) 7.8
   D) 8

8. Find $0.12 \div 1.0$.
   A) 12
   B) 1.2
   C) 0.12
   D) 0.012

9. $6 \times 0 \times 5$ equals:
   A) 30
   B) 11
   C) 25
   D) 0

10. If a rectangular field has a perimeter of 44 yards, and a length of 36 feet, what is the field's width?
    A) 30 feet
    B) 28 yards
    C) 18 feet
    D) 42 feet

11. Adam is painting the inside walls of a 4-walled shed. The shed is 5 feet wide, 4 feet deep, and 7 feet high. How much paint will Adam need?
    A) 126 ft²
    B) 140 ft²
    C) 63 ft²
    D) 46 ft

12. 35% of what number is 70?
    A) 100
    B) 110
    C) 150
    D) 200

13. A car dealer sells an SUV for $39,000, which represents a 25% profit over the cost. What was the actual cost of the SUV to the dealer?

A) $29,250

B) $31,200

C) $32,500

D) $33,800

14. At a bake sale, muffins are priced at $1.50 each and cookies are priced at $1 for two. If 11 muffins are sold, and the total money earned is $29.50, how many cookies were sold?

A) 12

B) 13

C) 23

D) 26

15. During a five-day convention, the number of visitors tripled each day. If the convention started on a Tuesday with 345 visitors, what was the attendance on that Friday?

A) 9,315

B) 1,035

C) 1,725

D) 3,105

16. The floor of Mark's bedroom measures 11 feet by 13.5 feet. What is the area of his bedroom in square meters? (1 meter = 3.28 feet)

A) 3.8 m²

B) 13.80 m²

C) 148.5 m²

D) 958 m²

17. Jim works for $15.50 per hour at a health care facility. He is supposed to get a $0.75 per hour raise after one year of service. What will be his percent increase in hourly pay?

A) 2.7%

B) 3.3%

C) 133%

D) 4.8%

18. What is the least common multiple of 2, 3, 4, and 5?

A) 30

B) 60

C) 120

D) 40

19. $2 + 3|4n| = 26$. Which of the following are the values of n?

A) (1, 2)

B) (−2, 2)

C) (3, 4)

D) (−1, −4)

20. If $|2r + 1| - 10 = 13$, which of the following values of r satisfies the given equation?

A) (12, −2)

B) (11, −11)

C) (12, −11)

D) (−12, 11)

21. $\frac{3}{4} \times \frac{4}{5} \times \frac{5}{3} =$

A) 1

B) $\frac{6}{5}$

C) 2

D) $\frac{12}{23}$

22. Which inequality is equivalent to $3x + 33 > -6x + 3$?

A) $2x < 10$

B) $3x > -10$

C) $x > 11$

D) $4x > 31$

23. $\frac{100}{30} \times \frac{3}{6} \times \frac{300}{50} =$

A) 10

B) 12

C) 15

D) 8

24. $\frac{2}{3} + \frac{4}{5} - \frac{5}{6} =$

A) $\frac{11}{14}$

B) $\frac{19}{30}$

C) $\frac{1}{2}$

D) $\frac{2}{3}$

25. $\frac{11}{22} + \frac{22}{44} + \frac{1}{2} =$

A) $\frac{2}{3}$

B) $\frac{17}{34}$

C) $\frac{5}{2}$

D) $\frac{3}{2}$

26. $\frac{13}{4} + \frac{5}{8} =$

A) $\frac{31}{8}$

B) $\frac{3}{2}$

C) $\frac{9}{4}$

D) $\frac{21}{8}$

27. David had 12 chocolates, which he decided to distribute among his friends. Alex got $\frac{2}{3}$ of the total chocolates. How many chocolates did he get?

A) 2

B) 4

C) 8

D) 9

28. Which inequality is equivalent to $4x - 12 < 12$?

A) $2x < 12$

B) $x > 12$

C) $x > 11$

D) $x > 21$

29. Convert 240 to roman numerals.

A) CCL

B) DXL

C) CCXXX

D) CCXL

30. Convert the following into decimal form:
$2\frac{1}{2} - 1\frac{1}{4}$

A) 1.5

B) 2.25

C) 1.25

D) 0.25

31. Convert 0.55 into a fraction.

A) $\frac{11}{20}$

B) $\frac{5}{9}$

C) $\frac{5}{10}$

D) $\frac{11}{50}$

CONTINUE

32. Convert $\frac{7}{20}$ into a decimal form.

A) 0.45

B) 0.35

C) 0.28

D) 0.65

Use the chart below to answer the next two questions.

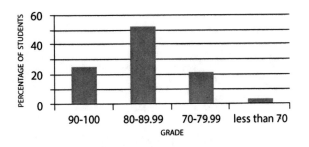

33. Referencing the chart, if scores below 70.0 are considered failing, what percentage of students passed this exam?

A) 51%

B) 22%

C) 3%

D) 97%

34. A score of 70 or higher is passing. A score of 70 to 79.99 earns a C. A score of 80-89.99 earns a B. A score of 90-100 earns an A. Based on the above chart, which of the following must NOT be true?

A) Over half the class passed.

B) Less than 30% earned an A.

C) More students earned a B than any other score.

D) Only 75% of the class passed.

1. When measuring blood pressure, the numbers represent:

   A) the systolic and diastolic pressures, respectively

   B) the diastolic and systolic pressures, respectively

   C) the pressure in the arteries and the veins, respectively

   D) the pressure in the veins and arteries respectively

2. The superior vena cava—

   A) ascends from the right atrium

   B) ascends from the left atrium

   C) descends from the right atrium

   D) ascends from the left ventricle

3. A scientist has isolated Fe (III), a variant of iron that has a charge of 3+. Which of the following compounds could be created from this element?

   A) FeO_2

   B) $FeCl$

   C) $FeCa_3$

   D) Fe_2O_3

4. What is the VSEPR structure of a PO_4 (phosphate) molecule?

   A) tetrahedral

   B) octahedral

   C) linear

   D) trigonal bi-planar

5. The rectum is a part of—

   A) the anus

   B) the large intestine

   C) the small intestine

   D) the genitourinary system

6. Where does digestion start?

   A) the stomach

   B) the small intestine

   C) the mouth

   D) esophagus

7. The large intestine's primary function is to—

   A) absorb water

   B) digest food

   C) move the food from the esophagus to the small intestine

   D) absorb nutrients

8. What type of reaction is the following?

   $CaCl_2 + 2NaOH \rightarrow Ca(OH)_2 + 2NaCl$

   A) single replacement

   B) double replacement

   C) synthesis

   D) acid-base

9. What are the products of the following reaction?

   $NaOH + HCl \rightarrow$

   A) dihydrogen monoxide and sodium chloride

   B) sodium hydride and chlorohydroxide

   C) hydrochloride and sodium monohydroxide

   D) sodium chloride and sodium hydroxide

10. In the following chemical reaction, what is the correct stoichiometric coefficient for silicon dioxide?

   $4Si + 2O_2 \rightarrow Si + SiO_2$

   A) 1

   B) 2

   C) 3

   D) 4

→

CONTINUE

11. When you notice that a chemical reaction equation is not balanced, which of the following can be performed to balance the equation?

    A) change the formula of the products

    B) change the subscripts of the molecular formulas

    C) change the coefficients of the reactants or products

    D) change the reaction type

12. A scientist places mercury oxide (HgO) into a sealed chamber and heats it to 400°C, causing a reaction to occur. When she opens the chamber, she notices liquid mercury has formed as well as oxygen gas. This reaction is an—

    A) endothermic synthesis reaction

    B) exothermic combustion reaction

    C) endothermic decomposition reaction

    D) exothermic replacement reaction

13. What is the name of the process that happens in the red bone marrow?

    A) hematopoiesis

    B) bone fusing

    C) calcification

    D) meiosis

14. The vertebral column protects the—

    A) brain

    B) heart

    C) spinal column

    D) peripheral nerves

15. Which unit of measurement is NOT used in the International System of Units?

    A) centimeters

    B) milliliters

    C) grams

    D) inches

16. A conclusion reached on the basis of evidence and reasoning is a/an—

    A) theory

    B) conclusion

    C) inference

    D) hypothesis

17. Plants are autotrophs, meaning that they—

    A) consume organic material produced by animals

    B) produce their own food

    C) are able to move by themselves

    D) can automatically transform from a seed into a plant

18. Which of the following is not true of a virus?

    A) Viruses have DNA or RNA.

    B) Viruses do not have a nucleus.

    C) Viruses cannot survive without water.

    D) Viruses can be infectious.

19. In the digestive system, the majority of nutrients are absorbed in the—

    A) esophagus

    B) stomach

    C) small intestine

    D) large intestine

20. How many pairs of human chromosomes exist?

    A) 17

    B) 22

    C) 23

    D) 46

21. Animals engaging in a symbiotic relationship will do which of the following?

    A) help each other survive

    B) take one another's food

    C) attack one another

    D) eat each other

22. What are the motor units made of?

A) motor neurons

B) muscle cells

C) tendons

D) bones

23. What is the name of a state of constant muscle contraction caused by rapid successive nerve signals?

A) tetanus

B) muscle tone

C) temporal summation

D) hypotony

24. Which of the following can be found in abundance in a fatigued muscle?

A) glucose

B) lactic acid

C) ATP

D) HCO^{3-}

25. Which of the following produces a gas from a solid?

A) melting

B) plasmification

C) condensation

D) sublimation

26. A student isolates a substance, and succeeds in purifying it. She then puts it into the lab refrigerator, at 4°C. When she comes back the next day, she notices that it has solidified! Which of the following statements should be true about the substance?

A) It has a melting point below 4°C.

B) It has a boiling point less than that of water.

C) It has a freezing point higher than that of water.

D) It has a vaporization point at around 90°C.

27. The specific heat of water is 1 calorie/gram × °C. How much energy is needed to heat 2 kg of water from 20°C to its boiling point?

A) 80 calories

B) 160 calories

C) 200 kilocalories

D) 160 kilocalories

28. In science, an educated guess is called a/an

A) observation

B) question

C) conclusion

D) hypothesis

29. In an experiment, what do you call the variable that is changed?

A) controlled variable

B) dependent variable

C) independent variable

D) experimental variable

30. What organ system contains your skin?

A) the respiratory system

B) the epithelial system

C) the lymphatic system

D) the integumentary system

31. If a gene is expressed, then that means that:

A) It is influencing a phenotype trait.

B) It is being copied into another set of DNA.

C) It will be passed on from mother to son.

D) The gene will produce some hormones.

32. Which of the following structures is found in eukaryotes but not in prokaryotes?

A) a cell wall

B) flagella

C) a nuclear membrane

D) ribosomes

⟶

CONTINUE

33. Which of the following is NOT a kind of genetic mutation?

    A) missense mutation

    B) nonsense mutation

    C) frameshift mutation

    D) uncover mutation

34. Which of the following does NOT correctly match the endocrine system organ with its function?

    A) hypothalamus: regulation of pituitary gland

    B) pancreas: control of blood sugar through production of insulin and glucagon

    C) testes: testosterone and estradiol production

    D) pituitary: production and regulation of cortisol, adrenaline, and melatonin

35. Which part of the PNS is accountable for the fight or flight reaction?

    A) the parasympathetic

    B) the sympathetic

    C) the ENS

    D) afferent nerves

36. People who suffer from Type I diabetes are lacking function in which organ?

    A) liver

    B) pancreas

    C) stomach

    D) heart

37. One of the primary differences between fungi and plants is that:

    A) Fungi can produce their own food and plants cannot.

    B) Plants have chlorophyll and fungi do not.

    C) Fungi are able to grow without water and plants cannot.

    D) Fungi and plants have no major differences.

38. Which is TRUE?

    A) Deoxygenated blood enters the left atrium.

    B) Deoxygenated blood leaves the right ventricle.

    C) Oxygenated blood enters the right atrium.

    D) Deoxygenated blood leaves the left ventricle.

39. In our atmosphere, nitrogen is the most common element, and makes up approximately what percentage?

    A) 25%

    B) 51%

    C) 65%

    D) 78%

40. Why is it ill-advised for patients to have surgery while on aspirin?

    A) It increases the likelihood of bleeding due to weakening of small vessels.

    B) It decreases respiratory rate.

    C) It increases bleeding time by interfering with normal platelet function.

    D) It causes increased clotting which can lead to increased bleeding and stroke.

41. Which of the following is correct regarding an aqueous substance?

    A) It is soluble in water.

    B) It is very reactive.

    C) It is soluble in hydrocarbon.

    D) It is able to dissolve most other compounds.

42. In order for work to be performed, a force has to be—

    A) applied to an object

    B) applied to a surface

    C) applied to a moving object

    D) applied over a distance to an object

43. According to electron theory, what is the maximum number of bonds a carbon atom can have?

    A) 2

    B) 3

    C) 4

    D) 5

44. If a rowboat weighs 50 kilograms, how much water needs to be displaced in order for the boat to float?

    A) 25 liters

    B) 50 liters

    C) 100 liters

    D) 500 liters

45. Where are the cilia found?

    A) smaller bronchioles

    B) in the alveoli

    C) in the trachea

    D) sperm

46. The tidal volume is the amount of air moved during—

    A) deep breathing

    B) shallow breathing

    C) coughing

    D) none of the above

47. A ball with a mass of 0.5 kg is moving at 10 m/s. How much kinetic energy does it have?

    A) 15 Joules

    B) 25 Joules

    C) 50 Joules

    D) 55.5 Joules

48. The temperature at which all molecular motion stops is—

    A) −460°C

    B) −273 K

    C) 0 K

    D) 0°C

CONTINUE

1. Which of the following sentences is punctuated correctly?

    A) They were scheduled to attend the lecture, but they were unable to be there due to illness.

    B) They were scheduled to attend the lecture but they were unable to be there due to illness.

    C) They were scheduled to attend the lecture but they were unable to be there, due to illness.

    D) They were scheduled to attend, the lecture, but they were unable to be there, due to illness.

2. Which of the following is a simple sentence?

    A) Take the car to the car wash.

    B) He was going to wash the car, but he didn't have time.

    C) You need to wash the car because we are leaving in the morning.

    D) The car is dirty, so it needs to be washed.

3. Good hygiene is _____ to a safe and healthy hospital.

    Which word best completes the sentence?

    A) essentel

    B) essentiall

    C) assential

    D) essential

4. The play was watched by John, Mary, and Tim.

    Which of the following sentences changes the sentence above from passive voice to active voice?

    A) The play watched John, Mary, and Tim.

    B) The play is watching John, Mary, and Tim.

    C) John, Mary, and Tim watched the play.

    D) The play was viewed by John, Mary, and Tim.

5. Which of the following sentences follows the correct rules of capitalization?

    A) The patient is ready for his MRI.

    B) The Patient, Mr. smith, is ready for his MRI.

    C) The patient, Mr. Smith, is ready for his mri.

    D) The patient is ready for his mri.

6. Which of the following sentences is punctuated correctly?

    A) Take a right at the gas station, and then drive two miles to the parking lot.

    B) Take a right at the gas station then drive two miles to the parking lot,

    C) Take a right at the gas station and then drive two miles to the parking lot.

    D) Take a right at the gas station; then drive two miles to the parking lot.

7. The patient had suffered from chronic coughing for several years.

    Which of the following is the meaning of *chronic* in the sentence above?

    A) new

    B) ongoing

    C) severe

    D) mild

8. I heard that jane was sick last week and had to go to the doctor.

    Which word in the sentence above should be capitalized?

    A) Sick

    B) Doctor

    C) Jane

    D) Week

9. Which of the following sentences contains a correct example of subject-verb agreement?

   A) Mr. Smith has been experiencing a variety of symptoms.

   B) Mr. Smith were having a variety of symptoms.

   C) Mr. Smith have a variety of symptoms.

   D) Mr. Smith experience a variety of symptoms.

10. Nursing school can be difficult, and you will need to _____.

    Which of the following words best completes the sentence?

    A) pernicious

    B) persevere

    C) perverse

    D) perpetuated

11. _____ the Eiffel Tower when he visited Paris.

    Which of the following best completes the sentence?

    A) They saw

    B) He seen

    C) They seen

    D) He saw

12. Which of the following sentences is punctuated correctly?

    A) Make a study plan to learn the parts of the respiratory system, the muscles, and the heart.

    B) Make a study plan to learn the: parts of the respiratory system, the muscles and the heart.

    C) Make a study plan to learn the parts of the respiratory system the muscles and the heart.

    D) Make a study plan to learn the parts: of the respiratory system, the muscles and the heart.

13. Which of the following is an example of the appropriate use of an apostrophe?

    A) could'nt

    B) shouldn't

    C) shaln't

    D) youl'l

14. Which of the following sentences is an example of the third-person point of view?

    A) She carried the tools up the stairs.

    B) Carry the tools up the stairs.

    C) I carried the tools up the stairs.

    D) You carried the tools up the stairs.

15. The _____ professor was asked to give speeches at many different universities.

    Which of the following is the correctly spelled word to complete the sentence?

    A) illustrious

    B) illustrius

    C) illustros

    D) illustries

16. The nurse was asked to _____ the patient for signs of improvement.

    Which of the following is the correctly spelled word to complete the sentence?

    A) examane

    B) examine

    C) eximine

    D) examaine

17. The student was thorough and worked through every problem on the test.

    Which of the following is the meaning of *thorough* in the sentence above?

    A) stationary

    B) sluggish

    C) incomplete

    D) meticulous

→

CONTINUE

18. Which of the following sentences is the most clear and correct?

A) After a thorough examination, the patient were released.

B) After a thorough examination, the patient was released.

C) After a thorough examination the patient was released.

D) After a thorough examination, the patient was release.

19. Which of the following sentences follows the correct rules of capitalization?

A) I finished reading the introduction to the history of medicine.

B) I finished reading the Introduction to the History Of Medicine.

C) I finished reading the introduction to the History of Medicine.

D) I finished reading the introduction to the History Of Medicine.

20. If you miss a lab, ten points will be deducted off your final grade.

The word *deducted* serves as which of the following parts of speech in the sentence above?

A) adverb

B) noun

C) verb

D) adjective

21. The patient came to the emergency room complaining of a keen pain in her stomach.

Which of the following is the meaning of *keen* in the sentence above?

A) mild

B) sharp

C) nonexistent

D) intermittent

22. Which of the following is a complex sentence?

A) He turned his homework in to his teacher.

B) He turned his homework in today, because he would not be in class the next day.

C) He turn in his homework.

D) He turned in his homework at the beginning of class.

23. Which of the following sentences contains a correct example of subject-verb agreement?

A) The homework assignment are due on Monday.

B) The homework assignment dues on Monday.

C) The homework assignment is due on Monday.

D) The homework assignments is due on Monday.

24. Take the laundry _____

Which of the following allows the above sentence to be completed as a simple sentence?

A) to the laundry room in the basement.

B) to the laundry room, so you can finish cleaning your room.

C) to the laundry room, and don't forget the detergent.

D) to the laundry room because it's your turn to do the chores.

25. The damage to the car after the accident was _____.

Which of the following is the correctly spelled word to complete the sentence?

A) minimal

B) minimle

C) minimile

D) minimale

26. Because the speakers weren't working properly, her voice was _____.

Which of the following is the correctly spelled word to complete the sentence?

A) unintelligable

B) uninteligible

C) unintelligible

D) uninttelligible

27. Which of the following sentences contains a correct example of subject-verb agreement?

A) The doctor's office is booked with appointments all day.

B) The doctor's office are booked with appointments all day.

C) The doctors' offices is booked with appointments all day.

D) The doctor's office booked with appointments all day.

28. _____ patients are more likely to seek medical care because they aren't deterred by the cost.

Which word best completes the sentence?

A) Ensured

B) Insured

C) Innsured

D) Ennsured

29. The injury was grave, but the doctors were optimistic about the patient's recovery.

Which of the following is the meaning of *grave* in the sentence above?

A) severe

B) accidental

C) unlikely

D) ongoing

30. Which of the following sentences is the most clear and correct?

A) Patient care is a much important part of the job of a nurse.

B) Patient care is the most important part of a nurse's job.

C) Patient cares are the most important part of a nurse's job.

D) Caring for patients are the most important part of a nurse's job.

31. _____ programs are designed to provide end-of-life care.

Which word best completes the sentence?

A) Hospital

B) Hospice

C) Hopeful

D) Heritage

32. Which of the following sentences is punctuated correctly?

A) The orthopedic hospital offers, a calm and well-organized environment.

B) The orthopedic hospital offers a calm and wellorganized environment.

C) The orthopedic hospital offers a calm and well-organized environment.

D) The orthopedic hospital offers a calm and well-organized environment;

1. B)	13. A)	25. C)	37. A)
2. B)	14. D)	26. A)	38. B)
3. B)	15. B)	27. C)	39. A)
4. A)	16. D)	28. C)	40. A)
5. D)	17. B)	29. B)	41. C)
6. A)	18. C)	30. B)	42. A)
7. D)	19. A)	31. B)	43. D)
8. A)	20. B)	32. C)	44. C)
9. C)	21. C)	33. C)	45. B)
10. D)	22. D)	34. D)	46. D)
11. C)	23. D)	35. B)	47. A)
12. C)	24. B)	36. B)	48. C)

Answer Key – Mathematics

1. D)

We need to remember the order of operations (PEMDAS) to solve this question. First of all, we solve the problem inside the parentheses, and then the exponents. In this particular question, 4^3 is within the parentheses so we solve it first. $4^3 = 64$.

Now, multiplying it by 2 to solve what is inside the parentheses, it becomes $64 \times 2 = 128$.

So, the expression becomes $3 \times 128 \div 4$. Following PEMDAS, we multiply 128 by 3, and then divide the answer by 4.

This gives us $384 \div 4 = 96$.

2. A)

This question also involves the order of operations (PEMDAS). To solve this question, we solve the problem inside the parentheses first, and then multiply the answer by 1.

After that, we add 5 to get our final answer. $(5 \times 3) = 15$, so the expression becomes $15 \times 1 + 5 = 15 + 5 = 20$.

3. B)

First of all, we find the value of 5^3 to solve what is inside the parentheses (remember PEMDAS). As we know that $5^3 = 5 \times 5 \times 5 = 125$, the expression becomes $(125 + 7) \times 2$.

We solve what is inside the parentheses first because it is given more preference in PEMDAS; it becomes 132×2.

By multiplying these two numbers, we get our final answer which is 264.

4. C)

Substitute 5 for x:

$4(5) \div (5 - 1) = 20 \div 4 = 5$

5. C)

We are asked to round 707.456 to the nearest tenths place. As the hundredths place in 707.456 is 5, we get 707.5.

6. A)

When we subtract 45.548 and 67.8807 from 134.679, we get 21.2503. Applying the rounding rules, we get 21.3 (note that we were asked to round up to the nearest tenth place only).

7. D)

In order to find the median of any given list, we need to check if the numbers are arranged in ascending order. In this case, the given numbers are already arranged in order. Secondly, we need to check if the total number of entries in the list is even or odd. Since the total number of entries in this list is 6, and 6 is an even number, the median of this list equals the average of two entries which are at the middle of this list, i.e.:

Median → $\frac{(7+9)}{2} = 8$

8. C)

Any number divided by 1 gives the same number as a result.

Therefore, $\frac{0.12}{1} = 0.12$

9. D)

Anything multiplied by zero gives zero as the answer. We are multiplying 0 by 5 and 6, so the answer is still 0.

10. A)

Please note that this is a tricky question. The perimeter of the rectangular field is given as 44 yards, and the length of the field is given as 36 feet (units are different).

1 yard = 3 feet

44 yards = 132 feet

We know the perimeter of the rectangular field is:

Perimeter = 2 × (length) + 2 × (width)

132 = 2(36) + 2 × width

Width = $\frac{132 - 72}{2}$ = 30 feet

11. A)

Find the area of all of the sides of the shed. Two walls measure 5 feet by 7 feet; the other two walls measure 4 feet by 7 feet:

$A = 2l_1 w_1 + 2l_2 w_2$

$A = 2(5 \text{ ft})(7 \text{ ft}) + 2(4 \text{ ft})(7 \text{ ft})$

$A = 70 \text{ ft}^2 + 56 \text{ ft}^2 = 126 \text{ ft}^2$

12. D)

Let's suppose that the unknown number is x. So, 35% of x is equal to 70:

$(35 \div 100) \times x = 70$

$x = \frac{70}{0.35}$

$x = 200$

13. B)

First of all, you should know that 25% profit on the actual price means that we have multiplied the original price by 1.25: (1 + 0.25).

So, in order to find the actual price of the SUV, we divide it by 1.25:

$39000 \div 1.25 = \$31,200$ which is the original price of the SUV.

14. D)

Build an equation. Use m for muffins and c for cookies. The money earned for muffins is equal to the number of muffins times \$1.50:

$1.5m$

The money earned for cookies is equal to the number of cookies divided by two times \$1:

$\frac{c}{2}$

The total money earned is the sum:

$t = 1.5m + \frac{c}{2}$

Set the total equal to \$29.50 and plug in the number of muffins to solve for c:

$29.5 = 1.5(11) + \frac{c}{2}$

$13 = \frac{c}{2}$

$c = 26$

15. A)

The number of people on Tuesday is 345. Every day the number of people triples. On Wednesday, it becomes 3 × 345 = 1035.

On Thursday, the number of people who came to this convention became 3 × 1035 = 3105.

On Friday, the number of people who came to this convention became 3 × 3105 = 9315.

16. B)

First, convert the dimensions from feet to meters:

$11 \text{ ft} \times \frac{12 \text{ in}}{1 \text{ ft}} \times \frac{2.54 \text{ cm}}{1 \text{ in}} \times \frac{1 \text{ m}}{100 \text{ cm}} = 3.3528 \text{ m}$

$13.5 \text{ ft} \times \frac{12 \text{ in}}{1 \text{ ft}} \times \frac{2.54 \text{ cm}}{1 \text{ in}} \times \frac{1 \text{ m}}{100 \text{ cm}} = 4.1148 \text{ m}$

Next, multiply the dimensions to find the area:

$3.3528 \text{ m} \times 4.1148 \text{ m} = 13.796 \text{ m}^2$

17. D)

His new hourly salary would become $15.50 + \$0.75 = \$16.25$

Percentage change =

$\frac{final\ value - original\ value}{original\ value} \times 100$

$\frac{16.25 - 15.50}{15.50} \times 100$

$\frac{0.75}{15.50} \times 100 = 4.8\%$

18. B)

Find all the prime numbers that multiply to give the numbers.

For 2, prime factor is 2; for 3, prime factor is 3; for 4, prime factors are 2; for 5, prime factor is 5. Note the maximum times of occurrence of each prime and multiply these to find the least common multiple.

The LCM is $2 \times 2 \times 3 \times 5 = 60$.

19. B)

Rearranging the given equation, we get:

$3|4n| = 26 - 2$

$3|4n| = 24$

$|4n| = 8$

$+4n = 8$ or $-4n = -8$

Therefore, $n = 2$, or $n = -2$

20. D)

The given equation can be rewritten as:

$|2r + 1| - 10 = 13 \rightarrow |2r + 1| = 23$

$+(2r + 1) = 23 \rightarrow r = 11$

$-(2r + 1) = 23 \rightarrow -2r - 1 = 23 \rightarrow -2r = 24 \rightarrow$

$r = -12$

Therefore, $r = 11, -12$

21. A)

If we observe closely, we note that for every number in the numerator, there is an equivalent denominator which cancels the numerator. Therefore the net result of this multiplication comes out to be 1.

22. B)

Consider the given inequality:

$3x + 33 > -6x + 3$

Add 6x on both sides:

$3x + 33 + 6x > -6x + 6x + 3$

$9x + 33 > 3$

Subtract 33 on both sides:

$9x > 3 - 33$

$9x > -30$

Divide by 3 on both sides:

$3x > -10$

23. A)

As explained in the previous questions, you need to look for the numbers which can be cancelled with each other in the numerator and denominator.

$\frac{300}{30} = 10$. Also, $\frac{100}{50} = 2$, and $\frac{3}{6} = \frac{1}{2}$

So, $\frac{1}{2} \times 10 \times 2 = 10$

24. B)

In this question, we find the sum of the given fractions first, and then subtract $\frac{5}{6}$ from that sum:

$\frac{2}{3} + \frac{4}{5} \rightarrow \frac{10+12}{15} = \frac{22}{15}$

Now, subtract $\frac{5}{6}$:

$\frac{22}{15} - \frac{5}{6} \rightarrow \frac{22(6) - 5(15)}{90} = \frac{19}{30}$

25. D)

We know that $\frac{11}{22}$ can be written as $\frac{1}{2}$.

Similarly, $\frac{22}{44}$ equals $\frac{1}{2}$. Therefore, the expression becomes:

$\frac{1}{2} + \frac{1}{2} + \frac{1}{2} = \frac{3}{2}$

26. A)

Add the given fractions:

$\frac{13}{4} + \frac{5}{8} \rightarrow \frac{13(2) + 5}{8} \rightarrow \frac{26+5}{8} = \frac{31}{8}$

27. C)

$\frac{2}{3}$ of the number of chocolates means that Alex got:

$12 \times \frac{2}{3} \rightarrow 4 \times 2 = 8$ chocolates

28. A)

Consider the given inequality:

$4x - 12 < 12$

$4x < 12 + 12$

$4x < 24$

Divide by 2 on both sides, we get:

$2x < 12$

29. D)

C = 100, X = 10, L = 50. Since X is before L and X is a smaller value than L, this means that you subtract instead of add. So you could visualize it as 100 + 100 − 10 + 50 = 240. This allows you to avoid having to write XXXX to equal 40.

30. C)

$2 \times \frac{1}{2} = 2.5$

$1 \times \frac{1}{4} = 1.25$

$2.5 − 1.25 = 1.25$

31. A)

0.55 equals $\frac{55}{100}$. The lowest common denominator of $\frac{55}{100}$ is 5.

$\frac{55}{5} = 11$ and $\frac{100}{5} = 20$.

32. B)

7 divided by 20 is .35.

33. D)

There is additional information provided in the question that is irrelevant to the answer you need to find. The question wants to know how many people passed the exam, and only scores above 70.0 are considered passing. Approximately 3% scored below 70, so that means 97% passed.

100% − 3% = 97%.

34. D)

Choice A is true; approximately 96% of the class passed the test. Choice B is true; only about 23% of students made an A. Choice C is true; B was the most popular grade; Choice D is false because only about 3% of the class scored less than 70.

CONTINUE

Answer Key – Science

1. A)	13. A)	25. D)	37. B)
2. A)	14. C)	26. C)	38. B)
3. B)	15. D)	27. D)	39. D)
4. A)	16. C)	28. D)	40. C)
5. B)	17. B)	29. C)	41. A)
6. C)	18. C)	30. D)	42. D)
7. A)	19. C)	31. A)	43. C)
8. B)	20. C)	32. C)	44. B)
9. A)	21. A)	33. D)	45. C)
10. B)	22. B)	34. D)	46. B)
11. C)	23. A)	35. B)	47. B)
12. C)	24. B)	36. B)	48. C)

Answer Key – English and Language Usage

1. A)	9. A)	17. D)	25. A)
2. A)	10. B)	18. B)	26. C)
3. D)	11. D)	19. C)	27. A)
4. C)	12. A)	20. C)	28. B)
5. A)	13. B)	21. B)	29. A)
6. C)	14. A)	22. B)	30. B)
7. B)	15. A)	23. C)	31. B)
8. C)	16. B)	24. A)	32. C)

CPSIA information can be obtained at www.ICGtesting.com
Printed in the USA
LVOW09s2027040516

486708LV00007B/108/P

9 781941 759486